Indigenous Identity Fo
in Chilean Education

This book offers rich sociological analysis of the ways in which educational institutions influence indigenous identity formation in Chile. In doing so, Webb explores the mechanisms of new racism in schooling and demonstrates how continued forms of exclusion impact minority groups.

By drawing on qualitative research conducted with Mapuche youth in schools in rural and urban settings, and in private state-subsidised and public schools, this volume provides a comprehensive exploration of how national belonging and indigeneity are articulated and experienced in institutional contexts. Close analysis of student and teacher narratives illustrates the reproduction of historically constructed ethnic and racial criteria, and demonstrates how these norms persist in schools, despite apparently progressive attitudes towards racism and colonial education in Chile. This critical perspective highlights the continued prevalence of implicit racism whereby schooling produces culturally subjective and exclusionary norms and values.

By foregrounding contemporary issues of indigenous identity and education in Chile, this book adds important scholarship to the field. The text will be of interest to researchers, academics, and scholars in the fields of indigenous education, sociology of education, and international and comparative education.

Andrew Webb is Associate Professor of Sociology at Pontificia Universidad Católica de Chile, Chile.

Routledge Research in Educational Equality and Diversity

For more information about this series, please visit: www.routledge.com/
Routledge-Research-in-Educational-Equality-and-Diversity/book-series/
RREED

Indigenous Identity Formation in Chilean Education

New Racism and Schooling Experiences of Mapuche Youth

Andrew Webb

Routledge
Taylor & Francis Group

NEW YORK AND LONDON

First published 2022
by Routledge
605 Third Avenue, New York, NY 10158

and by Routledge
2 Park Square, Milton Park, Abingdon, Oxon, OX14 4RN

*Routledge is an imprint of the Taylor & Francis Group, an
informa business*

Library of Congress Cataloging-in-Publication Data
A catalog record for this title has been requested

ISBN: 978-0-367-54814-8 (hbk)
ISBN: 978-0-367-54815-5 (pbk)
ISBN: 978-1-003-09070-0 (ebk)

DOI: 10.4324/9781003090700

Typeset in Sabon
by SPi Technologies India Pvt Ltd (Straive)

For my loving parents, Roger and Christine

Contents

Figures

Abbreviations

CEPI	Special commission of indigenous peoples
CONADI	National corporation of indigenous development
CONFECH	Chilean student confederation
FEMAE	Federation of Mapuche students
IBE	Intercultural bilingual education
LGE	General law of education
LOCE	Constitutional organic law of education
MIDES	Ministry of social development and family
MINEDUC	Ministry of education
NGO	Non-governmental organization
OEI	Organisation of Ibero-American states for education

About the Author

Andrew Webb is Associate Professor at the Instituto de Sociología, Pontificia Universidad Católica de Chile. He received his PhD in Sociology from Cambridge University in 2010 and in 2014 took up his current post at the Instituto de Sociología. His research focuses on schooling and inequalities in contexts of ethnic diversity, drawing on sociological theories of race and ethnicity, in combination with the work of Pierre Bourdieu and Norbert Elias. He has researched issues relating to school segregation, institutional racism, teacher expectations, peer groups and discrimination, school climate, interculturality/multiculturalism and youth identities using qualitative methodologies in primary, secondary, and tertiary education settings. He has published in journals such as *Race, Ethnicity and Education, International Journal of Inclusive Education, Ethnic and Racial Studies*, and *Equity and Excellence in Education*.

Acknowledgements

First and foremost, I would like to acknowledge the good will of all the students and staff at the 16 schools involved in the research. Without them, their willingness to speak openly to an outsider and their ethical consent, none of this would have been possible. Many gave up their free time to speak to either myself or a research assistant, so I am indebted to their kindness and generosity.

Second, I owe an enormous debt to Sarah Radcliffe, who was the principal investigator on the 2012 project. She gave me the opportunity to work with her as a postdoctoral researcher, on a proposal that we co-wrote. I learnt an enormous amount from her guidance, especially about how to publish academic articles, and my academic career would not have progressed in the way it has without her input. I would also like to thank David Lehmann for supervising my PhD and for his friendship and support throughout.

Third, I wish to recognise that the research could not have been successful without the help of the different researchers who assisted me on the various projects. In 2012, Natalia Caniguan travelled long distances each day to reach the research schools to carry out classroom observations and interviews. Alejandro Herrera was director of the Instituto de Estudios Indígenas in Temuco at the time of the postdoctoral project, and I thank him for his good will and amiability. In 2015, Rukmini Becerra and Simona Mayo carried out interviews in some remote schools which were feasibly impossible for me to reach at the time, so I wish to acknowledge their contribution in generating the data from the Acevedo, Quelentaro, Linterna, and Castañeda schools. In 2017, Macarena Sepulveda was instrumental in helping find and locate Mapuche students in post-secondary education, using snowballing techniques. She and Santiago Irribarra have been instrumental in generating data in elementary schools in Santiago on the most recent project (2019–2020).

Some of the material – interview data – was previously cited in published articles. In the endnotes of each chapter, I specify and reference the relevant papers. However, I would like to formally acknowledge the contribution of my co-authors on those papers: Sarah Radcliffe on two papers, Rukmini Becerra and Andrea Canales on another, and finally Denisse Sepulveda on another. I have enjoyed collaborating with my colleagues on each.

I would like to acknowledge the funding bodies that made the research possible. I am grateful to the ESRC for funding the postdoctoral project (RES-062-23-3168) "Intercultural Bilingual Education in Chilean Classrooms: An exploration of youth identities, multiculturalism and nationalism." I am also indebted to the long-term support offered by the Center for Intercultural and Indigenous Research (CIIR) under [Grant FONDAP 15110006], through which Macarena Sepulveda's valuable assistance was financed. The most recent research on discrimination and school climate has been funded by Fondecyt Regular (No.1190604). The ANID Millennium Science Initiative Program (Code NCS17_062) has also provided me with intellectual input from colleagues on the accumulative aspects of vulnerability.

Last, but certainly not least, I would like to thank my wonderful family, Carolina, Isabel, and Ana for allowing me to take time away from them to write this book. They are all a blessing to me.

Introduction
Racialised Effects of Schooling

As we enter the second decade of the twenty-first century, issues of unequal educational opportunities, institutional racism, segregation, and exclusion seem time worn. Histories of colonial education have taught us about the unapologetically explicit mechanisms of coercive imperialism carried out with the aim of establishing and imposing (among other things) ideational empires at the expense of the conquered. Today, similar talk of the subjugation, domination, and subordination of the disempowered in education seem unthinkable and certainly offend our liberal sense of progress and civilisation. Indeed, schools stand (theoretically at least) as bastions of formative education and training, knowledge, truth, and positive social values. Yet empirical research suggests that across much of the world, ethnic minority social groups continue to experience school unequally when compared to majority groups. Two questions seem befitting of this present-day quandary: first, how is it that these unsavoury and deeply undemocratic processes continue to prevail in institutional settings like schools during an era of heightened sensibilities and aversions to patent inequality? Second, and an equally pressing question, is how do such processes affect the self-identification and educational experiences of ethnic minority students in their day-to-day lives in schools?

Answers to these questions cannot solely be sought by looking to national education policies, or educational outcomes. It is also important to examine school contexts in which ideas about difference and normality are played out and given credence or acceptance. Part of the answer to how these inequalities prevail lies in deep-seated, routine, and (usually) unconscious ways of thinking about, and categorising, human groupings that are in some way interdependent on, or connected to, our own social identity. Studies of ethnicity often meet at a crossroads with the sociology of education to broadly demonstrate how institutions reproduce and legitimise specific values and norms which maintain racialised hierarchies. This process occurs across various school spaces and through administrative and organisational activities: curricular design and content, general school culture, the establishment's specific mission or educational vision, the school's ethnic composition,

DOI: 10.4324/9781003090700-1

the shared and conflicting values among staff and students, pedagogic styles and techniques, and particular forms of social interaction in the classroom and beyond. Scholarship examining racial inequalities and hierarchies in schools from micro-perspectives provide a vital glimpse into the ways identities are affirmed and transformed by these practices, and how ideas about race are mirrored in everyday talk (Lewis, 2003; Pollock, 2005; Castagno, 2008).

Although race is acknowledged to be a spurious analytical term, having no biological basis, racism and racialisation remain crucial analytical tools for understanding the underlying implications and effects of categorising and treating people as belonging to monolithic groupings. While racism is a commonplace term in media and in politics, crucially it is also a process that also occurs in daily interactions without being identified or sanctioned. Theories of new racism propose that continuities of racial inequality are systemically implemented across networks and institutions, but that they exist in more covert, and even apparently non-racial forms, compared to those of the past (Bonilla-Silva, 2006). Rather than drawing on discredited biological explanations for differences, cultural explanations are imposed to rationalise the status of minority groups. In particular, colour-blind racism proposes that all individuals are essentially the same and should be treated alike, thereby establishing culturally naturalised justifications for their inferior educational achievements or labour market prospects.

When analysing new racism, it is urgent to move beyond merely confirming the existence or presence of these contemporary forms of discrimination, towards an understanding of how these processes affect minority groups (Burke, 2016). That is to say, there are serious consequences associated with ignoring or explaining away discriminatory and racist issues, whether in schools or in wider society (Haney López, 2011; Modica, 2015; Pollock, 2005). Throughout this book, I address one minority group's experiences of school, relationships with peers, self-esteem, and their own sense of belonging. I offer a sociological analysis of schooling processes in Chile and how educational institutions influence indigenous identity formation through everyday and seemingly non-racial practices.

The research focuses on the narratives of Mapuche youth – the largest of nine indigenous peoples in the country – as well as school staff, across a range of educational establishments. I explore the ways national belonging and indigeneity are articulated and reformulated in these institutionalised contexts. My intention is to describe and analyse some of the ambivalent outcomes of these tensions at the micro-level of Chilean schools. The analysis relies on extensive research carried out in multiple sites covering urban and rural state-funded private schools and higher education institutes. The evidence presented comes from qualitative interviews and focus groups, with some additional ethnographic observations of research sites.

Researching inside these schools, over the years, has led me to the conclusion that there is a very big elephant in the classroom, the inequalities
facing indigenous students. Most of the schools have at least one-third
indigenous student enrolments, and many are located close to indigenous
communities. Yet Mapuche identity is an issue reserved for second grade
history classes, yearly symbolic nods to Mapuche New Year celebrations,
or in the best-case scenarios, to specific intercultural "bilingual" classes.
However, even with these procedures and considerations in place, this
research was inspired by the question of what young people living out
institutionalised lives in these establishments (especially those students in
the Araucanía Region who reside at the schools during the week) make of
these arrangements. Is it enough for schools to acknowledge these identities in such compartmentalised and sporadic ways, and what are the
effects of doing so? Are there damaging effects from these omissions and
are schools in these contexts doing enough to educate about the political,
ethical, and cultural significance of Mapuche identities as a contemporary issue in Chile? Does the avoidance of these issues compare in any
way to colonial and explicit forms of racism, or equate to the permissive
acceptance of inequalities? Although the answers to these questions are
case-specific and cannot be generalised to all Chilean schools, it does
seem that if there is anywhere where they ought to be addressed, it is in
schools where indigenous youth are most represented. In short, I wish to
address the specific role that schools fulfil in reproducing specific ideals
(or ideologies) and values about indigenous identities, and how young
people in these institutional settings respond to these socialising norms.

This topic is important because every student deserves the opportunity
to study in positive school environments. Discrimination can take many
forms, and although explicit forms of racism and derogatory treatment
of indigenous youth seem (for the most part) to have been overcome or
eradicated, there remains a matter of how these students identify and
connect with their schools. A crucial issue, then, is to understand how
indigenous youth navigate school life within new racism structures. Subtle
forms of exclusion are also likely to impact on their well-being, their
motivation for studying, and their ability to form friendships (Juvonen,
Wang, & Espinoza, 2011).

Schooling

This chapter (and book) carries the term *schooling*, and I want to be
clear that I understand this process as something distinct from education.
The intrinsic value of education is clear to most, and it seems inconsis-
tent, even contradictory, to speak of this in conjunction with racism. It
is commonplace to think of education as an antidote or corrective to all
types of discriminatory ideas and practices. It is therefore appropriate to
distinguish those aspects of educational practice that lead to informative,

instructive, and positive social growth, from those mass organised institutional practices that are prosaic, standardised, and formal. My thinking on schooling has largely been influenced by three very different authors: John Dewey, Pierre Bourdieu, and Ivan Illich.

Almost a century ago, John Dewey identified this difference, noting that although schools are institutions charged with educating younger generations, the general tendency is for them to stunt or impede development ([1916] 2004, [1938] 1997). Dewey's work introduces a key difference between formal schooling, as a culturally and temporally specific form of instruction, and education, as an experience that opens continual possibilities for cognitive, personal, emotional, and social growth and renewal. Dewey's central criticisms of traditional institutions are their focus on imparting an organised and formal education, instructing and conditioning students for future responsibilities, and the imposition of disciplinary and external habit-forming. The disconnect between the school and students' everyday experiences is one of Dewey's central criticisms throughout his work. Schooling, from this perspective, has little opportunity to engage with student identities which tend to be left outside the school gates.

In similar manner, Bourdieu and Passeron – whose work I return to throughout – conceived of *the work of schooling* as those routinised institutional conditions and pressures that restrict an educational establishment's activities so as to self-reproduce a specific culture (1990, p. 57). This is distinguished from both *family education* and *diffuse education*, the latter referring to the way social interaction between proficient members of society leads to social formation (Jenkins, 1992). The work of schooling, then, is directly related to the inculcation of an enduring habitus through taken-for-granted mundane routines, which limits what one expects from one's education. Simply put, Bourdieu sees the repetitiveness of school activities as nullifying alternate possibilities of what receiving an education means, reducing it to a singular logic in which certain values are promoted as privileged and worthwhile.

Finally, Ivan Illich's (1983) seminal work on deschooling offers a critique of the psychological and emotional dependency that institutions such as schools create in modern consumerist society. The author claims that schools lead individuals to mistake teaching and credentials as synonymous with learning and education, and that the product of institutionalisation is detachment from, or the loss of, their own innate possibilities for independent skill acquisition, creativity, and inventiveness. Illich's socialist approach to understanding the problem of schooling underscores that inequalities are reproduced by a monopoly on resources and the conferring of a social status. By seeking solutions to poverty and educational disadvantage through institutional means, Illich proposes that working class dependence on the very systems that condemn them is exacerbated. Whilst one need not concur entirely with

Illich's counter-proposal of deschooling, his work amply demonstrates the dangers of over-reliance on, and the perverse consequences of, standardised and state legitimated learning as the only form of education. If we follow through with Illich's vision of schooling and a schooled society, possibilities for alternate world visions or ways of thinking and being which are outside the commodified norm are reduced or even negated by institutionalised rote learning.

Whilst none of Dewey, Bourdieu, or Illich's work explicitly addressed racism or racial projects in schools, a sociological perspective of schooling offers the possibility to identify aspects of formal institutional life that coincide with the reproduction of racial hierarchies. It also seems appropriate for addressing how indigenous youth identities are affected, and most importantly, excluded from Chilean schooling. My purpose is to look at the effects of formal arrangements in educational establishments and implicit racism in excluding indigenous students from a full and equal participation in Chilean schools. Beyond the formative and positive aspects of educating, I will argue that schooling simultaneously produces culturally subjective norms and values that may coincide with the remaking of race (Lewis, 2003); that is, it may confirm or alter people's ideas about racial belonging.

Schooling and Indigenous Identity Formation

Within existing national sociocultural and political structures, Latin American schools have played a key role in reproducing racialised hierarchies. In these spaces, white-European privilege is constructed relationally against indigenous and Afro-descent populations across a range of educational practices. This can occur through textbooks, curricular design, school relationships (teachers, administrative staff, and students), streaming, academic expectations, school activities and festivals, or the architectural and material conditions of schools. As part of a new racism era, national education curricula are presented as non-racial, hence one does not find explicitly racist criteria in many, if any, of these practices. Scholars' research in this field suggests that instead the "culture of whiteness" in schools needs to be interrogated as presenting the dominant national ethnic category as neutral, transparent, and universal (Giroux, 1997; McIntyre, 2002; McLaren, 2007). That is, indigeneity may be altogether absent, or placed alongside the dominant whitened category as a contrasting and disjunctured pre-modern past, or subordinate present. As Luykx puts it,

> Although multiculturalist rhetoric has largely replaced the racist ideology and aggressive assimilation policies of the past, ethnic stereotypes persist within the normal school curriculum. Sweeping generalisations about the innate characteristics of campesinos and

mestizos appeared frequently in classroom lectures, as did matter-of-fact assertions of the 'backwardness' and 'primitieveness' of nonliterate societies.

(1999, p. 146)

Culturally responsive schooling (see Vass 2017; Castagno & Brayboy, 2008) theorists argue that this unmarked and invisible superiority of the "non-ethnic" pervades all of education. Acknowledgement of cultural difference usually implies compensatory mechanisms or addendums that further relegate alternate knowledges into the margins of what is considered valid and legitimate. From this perspective these multicultural and anti-racist initiatives, regardless of their "good intentions," become complicit in adding to the normativity of this whitened and western epistemological standard (Gorski, 2008). This consolidates a new racism model as an overarching tendency to invisibilise and minimise continuing inequalities in education as non-racial or raceless (Moreno Figueroa, 2010).

Indigenous young people's responses to this kind of schooling have sometimes been withdrawal or resistance, by maintaining their own cultural integrity (Hare & Pidgeon 2011; Dehyle, 1995). That is, the values of western schooling may be rejected or critiqued by indigenous youth as a threat to their own ethical principles. Even if they accept these socialised values, the racialised landscape of school spaces ensures that indigenous students remain peripheral or marginalised in terms of power and status. The vast literature on ethnic minority student conduct and strategies in schools has amply demonstrated the tensions between home and school culture, but also to rebut the notion that "acting white" is the only alternative to school failure (Carter, 2005; Ogbu & Simons, 1998). Indigenous youth also learn to navigate the tensions of schooling that oscillate between oppression and emancipation (Beresford et al., 2003; Schissel & Wotherspoon, 2003; St. Denis, 2007).

Previous work in Latin America (Gustafson, 2009; Canessa, 2004 and Luykx, 1999 on Bolivia, Martinez Novo, & de la Torre, 2010 on Ecuador, Garcia, 2005 on Peru) demonstrates the way indigenous students are subject to exclusion and racialised values in and around schools, leading many indigenous young people to distance themselves from these categories. Martinez Novo and de la Torre (2010) discuss the intersecting effects of socioeconomic status and racial segregation through school selection processes and pejorative teacher attitudes in Ecuador. The authors demonstrate that the divide between private elite light-skinned mestizo (a term used to refer to both "racial" and cultural admixture) or white-majority education and predominantly indigenous and Afro-Ecuadorian public education create very different national and racialised subjects. The former schools place an overriding emphasis and value on all that is foreign, or of European and North American origin, whilst associating the national with degraded notions of indigeneity and mestizo-ness. They conclude that schools play a vital role in the denial and even self-hatred of the local identities that elite Latin American children carry within themselves. The segregation between the worlds of elite white and light-skinned Ecuadorian schoolchildren and darker-skinned mestizo, indigenous and Afro-Ecuadorians means there is little opportunity to escape the racially charged stereotypes and whitened ideals that this system perpetuates.

Canessa (2004) shows that in rural schools composed mostly of indigenous students and Aymara-speaking school staff, teachers eschew Indian culture and encourage students to embrace modern, clean, and civilised life. Numerous symbolic asymmetries are utilised in daily school life to drive home this dichotomy; using Spanish as the authoritarian and disciplinary language, an emphasis on personal hygiene and cleanliness from Indian dirt, the superiority of modern farming techniques over traditional ones, and the replacement of a wooden flagpole with a more "contemporary" metal one, on which to hang the Bolivian national flag. Canessa proposes that plurinationalism and multiculturalism remain issues that are debated and centred in urban discourse that continue to mark out the inferior status of the rural indigenous (2004, 2007).

Luykx (1999) emphasises the cultural reproduction of racial categories among indigenous trainee teachers in Bolivian Normal School. The author demonstrates the way "minute micro-level" discourses and practices interpellate these trainees in such routinised and repetitive fashion that they cannot avoid occasional lapses into mirroring these dominant and racially constructed categories; something she calls the "gentle tyranny of everyday practice" (1999, p. 124). Similarly, Levinson (2001) demonstrates how teacher–student relationships and peer relationships in Mexico socialise the normative and power-centred typologies of society, in which discrimination and victimisation can become part of an accepted interaction dynamic. Other research in the region has demonstrated the crucial role that textbooks play in reproducing social representations of indigenous peoples, often delimiting them to the past or to purely folkloric culture (Crow, 2006; Johnson, 2007).

These are just some of the diverse ways in which Latin American schooling operates upon indigenous youth identities. To these one could easily add school infrastructure, forms of authority and sanctions, and teacher–parent communication as other institutional effects that adjust young people's expectations about what to hope for from a racialised society. That is, students learn their place in an unequal society and adjust their future expectations to this social hierarchy.

In Chile research has been conducted on the identity constructs of young Mapuche (Oteíza & Merino, 2012), intercultural and bilingual pedagogic practices and alternate knowledges (Quintriqueo & Arias-Ortega, 2019), and (discriminatory) schooling experiences of indigenous students (Becerra et al., 2011, 2015; Luna, 2015; Marimán, 2008; Ortiz,

2009). Similar research has also been conducted on Aymara school students (Caqueo-Urízar et al., 2014; Martinez, 2002), and also on other ethnic minority populations such as Latin American migrants (Riedemann & Stefoni, 2015; Valoyes Chávez, 2017). Most offer critical accounts of a hegemonic and mostly monocultural norm in Chilean schools, and collectively they amount to considerable evidence for unequal schooling experiences for ethnic youth. Most of these studies are focused on the creation and implementation of intercultural programmes, and although this is a central component for overcoming racist schooling in Chile, I suggest there is also a need to examine school contexts where whitened norms are constructed without reference to these special programmes, as well as in those that do. That is to say, I do not believe that all our hopes should be pinned on developing interculturality, unless we first recognise that new racism is an impediment to achieving this goal.

I argue that in contemporary Latin American contexts, it is vital to consider the ways theories of "new racism" (Barker, 1981) might inform our understanding of indigenous identity formation and schooling. Classical understandings of schools' roles in producing second-class citizens or as excluding native populations represent more historically explicit forms of colonial racism. Today, we need to look at the more nuanced and subtler aspects of racism operating in schools, and how colour-blind racism among staff and in curricular content may also create more ambivalent identities among indigenous school students.

I take the case of Mapuche students and analyse how they formulate identities that are often caught between an accommodation to new racisms' contradictions and re-articulations its meanings. We know relatively little about how such inequalities impact the daily lives of ethnic youth and their identity formation, meaning that we are unable to say what impact these inequalities have beyond educational outcomes. We do not know, for example, the extent to which ethnic youth perceive these inequalities, whether they deny their ethnic identities on account of unequal schooling, or whether they resist discriminatory treatment.

Racialisation in Education Systems

The vital issue in relation to this previous point is *how* schooling reproduces the meanings of race, and what effects this has. Throughout the book, I refer to racialisation as the process of hierarchically categorising people into specific groupings whose defining features are thought to be predetermined by biological or cultural characteristics. As Barot and Bird (2001) note, racialisation has been a key sociological term because although race has no scientific basis, it allows people's assumptions about race to be examined in reference to the real consequences they have in the social world. Racialisation is therefore a relational concept that occurs at individual and collective (institutional and state level) levels, affecting the lived experience of people involved (both the racialiser–categoriser and the racialised–categorised). I view schools as critical sites for understanding ongoing processes of racialisation. That is, they are spaces in which structural forms give shape to underlying ideas, values, and norms about racial categories and their meanings. They operate within and participate in transmitting historically constructed racial meanings. However, schools are also sites of opportunity to transform or potentially dissipate racial categories. Racialisation is therefore a process that is neither predetermined, nor ever concluded, but always in tension between the past and the present.

Omi and Winant's (1994) work offers a *long dureé* perspective of racial formation, which is to say that categories of difference endure, but undergo subtle changes in meaning over time. Schools are inescapably caught up in these historic periods and the ways sociopolitical contestations or racial projects develop. They note, for example, that racial categorising has become increasingly hard to identify, since it has come to operate through consent and hegemony, rather than domination and coercion (1994, p. 67). Yet on the other hand, racial formation is an iterative process open to contestations and agency by individual actors caught up in institutional settings where racial projects are played out. From this perspective, racialisation should not be read as a unidirectional or automatic acceptance of racial categories and their meanings, but as a dialectical tension of signification (Miles & Brown, 2003) that is played out on school sites by social actors. In general, schools will reproduce institutionalised forms of social relations that obey these broader racial projects, but at the same time are sites that offer possibilities of gradual change over time. I argue that this means that the day-to-day activities in schools are a vital part of this process.

Racial inequality is not simply a predetermined outcome, but something accumulated and reproduced over years of ongoing socialisation that contributes to the way racial categories are constructed and turned into popular thinking. As Barot and Bird (2001) argue, it is vital that racialisation be removed from purely abstract theorising about racism, by taking into account the psychological implications of being categorised into racial constructs that are usually detractive, discriminatory, and devalued. Equally important is to avoid solely emphasising the detrimental effects of "racial projects" to the exclusion of evidence of progress or improvements brought about by real people (Wimmer, 2013). This is a central consideration of the book; how and why Mapuche youth construct their social identities in reference to schooling experiences.

Examples of racialisation can be found at structural and micro-levels of education. There is overwhelming empirical evidence that ethnic minorities experience persistent disadvantages across structural and organisational aspects of school systems around the world. These include segregation between schools – including unequal allocation of funds by residential district, streaming within schools, disciplinary sanctions, drop-out rates, absenteeism, and educational achievement (Roscigno, 1998; Van de Werfhorst & Mijs, 2010). It is also important to add that these inequalities operate between and within groupings, meaning certain minority ethnic groups are more disadvantaged or stigmatised than others in the same context – such as Turkish minorities in Germany, Belgium and Netherlands, or Pakistani ancestry students in UK and Norway (Heath & Brinbaum, 2007). Also, these inequalities intersect with other social identities including gender and class (among others).

That racialisation exists is made evident by what is commonly referred to as the "achievement gap" – though this terminology is generally criticised for espousing an apparently neutral or passive process. Since differences in attainment between ethnic groups cannot be attributed to biological explanations, research has focused on the sociocultural and socioeconomic contexts in which these groupings are clustered. Poorly mixed schools have been shown to have detrimental effects on minority ethnic groupings' educational outcomes, and according to immigrant status and time in a receiving country (Dronkers & Levels, 2007; Marks, 2005 on cross-national comparisons, Gillborn & Mirza, 2000 in UK; van Houtte & Stevens, 2009 in Belgium; Szulkin & Jonsson, 2007 in Sweden). North American literature is even more extensive. Mickelson et al. (2013) provide evidence that high ethnic-minority composition schools are detrimental contexts for various ethnic minorities across areas of the US and across school grades, whilst also increasing achievement gaps over time. Economists also emphasise the unequal distribution of highly qualified teachers and school funding in segregated contexts as being responsible for achievement differentials (Hanushek, Kain, & Rivkin, 2009).

Important qualitative and quantitative work has also been conducted to show the ways racialisation operates in education at micro-levels and in different school spaces. These are principally located in teacher–student relations, peer relationships, teacher expectations and labels, and curricular materials (Agirdag et al., 2012 in Belgium; Rubie-Davies, 2007 in New Zealand; Gillborn, 2008 in UK; Barajas & Ronkvist, 2007; Dickar, 2008 and Cooper Stoll, 2014 in US; van Ingen & Halas, 2006 and Brault et al., 2014 in Canada). Some authors have also drawn attention to the lack of ethnic matches between teachers and students in schools leading to cultural misunderstandings (Thijs, Westhof, & Koomen, 2012).

This is pivotal because it indicates that something is happening in schools – and beyond – that affects minority youth. It points not only to outcomes, but to experiences. Although every school is different, there is a structural issue that subordinates these young people's participation in those establishments to a shared inequality. Racialisation enables us to examine the ongoing material and ideational effects of daily life within institutions that is common to many. This does not depend on racist attitudes of individuals, but rather on the way societies are structured, preventing all students from experiencing equal opportunities to thrive. For example, the ways certain minority groups are clustered into poorer, underfunded public schools, compounded by the unequal distribution of highly qualified teachers into private schools serving elite white school populations.

Researching New Racism in Schools

New racism is one lens for interpreting contemporary forms of racialisation, and why the abundant evidence for structural inequalities is not recognised as such. The absence of visible and explicit forms of racism in today's society equivalent to those of colonial violence, slavery, or apartheid may lead to the supposition that racism is something belonging to the past or restricted to far-right nationalist sentiment. Most people see race and racism as stains on human history, as ugly taboo terms, that contradict some of the cornerstone values of a modern post-racial Western civilisation; liberalism, individualism, respect, tolerance, justice, and egalitarianism. Yet this does not mean that racial categorisations and meanings do not continue to be endorsed or invoked (Denis, 2015).

Bonilla-Silva (2006) argues that racial structures of inequality endure despite these apparent advances because they are orders of material, political, and symbolic privilege – like class and gender – that people struggle to maintain. New racism (including coterminous perspectives such as symbolic racism and modern racism) is a critical perspective that addresses the subtler ways racial projects are supported or reproduced by explaining away racism as something individual rather than systemic or institutional (Burke, 2017). This means ongoing inequalities may be reduced to uniquely class-based issues, and although (biological forms of) race may be overtly rejected as an explanatory factor, individual member attributes, failings, shortcomings, or deficiencies within these minority groupings are usually emphasised. Bonilla-Silva (2006) identifies four interconnected forms (frames) that new racism may take: liberal forms of choice, naturalisation of unequal outcomes, cultural explanations of difference, and the minimising of discriminatory practices. Each provides an example of how reasonable sounding arguments about individual life choices, upbringing, and opportunity bypass the centrality and responsibility of a racial system.

In short, non-racial or post-racial perspectives generally assume that racism is an individual, psychological, and irrational phenomenon. It invokes a certain innocence, of well-meaning, unintentional, or passive forms of discrimination, and generally downplays the historical and institutional continuity of inequalities. It also adheres to a certain thesis of civilising process, by which people's reprehensible behaviour has improved and been moulded by modernity's social sensibilities, confining aberrant racism to an issue of the past (Elias & Scotson, 1994). New racism challenges these frameworks by alluding to the structural factors that make racism a present and continual force, as interrelated to, but distinguishable from socioeconomic factors, affecting all members of society (whether positively or negatively) materially and ideologically.

New racism draws on two useful metaphors to explain how people from the dominant (white) majority group avoid addressing ongoing racial inequalities: colour-blindness and colour-mutism. The first, obviously related to vision, contemplates why people claim not to see difference, or treat all individuals as colourless. Of course, if we accept the premise that society has deeply ingrained systems of material and symbolic privilege running through it that favour dominant groups over others, it is clear why treating everyone the same will only allow the status quo to remain intact. Whilst there is much merit in the concept of colour-blindness, the emphasis on a person's willingness to acknowledge or see racism is somewhat troubling. This assumes, methodologically, that we are able to accurately capture people's "true" thoughts or motives about race. Bonilla Silva has distanced his thesis from this approach by stating that it should not attempt to capture individual psychological tendencies towards prejudice (racists), but only people's position within the prevailing racial order (2006, p. 15). That is, studies on colour-blind racism should be concerned with racial ideology and not personal prejudice. Scholarly research into these issues is not akin to a conspiracy theory of how individuals seek to discriminate, since one can be complicit in reproducing systemic racism without necessarily intending to.

This makes the complementary concept of colour-mutism even more powerful, since it focuses on the "purposeful silencing of race words" (Pollock, 2005, p. 3). This enables us to return to the central tenet of racial categorisation as an act of naming. Talking about race indicates something about an active construction embedded in language use, whether conscious or unconscious. I believe this approach – for qualitative researchers – is the most plausible, since it avoids assumptions about what is going on in people's heads (how people perceive or think about race) and focuses on the discursive decisions present in their race talk (Pollock, 2005). It is also useful since colour-mutism can be linked to the fear to name (Fine, 1993). Explicitly avoiding talking about race or a refusal to name it, has been one of the defining features of teacher practices, as I detail in Chapter 4.

Both colour-blind and colour-mute analyses have been important in educational studies. Education continues to be held up as "the great equaliser;" meritocracy and hard work are deemed to be of greater significance than the social grouping one comes from. Few teachers or school staff would claim to discriminate against minority students, or that students achieve according to biologically determined criteria, but evidence from scholarly sources is clear; even in the absence of explicitly racist language, racial meanings continue to be transmitted. The fear of appearing racist is one of the most prominent issues in this research field, and teachers often allude to the democratic and civic principles of education to justify their neutrality (Nieto, 1996; Solomona et al., 2005). This has led a number of scholars to investigate how teachers explain enduring differences (inequalities) between majority and minority students, concluding that most often they attribute them to individual-level or cultural problems rather than systemic discrimination (Cooper Stoll, 2014; Picower, 2009).

A caveat for applying colour-blind racism to Latin American contexts is the assumption that the term "white privilege" works for all contexts. Since the literature is mostly North American-focused, it is founded on a dichotomous white–non-white analysis. Bonilla-Silva (2006) recognises that biracial analysis must be superseded in North America, but for other countries there is no reason why white privilege should be an appropriate term since it further reifies Eurocentricity. In Chile, the social imaginary corresponds to a whitened ideal, based on a spurious purity of European settler ancestry, but the reality is a widespread national criollo mestizaje (not to mention its violent sociopolitical and sexually imposed history). I return to this issue in the next chapter.

Burke (2016, 2017) argues that sociological studies of colour-blind racism have become stagnant over the past decade by seeking merely to prove that such attitudes or practices exist. She proposes instead that scholars focus on the social and material relations that lead people to adopt and express them. This critique is a mainspring for the rest of the book in which I detail the ways Mapuche youth relationships with school staff, and indigenous and non-indigenous peers create ambivalent tensions around their indigenous identities. I try to present a balanced account of how these interactions produce very mixed results among different individuals or different spaces; on the one hand, resilience and critical resistance against racist structures, while on the other perfunctory compliance, resignation, and consent.

The Research Context

This book owes much to the theoretical richness that has emerged from this work on new racism, but I apply it to the very different circumstances of Chilean schools. Unlike North American or European contexts, ethnic diversity is considerably lower in Chile, though this demographic landscape is now changing with Latin American migrants and increasing recognition of the Afro-Chilean population. Indigenous populations are less clearly identifiable along ethnic lines than those first- and second-generation migrants of African, Asian, or Latino descent commonly studied in the literature cited in the previous sections.

Whilst the terms indigenous and Mapuche are used interchangeably throughout the book, this should by no means obfuscate the diversity of indigenous peoples in Chile. Indigenous peoples in Chile constitute approximately 9% of the national population, and the Mapuche comprise by far the largest (84.8%) of the nine groups (peoples) currently recognised (CASEN, 2017). Approximately 22% of Mapuche live in the Araucanía region, in which many of the historical Mapuche territories are located, and around 33% in Santiago, the Chilean capital (Cerda, 2017). However, given the differences in total population size, indigenous people are overrepresented in the Araucanía region (33%) compared to the Metropolitan Region in which Santiago is located (7%) (CASEN, 2017). Cerda, basing his data on the CASEN 2015 survey, suggests approximately three quarters of Mapuche reside in urban areas, up from around two-thirds in 2009 (Cerda, 2017).

The sociodemographic data from these surveys show the long-standing and ongoing nature of inequalities faced by indigenous people in Chile across a range of indicators such as poverty and income, employment, health, and education. For example, 2.9% of non-indigenous Chileans were in extreme poverty in 2015 compared to 6% of indigenous. This occurs within a process of improvement of aggregate numbers, falling from 11.9% and 22.7%, respectively, in 2006, but the difference between these populations remains approximately double. In education, indigenous peoples in Chile have on average one less year of education than the non-indigenous, lower literacy rates (96.5–95.5%), lower completion rates of secondary education (47% to 38%), and lower rates of participation in tertiary education (38% to 31%). These indicators are lowest among the older generations of indigenous and in rural areas (CASEN, 2017). Indigenous students are also among the most likely to repeat academic years, enter school late, and have lower retention figures (Cerda, 2017; McEwan, 2008).

Education outcomes also show differences between indigenous and non-indigenous. Fernandez and Hauri (2016) calculated average national test scores in 8th and 12th grade between 2010 and 2014 in mathematics and language for Mapuche and non-Mapuche students in the Araucanía Region, finding that in addition to the former having inferior test scores, those of rural students were also lower. This confirms earlier research conducted by McEwan who found that achievement differentials between Mapuche and non-Mapuche students (nationally) were between 0.3 and 0.5 standard deviations, though much of this was attributable to the socioeconomic status of Mapuche families (McEwan, 2008). Additionally, it is vital that we give thought to the fact that the quality of education provision in the Araucanía region is among the lowest in the country, reflected in regional test score averages (Figure 0.1). This shows the detrimental effects of studying in rural Araucanía schools;

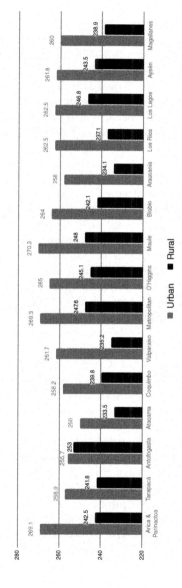

Figure 0.1 Average test scores by region 2013–2015

an issue that I focus on in Chapter 3. Whilst these statistics provide broad indications of some consistent forms of inequality, I propose that only micro-analytical perspectives will help us unravel some of these accumulative disadvantages.

Every year, between 150,000 and 190,000 Mapuche students pass through school doors (MINEDUC, 2017), but we know very little about their personal experiences of schooling. I will show that across levels of education, and types of educational establishment, young Mapuche attend institutions that reproduce structured inequality. Despite apparently more progressive attitudes towards indigeneity, and the implementation of educational systems of inclusion and intercultural curricula, and affirmative action policies, this book will demonstrate the tensions surrounding Mapuche youth identities whilst studying in institutions with underlying racialised ideas about difference.

To do so, I bring together results from my PhD and subsequent research projects over a combined 10-year period; the first conducted with Mapuche students in semi-rural late primary/elementary and secondary (7th–12th grade) schools in the Araucanía Region (discussed in Chapters 2 and 3), two subsequent projects with Chilean teachers in both the Araucanía Region and the Chilean capital (Chapter 4), and finally with Mapuche university students, also in Santiago, looking back at their educational trajectories (Chapter 5). Due to funding, pragmatic reasons (geographical distance), the research informing this book was carried out in schools where Mapuche student numbers were higher, but no other self-identified indigenous students (such as Quechua, Aymara, or Rapa Nui) were enrolled at these establishments. This is because Mapuche make up 99% of the indigenous population in the Araucanía region, and 94.7% in the Metropolitan region (CASEN, 2017).

Chilean education is well-known for its early neoliberal experiment during the 1980s when a voucher-based system was introduced by Pinochet. Responsibilities and funding were decentralised to local authorities in a bid to increase educational efficiency (Carnoy, 1998; Matear, 2007). Private schools were able to compete with public schools for state funding, allocated according to the number of enrolments each establishment could attract, thus creating a quasi-market effect which turned education provision from a social good into a market-good. This led to a rapid desertion of public-funded state schools among the growing middle-class population, thereby segregating Chilean education into a three-tiered system (Delannoy, 2000). Students from elite families are overrepresented in private schools, those from middle-class homes are concentrated into state-funded private schools,[1] which up until 2016 had higher parental contribution fees, and the highest achieving municipal schools (bicentenary state schools), while middle to lower income homes are mostly distributed across the lower-quality state-funded private establishments and municipal schools.

The schools involved in this research belong to the latter categories, serving families from the lowest socioeconomic quintiles in rural and urban sectors of the Araucanía and Metropolitan regions. Most of the secondary schools follow a technical vocational curriculum during the final two grades (11th and 12th). The schools selected from the Araucanía Region had Mapuche student compositions ranging between 18% and 88%. Those chosen in Santiago have large numbers of Latin American migrants and indigenous compositions ranging between 7% and 18%. Given that approximately 9% of the Chilean population self-identify as indigenous, these schools are examples of the segregated nature of the education system. For the most part, these schools are underfunded with somewhat dilapidated infrastructure and insufficient materials to maximise every student's learning opportunities, and struggle to attract better qualified teachers (Figure 0.2). Additional information on the research schools is available in the appendix.

Most of the Mapuche youth with whom I have worked speak little to no *mapuzungún*, the native language, though some heard it spoken by their grandparents during their childhood and could name isolated words. Most grew up (and some still lived at the time of the research), in rural homesteads in and around indigenous communities. Among all the participants, I found no more than ten whose parents had reached higher education. Most had incomplete secondary schooling, making this generation of young

Figure 0.2 A classroom at Raimilla school

Mapuche the first to manage family expectations of reaching university. Almost without exception the young people had participated in religious–cultural activities in these indigenous communities; most commonly the *nguillatún* (only some families abstained due to holding conflicting religious beliefs) and *we tripantu* (Mapuche New Year), and to a lesser extent *eluwün* (burials), *machitún* (healings performed by Machi shamans), and *llelipún* (prayer rituals). Approximately two-thirds of the Mapuche youth come from families composed of one Mapuche and one Chilean parent, and the other third have two Mapuche parents, representative of the entire Mapuche population (Valenzuela & Unzueta, 2015). Reasons for self-identifying as Mapuche were diverse (the subject of Chapter 1), but in most cases, it was related to blood ties, ancestry, family name, or ties to ancestral land. Yet these identifications were often discussed in relation to changes and situations where being or becoming Mapuche was an everyday option, depending on school, community, or home context.

Researcher Positionality

As a white British male, all the research, results, and discussion presented here are an outsider's perspective, centred around a eurocentric sociological analysis. This is an uncomfortable and unavoidable fact that I wish to make transparent, since some readers may object to this type of research on principle as further colonising the academy (Tuhiwai Smith, 1999). My motives for conducting the research began when working in a rural secondary school with Mapuche youth in the Araucanía Region, where I witnessed a number of educational inequalities that, as a sociologist, I felt warranted more research. As I began exploring this in other schools, I found recurring structural issues that afront justice and equal educational opportunities in Chilean schools. Whilst I would not claim that this automatically makes me an ally of indigenous researchers, I believe the study appeals to a universal moralism (or meta-ethics) of opposing structural inequalities in education. That is, I seek to challenge ongoing and often unspoken racism that exists within the Chilean education system.

To do so, I draw on the narratives of those involved in daily school life, but I do not speak for or define who is indigenous within the research. I have also compensated for my outsider status in other ways; on one of the research projects I worked with a self-identified Mapuche research assistant (Natalia Caniguan), whilst on the other three projects all the researchers and assistants were part of the Centre of Indigenous and Intercultural Studies (CIIR), with detailed knowledge of, and sensibilities towards, indigenous histories and culture. I also draw on research carried out by Mapuche scholars who are well positioned to understand the internal complexities of decolonial and representational politics to adjudge the veracity of my findings. There are, however, no easy answers to the ethical and political issues of speaking for others. The defence of researcher reflexivity is an easy one to cast, but I leave it to readers to make up their minds about the worthiness of the findings presented.

It is vital, based on this research background, and having introduced the key issues to be addressed, to emphasise what this book is *not* about. I conducted the research alongside school staff with sincere and good intentions, accompanied by deep moral convictions to provide a positive formative experience for their students. This book is not about identifying racists, or about vilifying teaching or administrative staff whose professions stand among those with the greatest social responsibility. Nor is it about reifying or amassing all Mapuche youth into one category as though describing an internally homogeneous collection of individuals. Borrowing from Augoustinos et al., I share the sentiment that, "the analytic site therefore is not the 'prejudiced' or 'racist' individual, but the rhetorical and discursive resources that are available within an inequitable society" (2005, p. 318).

During my time interacting with Mapuche youth, I have met some who participate actively in furthering indigenous rights and land recuperation, others who promote nuanced and culturally hybrid practices, such as Mapuche hip-hop, and others whose only affiliation is their surname and express a generally indifferent identity. The research does not capture those who reject their identity altogether since only participants who self-identified as Mapuche formed part of the sample.

Families often play a fundamental role in these young people's identity development, as do local communities, so I do not view schooling as an isolated process in this book. Nor are schools "to blame," since they are institutions that are part of a structural racial ordering. Rather the research is about the micro-level effects of structural and ongoing racial hierarchies in educational establishments, and the different ways young people respond to these. Staff may reproduce unintentional, and unconscious cultural values and attitudes across a range of administrative and pedagogical processes. Similarly, responses from young people are often ambivalent; sometimes celebrating indigenous identity, sometimes denying its relevance, or sometimes shifting its meaning according to personal preferences. I draw attention to these tensions as indigenous students work out their sense of place and belonging in the national context, their communities, and their families. In a country in which defining and knowing who is indigenous is deeply complex, subjective, and sometimes contested, it is vital to understand the racialising effects of schooling in the broader sociohistoric contexts of colonial education, and contemporary sociopolitical implications of neoliberalism.

The Organisation of the Book

Chapter 1 expands on various ideas presented here in the introduction by addressing the complexities of indigenous identities in Latin America and Chile in particular. This provides a backdrop to why new racism does not operate in exactly the same way as in the predominantly North American and European literature addressed in this introduction. Identities are precariously balanced in institutional contexts, such as schools, where racial criteria operate to reproduce colonial ideas of inferiority and backwardness but under a new guise of political correctness and tolerance. Simultaneously, the ethnic options available to young people are broader than ever, including access to global cultural artefacts, hyperconnectivity to social media, mass urban migration, and hybrid categories of belonging. These options suggest that indigenous identities, even within constraining institutional environments, are processes that are open to some negotiation and agency. I provide data from interviews and focus groups with Mapuche students to demonstrate the diversity and fluidity of these identity constructions.

Chapter 2 provides contextual information about Chilean education within historical processes of colonialism and neoliberal reforms from the 1980s. It includes a detailed analysis of how different policies affected indigenous populations during these periods; specifically, the creation of indigenous boarding schools, indigenous grants, and intercultural bilingual education programmes. I analyse the deeply unequal structure of the contemporary education system, and argue why, as well as being divided along class lines, it also has an implicit racial organisation. I incorporate literature which evidences inequalities between indigenous and non-indigenous groups in literacy rates, national test achievement, access to tertiary education, and experiences of racism. I finish the chapter by demonstrating some of the positive effects that certain formats of intercultural education have accomplished, from the young people's perspectives. These examples are used to contrast some of the issues addressed in later chapters.

Chapter 3 sets out empirical evidence of new racism among Mapuche students from 7th to 12th grades. I examine attitudes towards school-oriented issues such as school choice, relationships with teachers, peers, educational expectations, discrimination, and the inclusion of indigenous knowledges. Introducing a Bourdieusian perspective, I draw attention to the role that racialised habitus plays in the repetitive work of schooling to adjust young Mapuche students' expectations about normative education. I finish by providing examples of how a minority of students are able to resist these racial projects through critical narratives. I argue that indigenous identities are precariously balanced in institutional contexts, such as schools, where racial criteria operate to reproduce colonial ideas of inferiority and backwardness but under a new guise of political correctness and tolerance.

In Chapter 4, I continue addressing latent and implicit forms of new racism in the Chilean education system, this time from the perspective of school staff. I show the unwillingness of a majority of administrative and teaching staff to recognise specific forms of institutional inequality in schools with high density indigenous compositions. Following new racism literature, I argue that the Chilean education system reproduces a fear of talk or colour-mutism among teachers working in these areas, which obscures unequal social structures and opportunities for specific (class, gender, ethnic) groups in school contexts. Most teachers are non-indigenous and believe that, compared with historic forms of explicit discrimination against indigenous students, contemporary schooling has moved beyond this to offer a more equitable education.

Chapter 5 looks at the partial success stories from life history interviews with Mapuche students who went on to tertiary education. They are partial precisely because their testimonies reveal the personal strategies and resources that they have needed to draw on in order to remain in the education system, often at high costs. Enduring inequalities compared to more privileged families remain, such as choosing the institution and course that they would study on, since they are based on restricted information sources and prior knowledge, whilst the capital required to succeed in higher education is heavily biased towards higher socioeconomic backgrounds. This notwithstanding, the Mapuche youth also demonstrate spontaneous adaptations to work routines, managing crises, and the activation of other resources for staying in higher education. Emphasis is placed on the resilience expressed by these young people, as the first-generation from their families to access higher education, to negotiate cumulative disadvantages from low-quality educational establishments and poverty. Although indigenous people's access to higher education is beginning to improve, I argue that these changes misrepresent ongoing disadvantages in regard to experiencing university life under new racism.

The book concludes by bringing together the data discussed in the previous chapters to further consider the implications of new racism in contemporary Chilean schooling. I put forward the theoretical and empirical contributions developed throughout and suggest some practical recommendations for the future of Chilean education, especially in contexts of higher-than-average indigenous compositions.

Note

1 Throughout the book the terminology "state-funded private schools" and "state-subsidised private schools" (*escuelas particulares subvencionadas*) are used interchangeably to refer to privately owned and privately administered schools that under the voucher system became eligible to receive state subsidies (as part of government education expenditure), allocated according to the number of students enrolled at the school. These are supplemented by monthly parental contributions and enrolment fees which vary greatly according to each establishment, and donations from the founders – usually religious organisations or NGOs, although occasionally also a legally recognised consortium of individuals (*personalidad jurídica*). The Inclusion Law (*Ley de Inclusión*) introduced in 2016 has cut back many of these establishments that were previously profit-oriented, though most of my research in schools was conducted prior to this year.

They differ from private schools (*escuelas particulares*) which do not receive any state funding, and instead are funded solely from tuition fees. The terms "public schools" and "municipal schools" (*escuelas municipales*) are used interchangeably to refer to educational establishments that are state-owned, funded, and controlled, which cannot charge monthly fees, which since the 1980s have been decentralised under local municipal administration.

References

Agirdag, O., van Avermaet, P., & van Houtte, M. (2012). School segregation and math achievement: A mixed-method study on the role of self-fulfilling prophecies. *Teachers College Record, 115*, 1–50.

Augoustinos, M., Tuffin, K., & Every, D. (2005). New racism, meritocracy and individualism: Constraining affirmative action in education. *Discourse & Society, 16*(3), 315–340.

Barajas, H., & Ronkvist, R. (2007). Racialised space: Framing latino and Latina experience in public schools. *Teachers College Record, 109*(6), 1517–1538.

Barker, M. (1981). *The new racism*. London: Junction Books.

Barot, R., & Bird, J. (2001). Racialization: The genealogy and critique of a concept. *Ethnic and Racial Studies, 24*(4), 601–618.

Becerra, S., Mansilla, J., Merino, M. E., & Rivera, P. (2015). School violence against Mapuche indigenous students in Chilean secondary schools. *Procedia - Social and Behavioral Sciences, 197*, 1538–1543.

Becerra, S., Rivas, C., Cisternas, A., & Mera, J. (2011). Prejuicio y discriminación étnica docente hacia niños indígenas en la escuela. *Revista de Educación, Número Extraordinario, 2011*, 163–181.

Beresford, Q., Partington, G., & Gower, G. (Eds.). (2003). *Reform and resistance in aboriginal education: The Australian experience*. Crawley, WA: University of Western Australia Press.

Bonilla-Silva, E. (2006). *Racism without racists: Color-blind racism and the persistence of racial inequality in the United States* (2nd ed.). Oxford: Rowman & Littlefield Publishers.

Bourdieu, P., & Passeron, J.C. (1990). *Reproduction in education, society and culture* (2nd ed.). (R. Nice, Trans.). London: Sage Publications, Inc.

Brault, M.C., Janosz, M., & Archambault, I. (2014). Effects of school composition and school climate on teacher expectations of students: A multilevel analysis. *Teaching and Teacher Education, 44*, 148–159.

Burke, M. (2016). New frontiers in the study of color-blind racism: A materialist approach. *Social Currents, 3*(2), 103–109.

Burke, M. (2017). Colorblind racism: Identities, ideologies, and shifting subjectivities. *Sociological Perspectives, 60*(5), 857–865.

Canessa, A. (2004). Reproducing racism: Schooling and race in highland Bolivia. *Race Ethnicity and Education, 7*(2), 185–204.

Canessa, A. (2007). Who is indigenous? Self identification, indigeneity and claims to justice in contemporary Bolivia. *Urban Anthropology, 36*(3), 195–237.

Caqueo-Urízar, A., De Munter, K., Urzúa, A., & Saiz, J. (2014). Entre lo aymara y lo chileno: Escala de involucramiento en la cultura Aymara (eica). Una aproximación interdisciplinar a la dimensión aymara en la vivencia intercultural de estudiantes de enseñanza básica del norte de Chile. *Chungará (Arica), 46*(3), 423–435.

Carnoy, M. (1998). National voucher plans in Chile and Sweden: Did privatization reforms make for better education? *Comparative Education Review*, 42(3), 309–337.

Carter, P.L. (2005). *Keepin' it real: School success beyond black and white*. New York, NY: Oxford University Press.

CASEN. (2015). *Encuesta de caracterización socioeconómica Chile*. Santiago: Gobierno de Chile.

CASEN. (2017). *Encuesta de Caracterizacion Socioeconomica*. Santiago, Chile: Ministerio de Desarrollo Social.

Castagno, A. (2008). "I Don't want to hear that!": Legitimating whiteness through silence in schools. *Anthropology & Education Quarterly*, 39(3), 314–333.

Castagno, A., & Brayboy, B.M.J. (2008). Culturally responsive schooling for indigenous youth: A review of the literature. *Review of Educational Research*, 78(4), 941–993.

Cerda, R. (2017). Situación socioeconómica reciente de los mapuches: 2009–2015. In I. Aninat, V. Figueroa, & R. Gonzaléz (Eds.), *El pueblo mapuche en el siglo XXI: Propuestas para un nuevo entendimiento entre culturas en Chile* (pp. 405–434). Santiago: Colección Centro de Estudios Públicos.

Cooper Stoll, L. (2014). Constructing the color-blind classroom: Teachers' perspectives on race and schooling. *Race Ethnicity and Education*, 17(5), 688–705.

Crow, J. (2006). *Rethinking national identities: Representations of the Mapuche and dominant discourses of nationhood in twentieth century Chile*. PhD Thesis, University of London.

Dehyle, D. (1995). Navajo youth and Anglo racism: Cultural integrity and resistance. *Harvard Educational Review*, 65(3), 403–444.

Delannoy, F. (2000). Education reforms in Chile, 1980–1998: A lesson in pragmatism. In *Country studies education reform and management publication series*, 1(1). Washington, DC: World Bank.

Denis, J. (2015). Contact theory in a SmallTown settler-colonial context: The reproduction of laissez-faire racism in indigenous-White Canadian relations. *American Sociological Association*, 80(1), 218–242.

Dewey, J. [1938] (1997). *Experience and education*. New York, NY: Touchstone.

Dewey, J. [1916] (2004). *Democracy and education: An introduction to the philosophy of education*. New York, NY: Dover Publications.

Dickar, M. (2008). Hearing the silenced dialogue: An examination of the impact of teacher race on their experiences. *Race Ethnicity and Education*, 11(2), 115–132.

Dronkers, J., & Levels, M. (2007). Do School segregation and school resources explain the region-of-origin differences in the mathematics achievement of immigrant students? *Educational Research and Evaluation*, 13(5), 435–462.

Elias, N., & Scotson, J. (1994). *The established and the outsiders: A sociological enquiry into community problems*. London: Sage.

Fernandez, M.C., & Hauri, S. (2016). Resultados de aprendizaje en La Araucanía. La brecha de género en el Simce y el androcentrismo en el discurso de docentes de lenguaje y matemática. *Calidad en la Educación*, 45, 54–89.

Fine, M. (1993). *Framing dropouts: Notes on the politics of an Urban public high school*. New York, NY: State University of New York Press.

Garcia, M.E. (2005). *Making indigenous citizens: Identities, education, and multicultural development in Peru*. Stanford, CA: Stanford University Press.

Gillborn, D. (2008). *Racism and education: Coincidence or conspiracy?* London: Routledge.

Gillborn, D., & Mirza, H.S. (2000). *Educational inequality: Mapping race, class and gender. A synthesis of research evidence.* London: Ofsted Working Paper.

Giroux, H. (1997). Re-writing the discourse of racial identity: Towards a pedagogy and politics of whiteness. *Harvard Educational Review, 67*(2), 285–320.

Gorski, P. (2008). Good intentions are not enough: A decolonizing intercultural education. *Intercultural Education, 19*(6), 515–525.

Gustafson, B. (2009). *New languages of the state: Indigenous resurgence and the politics of knowledge in Bolivia.* London: Duke University Press.

Haney López, I.F. (2011). "Is the 'post' in post-racial the 'blind' in Colorblind?" *Cardozo Law Review, 32*(3), 807–831.

Hanushek, E., Kain, J., & Rivkin, S. (2009). New evidence about Brown v. Board of Education: The complex effects of school racial composition on achievement. *Journal of Labor Economics, 27*(3), 349–375.

Hare, J., & Pidgeon, M. (2011). The way of the warrior: Indigenous youth navigating the challenges of schooling. *Canadian Journal of Education / Revue canadienne de l'éducation, 34*(2), 93–111.

Heath, A., & Brinbaum, Y. (2007). Guest editorial explaining ethnic inequalities in educational attainment. *Ethnicities, 7*(3), 291–305.

Illich, I. (1983). *Deschooling society.* New York, NY: Harper Colophon.

Jenkins, R. (1992). *Pierre Bourdieu.* London: Routledge.

Johnson, E. (2007). Schooling, blackness and national identity in Esmeraldas, Ecuador. *Race Ethnicity and Education, 10*(1), 47–70.

Juvonen, J., Wang, Y., & Espinoza, G. (2011). Bullying experiences and compromised academic performance across middle school grades.*The Journal of Early Adolescence, 31*(1), 152–173.

Levinson, B. (2001). *We are all equal: Student culture and identity at a Mexican secondary school, 1988–1998.* Durham, NC: Duke University Press.

Lewis, A. (2003). *Race in the schoolyard: Negotiating the color line in classrooms and communities.* Piscataway, NJ: Rutgers.

Luna, L. (2015). Construyendo 'la identidad del excluido': Etnografía del aprendizaje situado de los niños en una escuela básica municipal de Chile [Building up ´the Excluded's Identity´: Ethnography of Children Situated Knowledge in a Chilean Public Primary School]. *Estudios Pedagógicos, 41*, 97–113.

Luykx, A. (1999). *The citizen factory: Schooling and cultural production in Bolivia.* Albany, NY: State University of New York Press.

Marimán, P. (2008). La educación desde el programa del movimiento Mapuche. *Revista,* (2), 135–152.

Marks, G. (2005). Cross-national differences and accounting for social class inequalities in education. *International Sociology, 20*(4), 483–505.

Martínez, J. (2002). La construcción de identidades y de lo identitario en los estudios andinos (ideas para un debate). In J. Martínez (Eds.), *Identidades y Sujetos. Para una Discusión Latinoamericana* (pp. 89–112). Santiago: Ediciones Facultad de Filosofía y Humanidades, Universidad de Chile, Serie Estudios.

Martínez Novo, C., & de la Torre, C. (2010). Racial discrimination and citizenship in Ecuador's educational system. *Latin American and Caribbean ethnic studies, 5*(1), 1–26.

Matear, A. (2007). Equity in education in Chile: The tensions between policy and practice. *International Journal of Educational Development, 27*(1), 101–113.

McEwan, P. (2008). Can schools reduce the indigenous test score gap? Evidence from Chile. *Journal of Development Studies*, 44(10), 1506–1530.

McIntyre, A. (2002). Exploring whiteness and multicultural education with prospective teachers. *Curriculum enquiry*, 32(1), 31–49.

McLaren, P. (2007). *Life in schools. An introduction to critical pedagogy in the foundations of education* (5th ed.). Los Angeles: University of California.

Mickelson, R., Bottia, M., & Lambert, R. (2013). Effects of school racial composition on K–12 mathematics outcomes: A Metaregression analysis. *Review of Educational Research*, 83(1), 121–158.

Miles, R., & Brown, M. (2003). *Racism* (2nd ed.). London: Routledge.

Ministry of Education (MINEDUC). (2017). *Programa de Educación Intercultural Bilingüe, 2010–2016*. Santiago: Ministerio de Educación.

Modica, M. (2015). Unpacking the 'colorblind approach': Accusations of racism at a friendly, mixed-race school. *Race Ethnicity and Education*, 18(3), 396–418.

Moreno Figueroa, M.G. (2010). Distributed intensities: Whiteness, mestizaje and the logics of Mexican racism. *Ethnicities*, 10(3), 387–401.

Nieto, S. (1996). *Affirming Diversity: The Sociopolitical Context of Education*. New York, NY: Longman.

Ogbu, J., & Simons, H. (1998). Voluntary and involuntary minorities: A cultural-ecological theory of school performance with some implications for education. *Anthropology and Education Quarterly*, 29(2), 155–188.

Omi, M., & Winant, H. (1994). *Racial formation in the United States*. New York, NY: Routledge.

Ortiz, P. (2009). *Indigenous knowledge, education and ethnic identity: An ethnography of an intercultural bilingual education program in a Mapuche school in Chile*. Ann Arbor, MI: VDM Verlag.

Oteíza, T., & Merino, M. (2012). Am I a genuine Mapuche? Tensions and contradictions in the construction of ethnic identity in Mapuche adolescents from Temuco and Santiago. *Discourse and Society*, 23(3), 297–317.

Picower, B. (2009). The unexamined whiteness of teaching: How White teachers maintain and enact dominant racial ideologies. *Race Ethnicity and Education*, 12(2), 197–215.

Pollock, M. (2005). *Colormute: Race talk dilemmas in an American school*. Princeton, NJ: Princeton University Press.

Quintriqueo, S., & Arias-Ortega, K. (2019). Educación intercultural articulada a la episteme indígena en latinoamérica. el caso mapuche en chile. *Dialogo Andino*, 59, 81–91.

Riedemann, A., & Stefoni, C. (2015). Sobre el racismo, su negación, y las consecuencias para una educación anti-racista en la enseñanza secundaria chilena. *Polis*, 42 [online], 1–18.

Roscigno, V. (1998). Race and the reproduction of educational disadvantage. *Social Forces*, 76(3), 1033–1061.

Rubie-Davies, C.M. (2007). Classroom interactions: Exploring the practices of high-and low-expectation teachers. *British Journal of Educational Psychology*, 77, 289–306.

Schissel, B., & Wotherspoon, T. (2003). *The legacy of school for aboriginal people: Education, oppression, and emancipation*. Don Mills: ON: Oxford University Press.

Smith, L.T. (1999). *Decolonizing methodologies: Research and indigenous peoples*. London: Dunedin.

Solomona, R.P., Portelli, J., Beverly-Jean, D., & Campbell, A. (2005). The discourse of denial: How White teacher candidates construct race, racism and 'White privilege'. *Race Ethnicity and Education, 8*(2), 147–169.

St. Denis, V. (2007). Aboriginal education with anti-racist education: Building alliances across cultural and racial identity politics. *Canadian Journal of Education, 30*(4), 1068–1092.

Szulkin, R., & Jonsson, J. (2007). Ethnic segregation and educational outcomes in Swedish comprehensive schools. *Linnaeus Center for Integration Studies Working Paper No. 2007–2*. Stockholm University, Stockholm.

Thijs, J., Westhof, S., & Koomen, H. (2012). Ethnic incongruence and the student–teacher relationship: The perspective of ethnic majority teachers. *Journal of School Psychology, 50*(2), 257–273.

Valenzuela, E., & Unzueta, B. (2015). Parental transmission of ethnic identification in mixed couples in Latin America: The Mapuche case. *Ethnic and Racial Studies, 38*(12), 2090–2107.

Valoyes Chávez, L. (2017). Inequidades raciales y educación matemática. *Revista Colombiana de Educación, 73*, 127–150.

Van de Werfhorst, & Mijs, J.B. (2010). Achievement inequality and the institutional structure of educational systems: A comparative perspective. *Annual Review of Sociology, 36*, 407–428.

Van Houtte, M., & Stevens, P. (2009). School ethnic composition and students' integration outside and inside schools in Belgium. *Sociology of Education, 82*(3), 217–239.

Van Ingen, C., & Halas, J. (2006). Claiming space: Aboriginal students within school landscapes. *Children's Geographies, 4*(3), 379–398.

Vass, G. (2017). Preparing for culturally responsive schooling: Initial teacher educators: Into the fray. *Journal of Teacher Education, 68*(5), 451–462.

Wimmer, A. (2013). *Ethnic boundary making: Institutions, power, networks*. New York, NY: Oxford University Press.

1 Indigenous Identities in a New Racism Era

It is paramount, before addressing the racialising experiences of Mapuche youth in schools, to address the situated meanings of being indigenous. It is evident from the introduction, where I discussed ethnic minority inequalities, that this terminology is somewhat broader than indigeneity. In this chapter, I unpack some of the criteria that are particular to indigenous identity, whilst also demonstrating its commonalities with a more general ethnic identity literature. Having outlined these conditions, I provide evidence for the ways Mapuche youth articulate their indigenous belonging and their management of tensions between permanence (or being) and transition (becoming). This is never a purely internalised issue but a social one, referring to how individuals understand their place in racialised taxonomies and how they establish criteria of similarity and difference to others. In an era of new racism, difference is rarely constructed around biological or moral criteria of inferiority in contemporary Chilean society, having shifted – like most or all societies – towards cultural explanations of difference and individual merits. An initial question, then, is how indigenous youth express ideas about racial/ethnic difference having grown up under these conditions, especially in a national context in which mestizaje complicates simple, naturalised, categories of difference.

By using the term identity, I am entering into one of the broadest, most ambiguous, and highly contested areas in social science; so much so that some theorists have deemed it redundant (see Anthias, 2002; Brubaker & Cooper, 2000). Identity, even in its definition, throws up all manner of apparent contradictions; the Latin *identitas* (from the root idem) meaning absolute or exact likeness and sameness simultaneously expresses that which is distinguishable or enduringly different from another (Jenkins, 1996). Yet rather than making this concept unavailing, I argue that this shows its appropriateness for drawing out the dynamic, dialectic, often contradictory, and overlapping nature of the modern construct of self, which reveals deep-rooted needs and desires for inclusion, for finding similarity, and committing oneself to significant (and generalised) others whilst expressing creative difference, distinctiveness, and individualism

DOI: 10.4324/9781003090700-2

(Brewer, 1991; Jenkins, 1997). By speaking of identity or identification, I refer to the process of seeking one's place in the world; whether sameness to, or distinctiveness from others. As Jenkins (1992) notes, this is a socially constructed process caught between mutually entangled aspects of internal identification and external categorisation, that is, between personal choices and structurally imposed and ascribed identities.

The young people who participated in the research are of different ages, at various stages of their education, living in two very different parts of Chile, but they all share the same challenge of constructing an indigenous identity in a society, and institutions, that operate according to racial categories.

Racial, Ethnic, and Indigenous Identities

As I already argued in the introduction, race is an unsubstantiated concept for distinguishing between populations, which was discredited following the atrocities of Nazism (Fenton, 1999). Continued use of the term racial identity by some scholars mirror "naturalised" categorisations that occur in people's everyday talk, but numerous authors propose that social scientists should avoid replicating this (Brubaker, 2004; Miles & Brown, 2003). Hence, I include racism and racialisation as analytical points of reference for this book because they refer to structural issues of power that categorise individuals into positions of subordination and inferior status, but racial identity as an internalised identification seems an inappropriate term.

It is true that contrary arguments have also been raised, positing that it is (etymologically) impossible to have racialising factors without race. Like Bonilla-Silva (1997), I argue that since races are *treated* as natural phenomena, as modes of political, cultural, and social competition between groupings – much like class and gender – the consequences of these collective actions create an organising principle that has independent effects. The hierarchical structuring of people premised on *perceived* racial differences creates very real material and relational disparities between those categorised into these groupings. This feeds back into and moulds the identities that individuals share. A problem, however, is that racial identities then become somewhat inevitable, imposed and static categorisations that individuals have little control over.

An alternative is the concept of ethnic identity, which since the 1960s has become increasingly influential in scholarship. The classic definition of ethnic groupings or *ethnie* is that it describes relationships based on shared myths and historical memories, linguistic, religious or other common cultural traits, and connections to a homeland (Hutchinson, 1996; Smith, 1986). In a climate in which the mobilisation and interconnectivity of groups across the world is too great for tribal affiliations, and in which the nationalist narrative of citizenship has failed to break down smaller group affiliations, "ethnic groups" and *ethnic identities* have become vital to the language of social analysis (Eriksen, 2002). This is not only because it provides a less pejorative narrative of group differentiations than tribes or races, but equally important is its capacity to account for perceived cultural traits of similarity, beyond biological ones, and for opening up avenues of choice and identity negotiation (Guibernau & Rex, 1997; Waters, 1990).

These cultural traits are also susceptible to racialising categorisation so in this sense we might question how far ethnicity has taken us beyond the politically charged and sometimes violent use of race (Fenton, 1999). In this sense, we must avoid assuming race is exclusionary and ethnicity is inclusive, given specific histories of forced migration, ethnic violence, and the segregation of ethnic groupings (Wimmer, 2013). Yet one advantage is its plasticity; it can be used to analyse how individuals and communities conceive of, or use their social positioning (positionality), and the cultural/symbolic codes made available to them, to create a sense of belonging that changes over time and place (Jimenez, 2004).

Exactly how or why individuals "choose" ethnic identities is a matter of greater contention in the relevant literature. Theories of self-interest (instrumentalism) or decisions based on particular contexts (situationism) have been presented as constructivist accounts of identity management that contrast more essentialist or primordial forms; those perceptions of fixed similarity or commonality to others, usually premised on common descent (Wimmer, 2013). The former shares a common objective of capturing fluid conceptualisations of constructed difference by transcending dichotomous categories of difference, and the "fixities of identity and culture that are so prominent in racialized discourse" (Anthias, 2001, p. 619). A middle ground approach has been to suggest that both essentialist and situationist accounts of ethnic identity formation are valid (Brubaker, 2004). That is, perceptions of enduring similarity do not necessarily prevent possibilities of change, as Stuart Hall argued:

> Cultural identity ... is a matter of 'becoming' as well as of 'being'. It belongs to the future as much as to the past. It is not something which already exists, transcending place, time, history and culture. Cultural identities come from somewhere, have histories. But like everything which is historical, they undergo constant transformation.
> (1990, p. 52)

Nuanced approaches to understanding identity management therefore need to take into account both the external, structural imposition of categories of difference, as well as internalised boundary markings and meaning-making created by individuals (Jenkins, 1997). A particularly meaningful contribution to unravelling how ethnic identities are worked out is a focus on the everyday meanings and practices that contribute towards the construction of categories of similarity or belonging, as well as differences and exclusion (Brubaker et al., 2006; Edensor, 2002; Karner, 2007). The everyday marks an important lens for understanding when, where, and how categories of belonging are negotiated and experienced. This is crucial because it avoids the assumption that ethnic identity is always a relevant or salient feature of people's lives (Brubaker et al., 2006). It also provides relief from the exclusively politicised and nationalist versions of ethnic belonging and conflict, which pits groups against one another. Ethnic identity is always political to some extent inasmuch as it involves positioning oneself in relation to the other (Jenkins, 1997). However, "everyday ethnicity" can be distinguished from those narratives that politicise the boundary between an "us" and a "them" for the purposes of domination, since the former is more concerned with making sense of one's place in the world (Anthias, 2002). As Hale (2004) observes, this informs us about "the set of points of personal reference on which people rely to navigate the social world they inhabit, to make sense of the myriad constellations of social relationships that they encounter" (2004, p. 463). In short, a discussion of the banal or mundane "from below," helps us understand the ethnic choices that people make away from the "extraordinary, politically charged, and emotionally driven" (Billig, 1995, p. 44; Edensor, 2002; Fenton, 2003). This is particularly useful when addressing youth identities within routinised school life.

My concerns are directed towards assessing how individuals identify, discuss, and understand similarities and differences to significant others around them in school contexts where racialised meanings and categories may be imposed. Therefore, although my discussion of Mapuche identity is analytically framed by ethnicity, it is only in response to the practices of the respondents themselves in their daily lives. In this sense I concur that, "the idea of ethnicity is a concept of practice, not an analytical concept" (Eder et al., 2002, p. 14). For this same reason, the settings and events which transpire in daily activities are all the more important for understanding how and when ethnicity is "set off" or when it becomes salient (Fenton, 2003). Crucially, these ethnic criteria take place in social contexts already defined by hierarchical relationships of difference. This is why it is compatible to speak of ethnic identity within racialising structures; adapting the Marxian dictum, people act within the racialised and post-colonial circumstances not of their own choosing.

Throughout the rest of the book, I demonstrate the ways that Mapuche youth draw on ideas about their identities and cultural belonging to negotiate their school lives. I do so in direct reference to indigenous identity. As discussed above, *ethnic minority groups* is such an overarching term for a huge diversity of interdependent peoples on the planet. Even leaving aside intersecting identities formed by particular interest groups, sexual orientations, or physical/cognitive/sensory disabilities, we are still left with a bewildering array of cultural and religious properties that distinguish, or are imposed to distinguish, groupings of individuals from a numerical majority.

Eriksen argues that internal distinctions are necessary to differentiate the conditions in which these relational characteristics are formed, and although only ideal types, could encompass five variants: post-slavery, urban migrants, proto-nations, plural-societies, and indigenous peoples (Eriksen, 2002). The analytical decision to speak of indigenous identity, then, refers to ethnic criteria that are sociohistorically and politically specific, with differing consequences in how they are lived out in day-to-day contexts. Being indigenous is not experienced in the same way as, say, second-generation urban migrants, or how African descendants live out their own identities. Even so, ethnicity remains relevant as a concept inasmuch it appeals to culturalist explanations of difference that are often used to legitimise racial structures. As de la Cadena puts it, "race could be biology, but it could also be the soul of the people, their culture, their spirit and their language" (2001, p. 16).

Indigenous Identities in Latin America

Defining who is indigenous, how they come to be defined as such, and what social spaces they are to occupy has governed much of Latin American politics over the last century. A brief overview of these broader issues will not only demonstrate the ways in which the Mapuche case is common to other parts of the continent, but also its unique features that lead to specific identity constructions. Although there are no easy answers of how to define indigenous identity, or who "has it" (Weaver, 2001), it does provide a more politically precise contextualisation of the power struggles involved.

The etymology of *indigenous* refers us to peoples descended from original inhabitants, but Paine (2000) and De la Cadena and Stern (2007) argue that indigenous identity is never about the "untouched reality" of home territories. Instead, it encapsulates a historical relationship of asymmetrical power defining who one is by what the other is not. Paine (2000) argues that terms such as aboriginal or indigenous were originally invoked as a means of categorising others as backward, pre-modern, and even subhuman in order to legitimate the quasi-religious and political aspects of conquest. That is, indigeneity set up a moral order of superiority that justified the invasion of foreign lands, by which the "civilisers" would teach, enslave, or kill the barbaric. Naming the indigenous meant distinguishing those who were rooted and static in a territory, to be appropriated, and the non-indigenous as those charged with the "virtuous" and dynamic mission of relieving them from this state.

Saugestad (2001) has suggested that four criteria are crucial to the acknowledgement or condition of being indigenous: being autochthonous, or those to have first settled in a territory, non-dominance, cultural difference, and self-ascription. The latter three criteria fit with most other ethnic minority experiences, thus making "first-come" the key component. There is a moral element to being indigenous that super-sedes other ethnonationalist claims to a specific territory, which is the loss of lands and pre-existing ways of life. However, as Kuper (2003) notes, these terms always risk being essentialised to express a pristine, untouched primitivism. Instead, indigeneity must acknowledge colonial usurpation in conjunction with continual internal cultural change and adaptation.

In Latin America, often violent sexual relations imposed on African slaves and native peoples by Europeans led to racialised hierarchies of status, establishing white settler supremacy, which would be drawn on during independence periods to justify a new national identity (Telles, 2004). Historically speaking the integration of indigenous peoples into mainstream culture has been a process of acculturation, assimila-tion, or "whitening of the population" (Wade, 1997, p. 32). Like the majority of the Southern Cone, Chile's imitation of western models of modernisation and state building subscribed to the notion of being a country "without Indians" (Mitnick, 2004). European presence became the masqueraded feature of countries such as Argentina, Uruguay, and Chile, whilst indigenous presence, albeit less prominent than in high-land regions, was marginalised, excluded, and in some cases eliminated (Maybury-Lewis, 1991; Schneider, 2004). Yet whilst most creole elites expected the Indians of Latin America to disappear through assimila-tion and ethnonational citizenship regimes, the 1980s and 1990s dem-onstrated that, much like the melting pot theory of North America, this never happened (Bengoa, 2000; Stavenhagen, 2002). Instead, indigenous peoples have used platforms to voice new meanings to what it means to identify as such, asserting claims to collective rights (see Canessa, 2006). The historical context of colonialism throughout Latin America there-fore directs us to a politics of difference founded upon discrepant power relations, which undermine any attempt to "interpret culture from the standpoint of tradition or continuity over time" (Urban & Sherzer, 1991, p. 3). Like other countries in the southern hemisphere, Mapuche past and present must be understood in its hybrid and contested relation-ship to the nation state, its institutions, and dialectics that compete for autonomous spaces of difference.

It is therefore important, as De la Cadena and Stern (2007) argue, to move away from unilateral definitions and presuppositions about the condition of indigenous people's day-to-day lives, since,

> although poverty, discrimination and second-class citizenship very often shape indigenous lives today, notable exceptions also undercut any simple association of indigeneity with misery and marginaliza-tion – and the status of indigenous peoples as objects of sometimes condescending pity.
>
> (De la Cadena & Stern, 2007, p. 2)

Canessa (2006) argues that the different contextual meanings of indigeneity across multiple scales and sites need to be taken into account. Speaking an indigenous language in the city, he exemplifies, carries a very different status to doing so in rural areas. Urban areas have been "important cauldrons of growth for indigenous intellectuals," and spaces in which young adults attend universities, work for government agencies and NGOs (Postero & Zamosc, 2004, p. 15). This also marks an important rupture from previously dichotomous stereotypes between a non-indigenous modern urbanism and indigenous traditional rurality (Bengoa, 2000).

Mestizaje remains a locus of ambiguity and ambivalence surrounding indigenous identity and politics (Canessa, 2006; Postero & Zamosc, 2004). In many Latin American countries, definitions of indigeneity are complex due to three-tier social stratification hierarchies which exist between whites, mestizos, and Indians (sometimes termed differently in their respective countries). De la Cadena (2001) proposes that mestizaje disrupts phenotypical classifications but replaces them with an emphasis on intelligence, education, morality, and culture; something akin to the new racism perspective outlined in the introduction. Wade argues something similar:

> Mestizaje, while it appears to erase origins and primordial categories of race and culture, actually continually reconstructs them. It depends on the idea of original or parent races and cultures to constitute the very possibility of mixture.
>
> (2004, p. 356)

How people define themselves within existing Latin American racialised categories has been a matter of interest during the last decades. Studies examining national censuses have shown changing definitions and fluctuating affiliations to different types of category that take on different importance according to local context (Telles et al., 2014). There are a plethora of features and traits around which people can self-identify, whether indigenous language, mixed heritage (*mestizaje*), the mobilisation of political indigenous rights, affirmative action policies, skin colour and other phenotypical features, family name, shared history, or claims to land. Ethnic identification in Latin American states, then, is open to multiple "options" and in many cases holds a close relationship to socioeconomic status (Telles, 2004). Yet, simultaneously, power relations remain firmly founded upon national ideals of Europeanness and its associated values of modernity, rationalism, technology, and democracy. Since degrees of whiteness are socially produced in relation to particular political histories, racial categories of whiteness, indigeneity, and mestizo-ness also result in similar patterns of social hierarchy, wealth, privilege, and status (Telles & Flores, 2013).

Mapuche Youth Identities

Given what has been outlined above, it will be already apparent that indigenous identity formation, for Mapuche youth, is an open-ended, fluid, and nebulous issue. It cannot depend solely on the "ethnic options" selected by these social actors, or only on the types of identity that can be imagined or negotiated. Categories and asymmetries imposed from outside, as well as the broader sociohistorical and political contexts of indigenous-state relations in their local area, are also relevant and very real in people's lived experiences. For this reason, in an era of new racism, in which educational opportunity and racial egalitarianism are emphasised (Bonilla-Silva, 2006), it is important to know how young people make sense of, and talk about, racial categories of difference (Pollock, 2005).

Below I provide a broad strokes introduction to some of the key tenets and principal issues that arose from discussions with participants about their indigenous identities. I present how self-identified Mapuche youth talk about indigenous classifications of belonging, and why they identify this way. All conversations took place in schools, but in this chapter I refrain from discussing these identities in relation to racialised schooling experiences (the subject of Chapter 3). This notwithstanding, the young people's narratives also make it clear that their interactions with one another in school, including peer victimisation, are constant sources of tension that influence how these identities are modified through time. Crucially, however, the young people do not shirk away from the complexities of racial taxonomies, but rather this chapter will show how they embrace its internal complexities.

Identities do not float freely in the air, but are negotiated and striven for within the pre-existing norms and rules of interaction of the social contexts in which they take place. Whilst there is undoubtedly space afforded to individuals to be creative within identities, they must be legitimated and accepted by all those located in and around the social boundary, and within both interaction and institutional orders (Jenkins, 1996). This is how nominal identity is established; stating that "I am Mapuche," marks a clear boundary of common affiliation to a specific community, and distinguishes itself from others, even though what one Mapuche person may understand by "being Mapuche" could differ from what others in the same community hold it to be. Although virtual identity, the lived experience of "becoming Mapuche," may vary (perhaps even greatly in some cases), providing that symbolically significant behaviour or language is presented for others to see and hear, nominal identity will remain intact (Jenkins, 1996).

I am not attempting to state what the young people's identities (objectively) "really" are, or what causes them to be such, rather I am interested in the narratives that participants use to make sense of the world around them and their identities within it. Following authors who stress the importance of "race talk" (Pollock, 2005), and everyday meanings that people attribute to ethnicity (Brubaker et al., 2006), I present how the Mapuche youth discursively constructed ideas about their indigenous status and their classifications of other indigenous and non-indigenous peers around them. In particular, I emphasise how they construct an identity that is sufficiently inclusive to encompass *mestizaje* and national Chileanness, whilst separating themselves from non-indigenous or white identities by drawing on cultural or physical traits, surname, claims to bloodline or ancestry, place of residence, or state-authorised documentation.

This narrative encapsulates the problem of mutual recognition and simultaneous differentiation; that is, everyday life of ethnic boundary maintenance (Wimmer, 2013). Although I subscribe to a constructionist and situationist approach to understanding indigenous identity, and ethnic options more generally, I was inquisitive about how ethnic boundaries are maintained. That is, whether individuals perceive the criteria of belonging to their indigenous communities as something fixed and permanent, or as transient and changeable. Bendle has observed a "crisis of identity theory" within the social sciences (and beyond) "between a valuing of identity as something fundamental that it is crucial to personal well-being ... and a theorisation of 'identity' that sees it as something constructed, fluid, multiple, impermanent and fragmentary" (2002, p. 2). He argues that despite the surging popularity of the term "identity" during the 1980s and 1990s, the original sense of the term as a "subsisting self-sameness" (2002, p. 6) has been altogether excluded from these models. I therefore take issue with excessive versions of identity constructivism which "reject[s] the notion of a core altogether and see[s] identity as entirely a product of discourse and as inherently fragmented, multiple and transient" (Bendle, 2002, p. 5; Callero, 2003). Like Brubaker and Cooper, I suggest that this "clichéd constructionism" literature is now so expansive that "one reads (and writes) them virtually automatically. They risk becoming mere place-holders, gestures signalling a stance rather than words conveying meaning" (2000, p. 11).

Instead, I focus on ethnic identity as a contested boundary in which individuals seek to establish stable and enduring senses of belonging, despite internalised claims to individualism and distinctiveness. It will later become clear that this willingness to confront the complexities of racial taxonomies in Chile enables many of the young Mapuche to resist new racism in schools. While some students align to the oversimplified individualistic and universal egalitarianism that staff voice as part of a new racism paradigm, others are able to see through and critique the cultural racism that schools reproduce.

Whilst it is evident that class and gender identities cut across ethnic ones and that both are relevant to the young people's biographies and narratives, this research prioritises the latter. Following Bucholtz (2011),

I believe there is analytical value in addressing component sections of youth identities separately – despite them acting dependently and often simultaneously – because this draws out the distinctive features of ethnicity and the positionalities that it allows young people to take up.

By conducting the interviews and focus groups in schools, students were clustered together from similar socioeconomic backgrounds. All but two of the schools have enrolments from the bottom two quintiles (measured by the school's vulnerability index). Hence although I do not discuss social class directly, many of the meanings that the young people attribute to being Mapuche interconnect with histories of poverty. In particular, many have been brought up in homes that reiterate generational changes and new opportunities in Chile. Many of the focus groups were filled with narrated episodes about their parents walking to school without shoes, or having only one book at home, and an overwhelming majority of the participants are the first from their families on course to complete secondary school.

Regarding the significance of gender in the research, Mapuche women are doubly marginalised on individual and institutional levels as a consequence of misogyny, chauvinism (machismo), and being Indigenous. On the other hand, the prominent role of the *machi* (shamans who are usually female) in both local and national politics, and surges of female Mapuche activism in recent years suggest that their positionality is not altogether fixed (Bacigalupo, 2004; Richards, 2003, 2005). The public representation of female Mapuche is therefore somewhat different from other indigenous groups in Latin America. Mapuche women are not, on the whole, considered the guardians of folk culture, language, or traditional dress to the same extent as in countries such as Bolivia, since men are equally active in maintaining these (wherever they are indeed maintained). Given the complexities and the dynamism of Mapuche gendered roles, I was particularly interested to know whether there would be differences in indigenous self-identification in my research. I did not question the students directly about this, but after analysing male and female responses to questions I did not find any meaningful differences. I have ensured that this is reflected in the results by purposively selecting responses from both male and female participants for each theme discussed. I nonetheless wish to emphasise that research specifically focused on the issue of gendered self-identification among Mapuche youth would be capable of going much further in exploring different role expectations, language tendencies, stereotypes, future expectations for future marriage and work, and so forth.

Other authors (Mapuche and non-Mapuche) have written about the identity construction process among young Mapuche (Carihuentro, 2007; Briones, 2007; Oteíza & Merino, 2012; Terwindt, 2009). This research shows the resourcefulness of Mapuche youth in constructing flexible contemporary identities, especially through virtual media and artistic expression for the purposes of political mobilisation. Mapuche heavy rock, hip-hop, and punk (called "Mapunky") groups incorporate a fusion between traditional and world music to express both their disaffected frustrations and anger at the sociopolitical situations they face (Briones, 2007). Other examples of poetry, art and graffiti, and social media networks are also common (Bengoa & Caniguan, 2011; Salazar & Cordova, 2008). Many are challenging the notion of the "real Indian" by de-essentialising traditional and normative categories and practices of belonging (Terwindt, 2009). This is expressly the case among the Mapurbe – urban residents – who find new ways of linking their daily lives in cities to the *mapu* (meaning land, which traditionally meant rural territories). Another study offers more banal and everyday explorations of Mapuche youth identities that reveal the importance of the normalisation of Chilean-Mapuche hybridity and downplaying experiences of discrimination (Oteíza & Merino, 2012). I see my research as complementary to these existing studies, since there is a clear need to situate these identity processes within institutional settings because so much of young people's time is spent in schools.

I draw mostly on data gathered during two separate studies in which students were asked directly about their indigenous identification in focus group conversations. The combined total of participants from both studies was 219 students (all names are pseudonyms) from seven schools.[1]

Talking about External Differentiation

The discussions below refer to interviewer-led questions about why the students had marked down that they self-identified as Mapuche, Chilean-Mapuche, or Mapuche-Chilean. Specifically, I asked about what made them different from non-indigenous Chileans. By far the most common answer offered by the young people was having a Mapuche surname. This marker of external differentiation is more complex than might first appear since in traditional Mapuche culture, surnames are highly valued due to their specific symbolic and identificatory significance. That is, surnames express a connection to the natural surroundings of the family's land as well as identifying the region or area from which the family originated (Carihuentro, 2007). Three examples from students who recognised this meaningful content when asked why they identified as Mapuche are provided below:

GASTÓN: "Our surname represents something which was of old, all our surnames, as mapuche, has something, I mean, that links us with nature or a typical animal from that region." (10th grade, Nacional School)

DIEGO: "The names of places or surnames of some people have meaning in mapuzungún, the sea, the heavens, so when a person dies he returns to the meaning, for example, Huenulaf could go to the heavens, things like that." (8th grade, Lihuén School)

XIMENA: "Because almost all Mapuche have surnames which represent something, like a 'hueche'; a new person, everything with a language like that." (8th grade, Tres Montes School)

Mapuche surnames connect individuals to a life force in an intimate union which, in traditional Mapuche spiritual belief, is a sacred "marriage" between man and land (*mapu*) (Sierra, 2000). Students who knew the meaning of their surnames were those who had been brought up speaking *mapuzungún*, or who had been brought up to value their family history. *Kupal* has traditionally had a prominent place in the Mapuche conceptualisation of both the being and becoming of personhood; in many ways it expresses the essentialised characteristics of descent, whilst in others it expresses behavioural and locational similarity to one's ancestors (Course, 2011; Ortiz, 2009). According to Carihuentro (2007), it refers to both an external identification (physical attributes) and an internal identification (psychological and spiritual), both transmitted via inheritance. Recognition of oneself as a Mapuche by virtue of one's surname is not therefore necessarily synonymous with a psychological and spiritual identification with one's own people and land. The latter requires individuals to be socialised into the culture so as to affiliate not only with their parents, but also with their people and their interests as a socially distinct group.

Mateo distinguished himself from many of the other students in his school by declaring that he had been brought up "in line with our culture." He had a very clear sense of his identity as coming from his ancestors and the land which they inhabited, as well as being conscious of the distinction between Mapuche culture and that of foreigners:

"I am a young Mapuche because I'm from here, from the Mapuche territory, as the Mapuche say, people of the earth, we are from here, we are not foreigners or westerners who came to invade us, so that's why we are Mapuche. We have a different culture."

(11th grade, Nacional School)

The student's emphasis on a group affiliation; an "us," marked out a boundary of belonging to both the land and his ancestors. This was notably absent in many students' conversations, who tended to speak of the Mapuche in the third person "they." During a focus group, Mateo suggested that having a Mapuche surname was not a sufficient expression of "Mapucheness" and challenged the definitions of his peers who claimed that this was the extent of their affiliation:

"They are Mapuche and they have no idea what it is to be Mapuche like us. How many have Mapuche surnames and have no idea how to carry out a ceremony like we have in the culture, or how long have they been living on those lands? A young person who has a Mapuche surname and you ask them who they are or what culture they belong to ... they can only tell you they are Mapuche."

Students in other schools made similar comments, claiming that indigenous identity requires a process of acquiring knowledge about one's roots and that a personal formation in cultural spheres of Mapuche communities was a requisite for a strong identity:

DAMIÁN: "[other students' indigenous identity] is weaker, I think, because they don't know where they are from, they don't know their roots, it's as if they don't know who their grandparents are. They are Mapuche, but in truth they won't feel Mapuche because they don't have any knowledge about the culture. Their identity is weaker; it's easier for it to break." (9th grade, Lihuén School)

Perhaps the most interesting thing about these young people's assertions is the implication of assimilation. In Mateo and these other students' narratives, the boundary between Mapuche and non-Mapuche is one that requires knowledge and cultural commitment. These students draw attention to the variety of socialisation practices and declining use of *mapuzungún* in their peers' homes as a means of questioning how authentic their identities are. However, as argued by St. Denis (2007), there is a danger of reducing indigenous identities to culturally fundamentalist prescriptions of behaviour that reinforce very static and monolithic forms of belonging. There is a fine balance between Mateo's legitimate frustrations about the loss of culture, and a rigid essentialising of identities. St. Denis proposes that cultural revitalisation can be divisive, by blaming individuals for their lack of cultural know-how, rather than critically understanding these processes as the outcomes of colonial histories.

For most students, their surname signifies otherness, but this is less clearly associated with a meaningful relationship to nature or their ancestor's territory. Instead, many of the young people articulated their surname as a reference to a "natural kind" of social category premised on shared essence of blood or biological ties. I cite participants from five different schools to show how common this type of response was:

INTERVIEWER: "Do you identify yourselves as Mapuche?"
EMILIA: "Not much in the social."
INTERVIEWER: "What do you mean by in the social?"

EMILIA: "I mean we don't distinguish ourselves from other [Chilean] people, so in the social, no, only in terms of the name and surname." (9th grade, Campaña School)

INTERVIEWER: "What makes the difference between a *winka* (non-Mapuche) and a Mapuche?"

MARCO: "The surname."

ANA: "Yes, the surname."

PAOLA: "Because of the surname, almost all who are Mapuche have a surname that represents something like a *hueche* – a new person, all with a language like that." (7th grade, Tres Montes School)

DANI: "I can have things, for example, a mobile phone, but I still continue to be conscious that I continue to be Mapuche, culture is preserved (*se conserva*) in the blood." (9th grade, Lihuén School)

INTERVIEWER: "Is it necessary to know much about Mapuche culture in order to be able to say that one is Mapuche?"

TOMÁS: "I think the surname is enough." (7th grade, Campaña School)

LORENA: "The Mapuche will never be lost, because blood is transmitted; from one generation to the next it will continue." (11th grade, Nacional School)

JAVIER: "Nobody can take out the Mapuche from within; the spirit (*espiritu*) of the Mapuche will never disappear. Even if you are brought up *winka*, nobody can remove the Mapuche (*sacarte lo Mapuche*); there will always be something there within." (10th grade, Campaña School)

BAYRON: "It's easier to tell if someone is Mapuche by their surname. If they are pure, Mapuche-Mapuche, they are dark skinned, but the mestizos are paler so it's harder to tell." (12th grade, Campos Verdes School)

The most central and significant issue that these narratives raise is that surnames act as an external marker of differentiation from non-Mapuche, establishing a clear boundary between an "us" and "them." For some, their identification as Mapuche draws on common-sense understandings of belonging through ethnobiological ties, especially in the absence of behavioural traits, shared values, or language. For some of these individuals, being Mapuche appears to be a racially ascribed and given (primordial) identity. In these instances, students seem to reproduce racialised oversimplifications of belonging. That is, there is recognition of the difficulties surrounding phenotype, and also upbringing that might not reflect a clear category of belonging, as Bayron and Javier allude to, but regardless of these elements, blood ties ensure one's place in the racial taxonomy is established. The notion that "culture is conserved in the blood," for example, indicates a belief that there is something genetically inherent, rather than social, about the way the Mapuche act. Surnames carry a permanence that ensures they will be recognised as such amidst other fluctuating criteria.

However, as I demonstrate below, this does not prevent the young people from modifying, negotiating, and working out the broader implications of such an identity in multifarious and dynamic ways which are appealing to their personal identity and life expectations (Gil-White, 2001). That is, race talk among the young people rarely plays by rigid or set rules.

Talking about Internal Differentiation

One of the main mechanisms by which internal hierarchies of being Mapuche are established were three terms used to distinguish different racial categories or statuses: *winka*, *Mapuchon*, and *champurria*. According to the Mapuche world vision, *winka* is an extensive term to refer to all that is non-Mapuche. It was originally a hostile term used in relation to the invading Inca civilisation who reached as far as northern Chile and which was then extended to incorporate the Spanish. *Winka* referred not only to the people themselves, but to their way of life, their behaviour, and their culture. However, for the youngsters who participated in the study, the term *winka* has a much more restricted usage, to individuals with no Mapuche surnames:

SIMÓN: "Well, the winka is whoever isn't Mapuche; without the surname."
INTERVIEWER: "Is it just because of the surname?"
ISABEL: "Yes, the surname."
SIMÓN: "Like Flores Flores." (9th grade, Campos Verdes School)

This is significant because it highlights the fused identities and blurred boundaries that the youngsters experience in their everyday lives, regarding Mapuche and Chilean culture. The participants did not consider Chilean culture to be separate from their own, and restricted the application of the term *winka* to notions of race and bloodline. The meaning of *winka* has therefore become increasingly restrictive so as to legitimate the adoption of non-Mapuche culture due to the declining practice of traditions. I also heard its antonym mentioned, *Mapuchon*. This was used as a term of racial "purity," meaning someone with two Mapuche surnames:

LESLIE: "When a person is very Mapuche."
CRISTIÁN: "Of the Mapuche race."
FRANCISCA: "Mapuche Mapuche."
LESLIE: "When all their family is Mapuche." (7th grade, Tres Montes School)
JAIME: "The thing is that there are virtually none left, the pure *Mapuchon*, there are only really some of our grandparents, and all the rest of us are mixed." (10th grade, Campos Verdes School)

This was contrasted by those students with only one Mapuche surname, who were labelled *champurria*, or as one student joked, "cider with water" (a diluted form). What was most revealing about the use of this term, was that, although it was applied in relation to racial mixture, it was assumed by the students that this had cultural effects such as "not being able to pronounce *mapuzungún* words properly," dressing more like a *winka*, wearing "decent shoes," and having "fancy hairstyles." To some degree, one's racial heritage was seen to influence or determine one's cultural tendencies as well as one's socioeconomic status. One student suggested those who are *champurria* tend to esteem themselves as better than "pure" Mapuche: "they think they're superior to us because they are mixed" (Evelyn, 9th grade, Nacional School).

Internal categorising plays a role in boundary maintenance in these young people's social relations in schools. In each case, the students insisted that the names given to each other were neither derogatory nor discriminatory; rather they were terms used for raillery. Nevertheless, it does set a precedent or norm by which internal identifications are measured as well as revealing ideas about racial mixing and how it was considered to limit or determine one's identity. There are no racists here, only a normative context in which complex ideas about race continue to be coded and utilised in day-to-day encounters.

"Race talk," due to miscegenation between Mapuche and non-indigenous in Chile, is difficult. It cannot be based singularly on physical attributes to distinguish individuals with mixed-race parents (champurria) from certain sections of the "non-indigenous" population. Pollock (2005) found a similar tension among the young participants from her study in the US surrounding belonging to "simple race groups." Students frequently utilised racial taxonomies to categorise others, but at the same time resisted being categorised in simplistic terms, resulting in what Pollock describes as "limitless complexity and pointed simplification" (2005, p. 40). Similarly in my case study, three students pointed out that there are very few concrete ways to identify "racial" differences:

ERNA: "In truth, all Chileans carry some Mapuche blood, even if they don't consider themselves to be Mapuche or don't have a surname they are still Mapuche." (8th grade, Mapocho School)

HENRY: "If you look at past culture, we're all mixed, no-one is a pure Chilean, even if they have two Chilean surnames and say they are pure, but their ancestors, they'd all be a mix and everyone has some indigenous blood, but people reject that and think they are superior because they have two Chilean surnames." (9th grade, Tres Montes School)

JAVI: "There's not much physical difference, in the face, because some people are Mapuche and look really white." (11th grade, Raimilla School)

This could plausibly explain why surname has come to be such an important identificatory device in who is Mapuche. Being *champurria* is an ambiguous category which requires a more complex process of identity management than those who are labelled *Mapuchon*. It is therefore consistent that the meaning of *winka* should be restricted, since it is no longer a useful categorisation of external differences from non-Mapuche because many Mapuche adopt similar behavioural traits. *Champurria* expands the identity boundary to account for this cultural assimilation (however partial). These linguistic devices function as important internal boundaries for the Mapuche youth to ease tensions surrounding racial purity and also as a legitimating device for differing levels of cultural practice. Being *champurria*, for example, means social expectations are lowered regarding one's cultural affiliations since it is assumed one will be influenced by Chilean ways of life, yet without compromising one's social acceptance as a nominal Mapuche. This provides an important degree of personal freedom for expressing the meaning of being and becoming Mapuche, which the students themselves were evidently conscious of:

SIMÓN: "Well, supposing a family has one Mapuche surname and another which is winka, I think that the desire to identify oneself as Mapuche or as winka will depend on the family; I think it will depend on their way of life and the interests that they have." (8th grade, Lihuén School)

Feeling Mapuche

Another aspect of discursively constructed indigenous identity was the replacement of external practices by internalised, private, and personalised feelings. Some students chose to emphasise that what made them Mapuche was the psychological acceptance of such a label and the ensuing emotional state provoked by this. This was most frequently drawn on when asked about participation in Mapuche religious rituals (*we tripantu* or *ngillatún*), or their linguistic competence with *mapzungún*. Shifting the emphasis away from *doing culture*, these individuals make indigenous identification a matter of tacit, latent, and intangible feelings:

SANDRA: "It's not about talking but about doing, you participate, even though everyone's involved in one thing and in the end it just happens by itself; you don't talk about the culture but rather you do what you have to do in certain religious activities." (9th grade, Lihuén School)
VICTOR: "I don't believe being Mapuche can be about surname or dressing like a Mapuche or knowing how to speak Mapuche, because for my part I do have the surname but I don't speak it and don't dress like Mapuche, but I do feel Mapuche and because of that feeling, I believe I am Mapuche." (10th grade, Raimilla School)

HUGO: "If one feels Mapuche that's enough, whether one knows how to speak Mapuche or not is just details."

INTERVIEWER: "Do you all agree with Hugo?"

JASMINE: "I do."

BRYAN: "I don't, because the Mapuche always have to show that they are who they say they are." (Focus group, 10th grade, Lihuén School)

This was a sensitive issue and a degree of negotiation took place among the discussants in order to neutralise certain contention. Students from every one of the participating schools had different ways of redefining or refocusing the central meaning of becoming Mapuche by emphasising a more pluralistic and incongruous way of being, such as "it's what one feels," "carrying one's Mapucheness within," "the way one tolerates certain things," "holding one's head up high,", and "not denying oneself."

Given the ambiguity surrounding the many meanings which can be attached to their indigenous identity, these Mapuche youths' narratives are indicative of how self-made definitions are adhered to. For some students then, expressing oneself through the traditional ceremonies and rituals is how one feels most Mapuche, but for others, whose lives are increasingly taken up by different activities and lifestyles, the nucleus of their identity is increasingly internalised and felt, rather than acted out. In one case, participants even acknowledged that non-Mapuche peers and teachers, who participated in intercultural events at the school, could also feel Mapuche; though they were emphatic that this did not alter the external boundary of belonging:

HENRY: "Even though they [students] aren't Mapuche, they feel it, and they participate as if they were."

MÓNICA: "Yes, even the teachers who aren't Mapuche also feel Mapuche, even though they don't have Mapuche blood, but they feel it by taking part." (12th grade, Lihuén School)

Eileen, a student at the Lihuén School confirmed this first-hand. She requested to participate in the focus group activity to which some of her classmates had been invited. Despite not having a Mapuche surname she claimed that by attending the school and learning about the culture, she had, in certain ways, come to identify herself as being Mapuche. This boundary-crossing shows how fluctuating and contextually defined Mapuche identity can be. Literature based on everyday ethnicity confirms that temporary instances of becoming experientially ethnic without being nominally so are plausible among certain groups (Brubaker et al., 2006). Among the participants there was no sense of the external boundary of belonging being altered by Eileen's affirmation, but in the contexts of intercultural practices carried out by the school, some degree of momentary inclusion is open to those non-Mapuche who show respect and choose to take part. The crucial issue here is that schools may be one of the few spaces in which this can occur, yet few of the schools from my research achieved this level of inclusion. As will be discussed in greater depth in the next chapter, Intercultural Bilingual Education (IBE) programmes have played an important role in opening up spaces for indigenous knowledges, and fostering indigenous identity, but are also prone to additive measures that can marginalise these identities.

The Lihuén School also fostered a "feeling" of being Mapuche for two students who had been brought up in homes that had lost most traditional cultural practices. These students described their experience as a process of awakening to their cultural, indigenous, or in some cases ethnonational identity as Mapuche:

JOHANNA: "For example in my case the school has been important, because it has taught me to see the world or society from a different point of view."
YERKO: "In my case it's been really useful for me, because I have come to value the culture, to recover different things which for me were not that special, but now I've realized that for others they are ... you could say, invaluable riches, but which are preserved in us alone, like being born anew, it's like they make us live things which others don't know about." (Focus group, 9th grade, Lihuén School)

This feeling of being Mapuche is directly connected to an additional boundary of difference between the Mapuche and Chileans, belonging to a morally superior community. Internalised differentiation is common where outward traits coincide between two social groupings (Elias & Scotson, 1994; Wimmer, 2013). Students referred to feelings of pride about being Mapuche because the community uphold certain principles of respect and solidarity, which they believed to be absent in non-indigenous settings:

JUAN: "Those who think they're pure Chileans try to discriminate against us, because they see us as being inferior, but we never do that, we treat all people as equal independent of their colour, race, or whatever, we treat all the same because we're all brothers (*peñis*)." (12th grade, Raimilla School)
BERNARDO: "The non-Mapuche (*winka*) don't care what happens to other people, but the Mapuche on the other hand are ... because traditions says that the ancestors always helped one another .... Humility. That will never disappear, because for generations humility has been maintained, conforming to what one has, that's the most important factor [about being Mapuche]; the communion between the people and the humility because that's the most valuable thing the Mapuche have." (11th grade, Campaña School)

STEPHANNIE: "The Mapuche respect their culture, but Chileans aren't bothered about that."

CAMILA: "The Mapuche preserve the things they do and respect nature." (Focus group, 10th grade, Lago Profundo)

Most students were not concerned about identifying as Chilean in regard to their nationality, or in reference to their day-to-day activities and lifestyles (see below). However, in regard to moral characteristics such as generosity, sociability, and kindness, the Mapuche participants almost unanimously described the Mapuche as superior. Being Chilean, in this regard, is connected to a colonial history, and continued practices of affecting indigenous lands:

ALONSO: "I can say I'm Mapuche and Chilean because the surname Mardones is a Chilean name, and I feel it [Chilean] but I'm also clear about this, I mean, who invaded who? I think that's clear." (12th grade, Campos Verdes)

FRANCISCA: "The Mapuche have something special; they aren't like the Chileans who destroy everything. If they need to destroy a field [to build on] they just do it whereas the Mapuche are more noble. The Chileans just take over everything." (11th grade, Raimilla School)

Despite changes within many Mapuche families in reference to more traditional socialisation and cultural practices, affiliations to the family and resultant ties remain extremely strong (see Course, 2011; Ortiz, 2009). While cultural practices may be declining from generation to generation, social values are still highly esteemed, adhered to, and are becoming increasingly important markers of difference for the internal identification of the group.

Being Chilean and Mapuche

Scholarly literature has indicated that ethnic identities and loyalties sometimes conflict with nationality, particularly in multi-ethnic states with assimilatory tendencies. In these instances, devotion to the nation may require a rejection, or putting aside the priorities, of ethnic minority interests (Kymlicka, 1995). However, other instances such as discrimination may make internal ties much closer, and boundaries between groups much stronger. Although the majority of participants self-identified as Chilean and Mapuche, when asked directly whether the students felt an affinity with their national identity, responses were mixed. Some considered that being Mapuche was almost synonymous with being Chilean, with the exception of having a different surname:

ANGELA: "Even though we're Mapuche we're still Chileans, and I don't think we need to be ashamed of being Chilean either." (10th grade, Lihuén School)

HELGA: "I couldn't say I'm not Chilean, having been born in this country and brought up here. Maybe my surname is different to the rest, but I'm Chilean all the same." (8th grade, Campos Verdes School)

SEBASTIÁN: "I think that the [Mapuche] customs are very different, but I think that we are all the same because we were born here."

EDGAR: "Still, we've [Mapuche] kept changing or acquiring another culture." (Campos Verdes School)

Upon pursuing this matter further, I asked about whether there was any incompatibility for indigenous youth to celebrate national holidays, particularly Independence day (given the Chilean republic's invasion of indigenous territories shortly after), and whether modern lifestyles conflicted in any way with the meaning of being Mapuche. In response to the first question, some students replied that the Mapuche New year (*we tripantu*) was more significant, whilst a larger proportion claimed there was no contradiction:

JUAN: "I don't see much sense in celebrating the 18th September, even though I'm Chilean I think the *we tripantu* is more important." (12th grade, Raimilla School)

MATÍAS: "Yes, it's [independence celebration] still important because we're with our family, we share, we dance cueca (traditional Chilean dance) it's fun and it's important because we feel part of Chile." (10th grade, Campos Verdes School)

In most areas of their daily activities, the students suggested that they were not at odds with Chilean culture, especially since much of its content corresponds to components that are attractive to young people, as these students pointed out:

EDUARDO: "Yes there is a difference, but always from the Mapuche point of view. I mean, we are always similar to other people in [our desire for] internet and television, but there are always differences when one speaks about their Mapuche culture, and they have a different point of view."

MICHELA: "Like any youngsters that's what we want; fun, to have a good time, instead of sitting down and talking with our parents, which might be both naturally and spiritually good for us, but we don't go down that route and as youngsters we prefer to watch television or see an important soap opera that's on or listen to music; that's technology."

VALENTINA: Some people may feel different because they speak Mapuche [*mapuzungún*] or dress traditionally but I don't share those things so I don't find myself too different to [non-indigenous] Chileans. (10th grade, Lago Profundo School)

In general, it is not necessary for these young people to construct boundaries or social markers of difference because the lived experience of being Mapuche is not sufficiently at odds with being Chilean to warrant them. Rather, the nominal label of Mapuche is sufficient as an in-group identifier, to identify the students with their family or community, without requiring outward behaviour that distinguishes them from their non-Mapuche peers. However, this choice is not altogether of their own making. Most students recognised the power and status asymmetries between being indigenous and non-indigenous, and the stigma attached to indigeneity, leading a limited number of students to try to hide their indigeneity:

SANTIAGO: "It's hard to say one is Mapuche. It's not just like you come out with it so easily and you just identify yourself that way, because it can be embarrassing, and can make you scared what others will say." (12th grade, Lihuén School)

Generally though, perhaps owing to the focus group format, students were reluctant to admit to personally "opting out" of their ethnic identity. Instead, more participants acknowledged this as a general practice among other indigenous students, claiming that they knew of others who prefer to "pass" as Chilean:

LUIS: "They act all ignorant if they do know (about their status as Mapuche), they hide their personality and pretend to be another person which is really sad and I've seen that happen to my course mates; I've seen them because people make fun of them, and then they says 'ah no, I'm not Mapuche'." (10th grade, Campaña School)

BEATRIZ: "There are those of us who feel proud to be Mapuche."

JOANNA: "That's right."

BEATRIZ: "On my part I feel really proud to carry my Mapuche surname, but there are other kids who are ashamed, as if saying 'no, no, I'm not Mapuche.'" (Campos Verdes School)

CLAUDIA: "Some people have surnames that are sort of Mapuche, sort of weird, and people who don't have [indigenous] surnames like that laugh at them, so those who are Mapuche, we feel kind of discriminated against and that's why young people are losing their identity." (10th grade, Tres Montes)

Discrimination comprises an explicit part of Mapuche youth identity which is both present and consciously perceived within their lifeworlds.

This was a topic that was raised by the students themselves in virtually every focus group and many interviews without prompting. That is, it is a central aspect of the tension between the structural effects of being Mapuche in a racialised sociohistoric context and the ethnic options that are provided by the ambivalence of mestizaje and hybrid forms of becoming. For this reason, it is an issue that I return to in Chapter 3.

Forming a Sense of Belonging

This initial outline of Mapuche youth identity shows the deeply complex, multiple, and fluctuating ideas about belonging. I have provided evidence of heterogeneous forms and expressions of Mapuche identity among the young people with a view to avoiding any type of dichotomous hierarchy between "traditional" and "assimilated" identities which tend to celebrate the former and denigrate the latter (St. Denis, 2007). As Wimmer (2013) observes, boundaries rarely remain static but are constantly negotiated and shifted, whether through expansion (the inclusion of new categories), contraction (lumping different cultural groups under one term), re-positioning (individuals who change their hierarchical position in regard to the boundary), or blurring (an emphasis on non-ethnic criteria that undermine racial criteria). The young people who participated in the research demonstrate some of these tendencies, and articulate Mapuche identity in varied and complex ways.

Focus groups are an excellent technique for addressing socially shared meanings, and many of the extracts presented here show how everyday life in shared spaces such as schools become relevant to this process of boundary maintenance. The young people compare themselves to other peers, and make comments about their identities and the social legitimacy of those affiliations. They also demonstrate how tensions are managed surrounding a lack of external markers (such as phenotype, linguistic competence, or cultural activities) by internalising Mapuche identity as something felt or something expressed as moral values.

Perhaps most important of all are surnames as biological cues that maintain differences from "non-Mapuche" others. Although many of the individuals understand their indigenous identity in relatively static ways – as an ancestral inheritance marked out through surname – they nonetheless act in ways which maximise acceptance into both national and indigenous milieux (with varying levels of commitment) as well as allowing for the expression of individuality. This carefully achieved equilibrium of optimum differentiation (Brewer, 1991) suggests the young people understand the different social expectations and roles attributed to being Mapuche-Chileans, as a hyphenated identity, growing up in an increasingly interconnected and globalised world. Many of the narratives suggest the students navigate somewhere in between these two worlds (Luna, 2007).

However, Wimmer (2013) also argues that individual actors are not entirely free to make decisions about which strategies to adopt, since boundaries exist within structurally pre-defined circumstances and constraints. In particular, boundaries of difference are historically situated in institutional settings that define power relationships and politics. Actors are only able to make "decisions" about their self-identifications premised on the conditions produced by institutional peculiarities. Returning to Omi and Winant's work on racial formation, identities are always caught up in broader racial projects that define who one can be. In this regard, the remainder of the book addresses the specific part that schools play in limiting the types of identity that are produced through everyday institutional life. New racism ensures that, despite attending higher-than-average indigenous composition schools, which are often underfunded establishments with below-average achievement, racism and inequality are rarely topics that are directly addressed across the schooling experience in relation to indigeneity. Indeed, many of the young people who participated in the research expressed surprise and, on occasion, consternation about why I would ask them questions of this nature.

If navigating these racial taxonomies and achieving acceptance and self-identification as Mapuche are such slippery and vacillating issues among the young people interviewed, then it stands to reason that the ways schools approach matters of discrimination and indigeneity will be influential in how the young people resolve or develop their identities, and how they experience these educational environments. In an era of new racism, there are few explicitly negative or bigoted associations with being Mapuche. In fact, indigenous grants and IBE programmes suggest the opposite. However, as I will detail over the coming chapters, structural and racialised inequalities continue to operate in these environments, in which there is a general reluctance to address these complex issues head on. At the very least, the young people display a willingness to destabilise racial taxonomies (Pollock, 2005). Yet identifying the racial projects in which they are located and interrupting the half-truths of neoliberal Chilean educational opportunity – as we will see – is less common among the participants, given how discreet and naturalised these forms are for those who are schooled in these contexts.

Note

1 Some of the data was previously cited in Webb (2013).

References

Anthias, F. (2001). New hybridities, old concepts: The limits of 'culture'. *Ethnic and Racial Studies*, 24(4), 619–641.

Anthias, F. (2002). Where do I belong: Narrating collective identity and translocational positionality. *Ethnicities*, 2(4), 491–514.

Bacigalupo, M.A. (2004). Shamans' pragmatic gendered negotiations with Mapuche resistance movements and Chilean political authorities. *Identities: Global Studies in Culture and Power, 11,* 501–541.

Bendle, M.F. (2002). The crisis of identity in high modernity. *British Journal of Sociology, 53*(1), 1–18.

Bengoa, J. (2000). *La emergencia indígena en América Latina.* Santiago: Fondo de Cultura Económica.

Bengoa, J., & Caniguan, N. (2011). Chile: Los Mapuches y el Bicentenario. *Cuadernos de Antropología Social, 34,* 7–28.

Billig, M. (1995). *Banal nationalism.* London: Sage.

Bonilla-Silva, E. (1997). Rethinking racism: Toward a structural interpretation. *American Sociological Review, 62*(3), 465–480.

Bonilla-Silva, E. (2006). *Racism without racists: Color-blind racism and the persistence of racial inequality in the United States* (2nd ed.). Oxford: Rowman & Littlefield Publishers.

Brewer, M. (1991). The social self: On being the same and different at the same time. *Personality and Social Psychology Bulletin, 17,* 475–482.

Briones, C. (2007). Our struggle has just begun: Experiences of belonging and Mapuche formations of self. In M. De la Cadena & O. Stern (Eds.), *Indigenous experience today.* Oxford: Berg.

Brubaker, R. (Ed.). (2004). *Ethnicity without groups.* Cambridge MA: Harvard University Press.

Brubaker, R., & Cooper, F. (2000). Beyond identity. *Culture Theory and Society, 29,* 1–47.

Brubaker, R. Feischmidt, M., Fox, J., & Grancea, L. (2006). *Nationalist politics and everyday ethnicity in a Transylvanian town.* Princeton: Princeton University Press.

Bucholtz, M. (2011). *White kids: Language, race, and styles of youth identity.* Cambridge: Cambridge University Press.

Callero, P. (2003). The sociology of the self. *Annual Review of Sociology, 29,* 115–133.

Canessa, A. (2006). Todos somos indígenas: Towards a new language of national political identity. *Bulletin of Latin American research, 25*(2), 241–263.

Carihuentro, S. (2007). *Saberes Mapuche que debiera incorporar la educación formal en contexto interetnico e intercultural según sabios Mapuche.* Masters Thesis in Education, Universidad de Chile, Santiago.

Course, M. (2011). *Becoming Mapuche: Person and ritual in indigenous Chile.* Urbana, IL: University of Illinois Press.

De La Cadena, M. (2001). Reconstructing race: Racism, culture and Mestizaje in Latin America. *NACLA Report on the Americas, 34*(6), 16–23.

De la Cadena, M & Stern, O. (Eds.). (2007). *Indigenous experience today.* Oxford: Berg.

Edensor, T. (2002). *National identity, popular culture and everyday life.* Oxford: Berg.

Eder, K., Giesen, B., Schmidtke, O., & Tambini, D. (2002). *Collective identities in action: A sociological approach to ethnicity.* Aldershot: Ashgate Publishers.

Elias, N., & Scotson, J. (1994). *The established and the outsiders: A sociological enquiry into community problems.* London: Sage.

Eriksen, T.H. (2002). *Ethnicity and nationalism: Anthropological perspectives* (2nd ed.). London: Pluto Press.

Fenton, S. (1999). *Ethnicity racism class and culture*. London: Macmillan Press.

Fenton, S. (2003). *Ethnicity*. Cambridge: Polity Press.

Gil-White, F. (2001). Are ethnic groups biological 'species' to the human brain? Essentialism in our cognition of some social categories. *Current Anthropology*, 42(4), 515–554.

Hale, H. (2004). Explaining ethnicity. *Comparative Political Studies*, 37(4), 458–485.

Hall, S. (1990). Cultural identity and diaspora. In J. Rutherford (Ed.), *Identity: Community, culture, difference*. London: Lawrence & Wishart.

Hutchinson, J., & Smith, A.D. (Eds.). (1996). *Ethnicity*. Oxford: Oxford University Press.

Jenkins, R. (1992). *Pierre Bourdieu*. London: Routledge.

Jenkins, R. (1996). *Social identity*. London: Routledge.

Jenkins, R. (1997). *Rethinking ethnicity: Arguments and explanations*. London: Sage.

Jimenez, T. (2004). Negotiating ethnic boundaries multiethnic Mexican Americans and ethnic identity in the United States. *Ethnicities*, 4(1), 75–97.

Karner, C. (2007). *Ethnicity and everyday life*. New York, NY: Routledge.

Kuper, A. (2003). The return of the native. *Current Anthropology*, 44(3), 389–395.

Kymlicka, W. (1995). *Multicultural citizenship: A liberal theory of minority rights*. Oxford: Clarendon Press.

Luna, L. (2007). *Un mundo entre dos mundos: Las relaciones entre el pueblo mapuche y el estado chileno desde la perspectiva del desarrollo y de los cambios socio-culturales*. Santiago: Ediciones UC.

Maybury-Lewis, D. (1991). Becoming Indian in lowland South America. In G. Urban & J. Sherzer (Eds.), *Nation states and Indians in Latin America*. Austin: University of Texas Press.

Mitnick, G.W. (2004). Chile: Indígenas y mestizos negados. *Política y Cultura*, 21, 97–110.

Ortiz, P.R. (2009). *Indigenous knowledge, education and ethnic identity: An ethnography of an intercultural bilingual education program in a Mapuche School in Chile*. Ann Arbor, MI: VDM Verlag.

Oteíza, T., & Merino, M. (2012). Am I a genuine Mapuche? Tensions and contradictions in the construction of ethnic identity in Mapuche adolescents from Temuco and Santiago. *Discourse & Society*, 23(3), 297–317.

Paine, R. (2000). Aboriginality, authenticity and the settler world. In A.P. Cohen (Ed.), *Signifying identities: Anthropological perspectives on boundaries and contested values*. London: Routledge.

Pollock, M. (2005). *Colormute: Race talk dilemmas in an American school*. Princeton, NJ: Princeton University Press.

Postero, N.G., & Zamosc, L. (Eds.). (2004). *The struggle for indigenous rights in Latin America*. Brighton: Sussex Academic Press.

Richards, P. (2003). Expanding women's citizenship? Mapuche women and Chile's national women's service. *Latin American Perspectives*, 30(2), 249–273.

Richards, P. (2005). The politics of gender, human rights and being indigenous in Chile. *Gender & Society*, 19(1), 199–220.

Saugestad, S. (2001). *The inconvenient indigenous. Remote area development in Botswana, donor assistance and the first people of the Kalahari*. Uppsala: Nordiska Afrikainstitutet.

Schneider, A. (2004). Rooting hybridity: Globalisation and the challenges of mestizaje and crisol de razas for contemporary artists in Ecuador and Argentina. *Indiana, 21*, 95–112.

Sierra, M. (2000). *Mapuche: Gente de la tierra. Donde todo es altar.* Santiago: Editorial Sudamericana.

Stavenhagen, R. (2002). Indigenous peoples and the state in Latin America: An ongoing debate. In R. Sieder (Ed.), *Multiculturalism in Latin America: Indigenous rights, diversity and democracy.* New York, NY: Palgrave Macmillan.

St. Denis, V. (2007). Aboriginal education and anti-racist education: Building alliances across cultural and racial identity. *Canadian Journal of Education / Revue canadienne de l'éducation, 30*(4), 1068–1092.

Telles, E. (2004). *Race in another America: The significance of skin color in Brazil.* Princeton, NJ: Princeton University Press.

Telles, E., & Flores, R. (2013). Not just color: Whiteness, nation and status in Latin America. *Hispanic American Historical Review, 93*(3), 411–449.

Telles, E., & the Project on Ethnicity and Race in Latin America. (2014). *Pigmentocracies: Ethnicity, race and color in Latin America.* Chapel Hill, NC: University of North Carolina Press.

Terwindt, C. (2009). The demands of the 'true' Mapuche: Ethnic political mobilization in the Mapuche movement. *Nationalism and ethnic politics, 15*(2), 237–257.

Urban, G., & Sherzer, J. (Eds.). (1991). *Nation states and Indians in Latin America.* Austin: University of Texas Press.

Wade, P. (1997). *Race and ethnicity in Latin America.* London: Pluto Press.

Wade, P. (2004). Human nature and race. *Anthropological Theory, 4*(2), 157–172.

Weaver, H.N. (2001). Indigenous identity: What is it, and who really has it? *American Indian Quarterly, 25*(2), 240–255.

Webb, A. (2013). Negotiating optimum distinctiveness: Cognitive tendencies toward primordialism among Mapuche youth. *Ethnic and Racial Studies, 36*(12), 2055–2074.

Wimmer, A. (2013). *Ethnic boundary making: Institutions, power, networks.* New York, NY: Oxford University Press.

Guibernau, M., & Rex, J. (Eds.). (1997). *The ethnicity reader: nationalism, multiculturalism, and migration.* Cambridge, MA: Polity.

Miles, R., & Brown, M. (2003). *Racism* (2nd ed.). London: Routledge.

Salazar, J. F., & Cordova, A. (2008). Imperfect media and the poetics of indigenous video in latin America. In P. Wilson & M. Stewart (Eds.), *Global indigenous media: Cultures, poetics, and politics* (pp. 39–57). Durham, NC: Duke University Press.

Smith, A. (1986). *The ethnic origins of nations.* Oxford: Blackwell.

Waters, M. (1990). *Ethnic options.* Berkeley, CA: University of California Press.

2 From Colonialism to Neoliberal Success

Chilean Education and Indigenous Participation

New racism is part of an ongoing, historically specific, and structural process through which racial categories come to be defined and reproduced (Omi & Winant, 1994). If we are to understand new racism's role in contemporary Chilean education, we must first address the development of this racial project over time. This chapter provides contextual information about how indigenous categories of belonging and modalities of schooling have been modified during progressive periods; from colonial through to neoliberal times. I do not provide a generalised historical overview of Mapuche-Chilean State relations, since these have been widely written about elsewhere (Bengoa, 1985; Boccara, 1999; Course, 2011; Mallon, 2005; Pinto, 2000; Richards, 2013 among others). Instead, I address how different educational reforms and policies were instigated, often on account of Mapuche intellectuals, politicians, and organisations' involvement during the twentieth century, ultimately furthering indigenous people's educational rights in Chile. Specifically, the creation of intercultural bilingual education (henceforth IBE) programmes, indigenous residential schools, and indigenous grants have been central components of these advancements. Paradoxically, I discuss how these very same policies fit into a new racism logic that allow enduring educational inequalities to continue unchallenged. As such, these educational programmes and initiatives are somewhat of a double-edged sword. I finish by considering the capacity of some IBE practices to bring about more equitable education for indigenous youth, by citing Mapuche students studying in two IBE schools where Mapuche knowledges were most centrally incorporated (Lihuén and Raimilla). Their narratives accentuate the possibilities of change, and how more critically aligned pedagogies and intercultural relationships can challenge inequitable monocultural education.

The appropriateness of new racism as a lens through which to address Mapuche young people's experiences of schooling comes more sharply into focus when it is contrasted with historic forms of colonial and post-colonial education. That is to say, approaches to indigenous people's education in Chile can only appear non-racial or progressive in view of formerly biologising, inferiorising, bigotted, and explicitly racist

DOI: 10.4324/9781003090700-3

educational practices and policies. Earlier phases included the total exclusion of indigenous Peoples, followed by unequivocally assimilatory education instilled through punitive sanctions for indigenous students (Vergara & Mellado, 2018). Intercultural and bilingual programmes seem to be an apex for indigenous rights only because traditional forms of education ignored all values, knowledges, and practices outside of Western, white, rationalist, scientific, nationalising, and hegemonic curricular activities. The absence of these explicitly racist forms of education enhances the belief that modernising progress (which is not the problem itself) has led to the eradication of ethnic-based inequalities. By addressing these historical advancements in Chile, it is possible to set the scene for how new racism has become an integral part of neoliberal schooling for the young people involved in this research.

The Pre-Independence Period

The history of education among the Mapuche in Chile is closely bound to the multiple processes of colonisation and othering carried out under various ideological vehicles. The first contact between Mapuche and Spanish was typified by eradication, cruelty, and slavery, and little effort was made to understand the indigenous inhabitants (Bengoa, 1985; Ortiz, 2009). Various soldiers, in the earliest chronicles, describe the Mapuche as pagan devil worshippers or as having animalistic social organisation and rituals; criteria that were used to justify the violent means for obtaining colonial sovereignty (Foerster, 1996). Soldiers involved in the conquest began to demand education for their children, but since no formal institutions offering instruction similar to those of Europe had been established in Chile, many of these children were sent to the Royal School (*Colegio Real*) in Lima, Peru (Cañulef, 1998). From 1598 Jesuit priests reached Chile with the mission of evangelising and schooling the Mapuche. Noggler (1972) cites one of the earliest letters written to the Spanish crown prior to their arrival as follows:

> I urge you, by request of the religious [priests] of your Order ... that you send these to the provinces of Chile where Captain Validivia is [located], and that they undertake the defense and protection of the Indians of that land, and their instruction in and conversion to our Holy Catholic Faith.

Unlike the first wave of conquistadors, the missionaries sought to establish the sovereignty of the crown (and therefore the Church) via non-violent means in what would become known as the "defensive war" (*La guerra defensiva*). The Spanish armies eventually conceded the futility of their previous conquest attempts, which after more than a century (beginning in 1536) had ended in failure, and signed a Peace accord with the Mapuche in 1641. Evangelism and education, from this moment, would form the two central axes of the civilising project aimed at transforming the social and moral behaviour of the Mapuche which would enable them to receive the Catholic faith (Foerster, 1996). Many of the Jesuit priests, most notably Luis de Valdivia and Diego de Rosales, were critical of the violent means employed by the first wave of colonisers. These political interventions were deemed to exceed their limits, and the Jesuits were expelled by the conquistadors in 1756 and replaced by the Franciscan priests.

The Franciscan priests were critical of the liberal stance taken by the Jesuits whose impact on the religiosity of the Mapuche was minimal (Foerster, 1993; Serrano et al., 2018) and insisted on a more systematic adherence to Catholic doctrines and moral codes. Consequently, the schooling of children was promoted to "guarantee their future faithfulness to the Church" (Foerster, 1996, p. 32 footnote 24). Until 1700, efforts to impose schooling and the Spanish language had failed due to the social structure of the Mapuche, who did not reside in the few towns that had been established and were too dispersed for this to be effective (Serrano, 1995). Consequently, the Spanish crown invested greater finances in establishing a residential school in Chillan (*Escuela Fide de Chillan* and later called *Colegio de Naturales*). Part of the crown's strategy was to eliminate any possible revolts by re-socializing the children of the most influential Mapuche leaders who were sent to be schooled there (Marimán, 1997; Noggler, 1972).

The Early Post-Independence Period

The work of the Franciscan and Capuchin missions would take on even greater importance in the build up to, and following, national independence in 1818. During the first government meeting of the newly formed Republic, public education was discussed as a critical means of integrating the nation and the importance of it being available to all its citizens. In 1832 the School of Chillan was reopened and became a centre for "centralising and coordinating the educational efforts of the State and the Church for the education and assimilation of the Mapuche youth into the ideology of the newly created Chilean nation" (Ortiz, 2009, p. 28). The Mapuche were now to be treated not just as allies, but as Chilean nationals, and any formerly special forms of education were replaced by a homogenising curriculum. The following year of 1833, the political constitution established that education was the responsibility of the State. In just 1 year, between 1834 and 1835, public spending in education rose from $22,377 pesos to $168,213 pesos despite overall public spending figures rising less substantially ($2,329,174 pesos to $3,566,260 pesos) (Serrano, 1995, p. 438). Rome also continued to send Italian Franciscan priests and Capuchin missionaries to reinforce work in missionary schools during this period as part of a coordinated effort to extend education coverage throughout the Republic (Foerster, 1996). This reflected a renewed commitment to the civilising project undertaken decades earlier, but now under a hegemonic discourse of nationhood. The Church would therefore become the State's main vehicle for achieving its assimilatory policies.

The Republic of Chile aspired to be a forerunner of economic success in Latin America, which also went hand in hand with educational preparation. From 1840 a national education system was devised, culminating in 1860 in the *Ley Orgánica de Enseñanza Primaria y Normal*; the first standardised single national curriculum (Canales Tapia, 1998). During the 1840s, infrastructure expanded rapidly with the founding of the University of Chile in Santiago, *Escuelas Normales* – teacher training institutions – and the construction of state schools (*escuelas fiscales*), sometimes even displacing missionary schools at the same time (Pinto, 2000, p. 179). As towns were established, so too were schools, yet the number of Mapuche students enrolled, despite the new laws, remained extremely low (Serrano, 1995).

From 1883, the Mapuche were violently usurped from their territories and confined to reservations on lands that were redistributed according to legal documents known as *Titulos de Merced*. This tumultuous period was marked by the reorganisation of all Mapuche society on just 6.4% of their original lands (Bengoa, 1985; Serrano, 1995). Mapuche economy, political structure, family, and community relations were all affected (Stuchlik, 1979). Likewise, the state's position regarding the Mapuche changed from a fairly detached assimilatory policy to a more intrusive and vigorous intervention (Pinto, 2000). The Mapuche had gone from being the "moral defenders" of the homeland – having fought alongside the criollos for independence – to "enemies of the Fatherland" (Stuchlik, 1979, p. 42). There was increased suspicion surrounding the future of the indigenous, and the state – no longer trusting in religious missions to achieve a moralising transformation (though these continued to function) – sought to ensure future generations of Mapuche would be more conforming. The number of schools within Mapuche territories (as well as Huilliche, Lafkenche, and Pehuenche) between the Biobío River and the Chiloé Island to the south increased from 159 in 1880 to 289 in 1888, an increase of 45% (Egaña, 2000). In the province of Cautín in the Araucanía region alone, this increase was even greater at the turn of the century, increasing from 15 schools in 1892 to 73 in 1910 (Serrano, 1995). These establishments aimed at providing homogenising instruction with a view to converting the Mapuche into productive rural Chilean peasants (*campesinos*) (Pinto, 2000).

Crucial to this project was the 1920 Compulsory Primary Education Law (*Ley de Instrucción Primaria Obligatoria*). Unlike many of the earlier missionary schools, state-governed establishments operated under the new law which prohibited the use of *mapuzungún* and punished pupils for its use.

Crow (2006) notes that indigenous cultures were still part of the primary education programmes of 1931 and 1949, in areas as diverse as mathematics, music, art, physical education, and humanities. However, the author emphasises that this "inclusion" was always directed towards educating how Chile was constituted, and what being Chilean meant. That is, far from being an early attempt at interculturality, it was a study of the ethnogenesis of Chilean nationality. The state had gradually moved from its emphasis on civilising the indigenous through the missions towards creating industrious citizens through the national education system (Serrano et al., 2018). Education thereby played a central and decisive role in the state's objective of creating monolingual and monocultural citizens during this period. All these measures ensured Mapuche schoolchildren would undergo a radical cultural shift, through the elimination of *mapuzungún*, decreasing time spent with the family, and training for working-class rural occupations.

During these early periods, schools operated according to explicitly assimilatory criteria first through religious ideology, and then paternalistic state wardship, as a means of civilising the indigenous. Education policies were oriented towards homogenising and unifying the nation, rather than towards providing equal social and economic opportunities for all its citizens. A more humanitarian and developmentalist approach would only be implemented from the mid-twentieth century onwards (Ortiz, 2009). Education remained mostly segregated, with most of the Mapuche taught in the rural Chilean school network established from the late nineteenth century. Through dichotomous principles – a European legacy of religious and cultural moral virtues and rationality on the one hand, and indigenous ambivalence and potential danger on the other – racialised taxonomies were ingrained into the national identity.

Resistance during the Twentieth Century

In response to the assimilatory discourses of this time, Mapuche organisations began to form to defend their rights. Some adopted compensatory politics – whether *indigenismo* (an intellectual movement promoting indigenous culture) or *desarrollista* (developmental) – such as the Sociedad Caupolican Defensora de la Araucania (the first post-reduction Mapuche organisation) formed in 1911. The movement, made up mainly of primary teachers, made two demands: the "defence of the race" and the need for education. It was thought that through education, Mapuche youth could better integrate into Chilean society and obtain better social status (Bengoa, 1985, p. 387; Foerster & Montecino, 1988). The society also petitioned grants for Mapuche teachers to be trained and assigned to schools in the Araucanía Region (Marimán, 1997).

Serrano (1995) observes that the acculturation process of schooling actually had the opposite effect on many of the Mapuche who had attended the missionary schools in Chillán and Concepción. Many of those sent to the *Escuela Normal* became teachers and organised demands for culturally and linguistically relevant curricula in Mapuche territories. Others formed political alliances in Chilean society with a view to defending indigenous rights. Among these, the most distinguished Mapuche intellectuals of the early-twentieth century were Manuel Manquilef who led the aforementioned *Sociedad Caupolican Defensora de la Araucanía*, Manuel Neculman, Manuel Aburto Panguilef and Venanacio Coñuepán (Bello, 1999; Crow, 2010; Foerster & Montecino, 1988). Coñuepán was elected to National Congress in 1945, and called for more radical measures to be taken, arguing for the need for separate indigenous schools able to teach indigenous knowledges to its students (Crow, 2010; Marimán, 1997). Many of these ideas would sow the seeds for later advances in culturally appropriate teaching. Perhaps Coñuepán's most lasting contribution to education was the agreement established between the organisation under his leadership (*Corporación Araucana*) and President Carlos Ibáñez to form the Management of Indigenous Affairs (*Dirección de Asuntos Indígenas*) (Vergara. Foerster & Gundermann, 2005). Two decades later, this would initiate the first indigenous grants to support students wishing to continue with their education.

Further political intervention was achieved in December 1935 when Mapuche leaders from different regions drafted a document for the President of the Republic, Arturo Alessandri. This document appealed for German missionary Fathers to be replaced by Mapuche Fathers (or mestizo Chileans) able to teach in the missions, and for permission to create autonomous schools within each Mapuche reservation, with materials in *mapuzungún* and Mapuche teachers (Cañulef, 1998). This would set a precedent for the decades to come, though crucially these grassroots initiatives would later be absorbed into a top-down state model of interculturality.

According to Foerster and Montecino (1988), this period was a political awakening for many Mapuche teachers who recognised that education could be a weapon against the state's ideological conquest (Foerster & Montecino, 1988, p. 60). In 1939, the Congress of Radical Teachers (Congreso de Profesores Radicales) sought educational rights such as teaching in *mapuzungún*, the designation of a Secretary of Indigenous Education, the establishment of an indigenous teacher training institute, and the creation of polytechnic state schools with curricula adapted to local economies of agriculture, horticulture, and farming in the Araucanía Region (Foerster & Montecino, 1988, p. 263). Mapuche teachers were at the centre of the progress consolidated during this period, making the schooling of indigenous children a visible political issue. In 1953, demands were made by the consolidated National Indigenous Association of Chile (*Asociacion Nacional Indigena de Chile*) for the state to provide grants to cover student expenditures (Marimán, 1997). From this initiative, the nationwide state fund called the Indigenous Grant was created (*Beca Indigena*).

Mapuche student political organisations also sprang up as a result of mass urban migration and attendance at residential/boarding schools in cities such as Temuco and Santiago. One example was the Centre of Araucano Nehuentuayn Students (*Centro de Estudiantes Araucanos Nehuentuayn*) whose members edited a magazine entitled "The Voice of Aracuanía" and petitioned for the creation of Mapuche Residential Homes that could house those wishing to study in urban areas. Likewise, the Modern Araucanian Youth (*Juventud Moderna Araucania*) were concerned about correcting the transmission of historical errors in Chilean classrooms, and the lack of Mapuche teachers qualified to teach on the reservations.

The most evident conclusion to be drawn from this period is that the assimilatory intentions of Chilean education from the earlier period were unsuccessful. Mapuche intellectuals, teachers, and students who had been socialised under these conditions utilised the educational platforms provided by these institutions to resist and re-vindicate Mapuche concerns and politics. Many of the contemporary reforms that the Chilean state has undertaken over the last three decades were sown by Mapuche organisations during this period.

However, this did not translate into universally positive experiences for Mapuche schoolchildren. Canales Tapia (1998) confirms that schooling continued to be defined by insults and inferior treatment from teachers and peers throughout the mid to late twentieth century. Based on these experiences (as well as workplace discrimination) many Mapuche parents chose not to transmit *mapuzungún* to their children to protect them from similar traumas, creating a seismic generational shift in cultural socialisation, and invisibilised identities.

Pre-Dictatorship Period

During the liberal and socialist governments of the 1960s and 1970s, indigenous demands for education began to come to fruition. Eduardo Frei's government (1964–1970) achieved universal primary education coverage and introduced greater flexibility to the national curriculum enabling schools to adapt to the regional and local sociocultural contexts (Cañulef, 1998). The Agrarian Reform of 1962 brought reforms to rural education, but there were few, if any, specific proposals for supporting indigenous populations in their education (Crow, 2006). Samaniego and Ruiz (2007) argue that the pejorative categorising of Mapuche as "rural peasants" or farmers during this period of liberal economic solutions was responsible. This interventionist/developmentalist government was effective in creating new social policies to organise and empower the rural poor, and substantial increases of aid and materials reached remote schools, but Mapuche and non-Mapuche were seen as one economically exploited class (Mallon, 2005).

Salvador Allende's impact was much greater. He had a long relationship with Mapuche leaders, and during his (unsuccessful) presidential campaign of 1964, Allende signed an agreement to support the protection of indigenous lands and provide indigenous language instruction in schools (Marimán, 1997). In 1972, the first Indigenous Law (17.729) was passed in parliament. Although the implementation of this policy was cut short by the coup d'etat, it created the Institute of Indigenous Development (*Instituto de Desarrollo Indígena*; DASI) under the existing Management of Indigenous Affairs, with seven rural Mapuche representatives (Vergara, Foerster, & Gundermann, 2005). Among its many functions, it allocated funding for Mapuche students, provided technical and vocational education, and the establishment of communal indigenous residencies (*hogares*) for rural students to facilitate access to higher education.

This period marks a shift in terms of the national discourse, from one of assimilation, towards indigenism (*indigenismo*) which is related to notions of the indigenous needing state help to develop and progress. As mentioned above, some of these initiatives were simply aimed at helping the working-class farmers utilise their lands to better effect and thereby strengthen the national economy. Ortiz (2009) notes that educational policies during this period took on a humanitarian and social policy focus to remediate and improve those categorised as helpless or deficient – for the good of the national whole. This marks an important moment in the introduction of new racism into Chilean education. That is to say, affirmative action was not incorporated on account of recognising the need to redress historic debts of colonial injustice, or to confront the structural barriers placing indigenous Peoples at a constant disadvantage, but rather to assist the shortcomings of indigenous individuals (Augoustinos et al., 2005).

The Dictatorship Period

During the period of the military government (1973–1990), demands for indigenous rights were silenced by the break-up of Mapuche organisations and political persecution. There were few governmental initiatives to benefit indigenous populations, though the programme for grants and student housing (*hogares*) were maintained (Vergara, Foerster, & Gundermann, 2005). Only certain social and cultural organisations, such as the Indigenous Cultural Centres (*los Centros Culturales Indígenas*), were able to function under the wing of the Catholic and Evangelical churches and NGOs, though most of these were dedicated to resisting the division of indigenous lands (Bello, 1999). The general position of the government was a "politics of omission" seeking neoliberal economic and social models of national growth and stability that only had space for one national identity (Serrano, 1995, p. 473).

However, there were a number of unexpected advances during this period. On the one hand, the Education Journal (*Revista de Educación*) published articles criticising the existing national curriculum for its assimilatory and traditional pedagogical design, causing indigenous students to attain lower academic results (Crow, 2006). Likewise, during the dictatorship a number of indigenous intellectuals with university education, many of whom worked under the organisation *Asociacion Nacional Mapuche Nehuen Mapu*, began working towards indigenous forms of education (Marimán, 1997).

In 1981 the organisation of the Chilean education system was overhauled with a national school voucher system "as a way to improve education under severe cost constraints and to decrease central bureaucracy by shifting financial and educational decision making to local governments and private households" (Carnoy, 1998, pp. 309–310). This was part of Pinochet's neoliberal free market model for the country, and the justification for these reforms was its capacity to promote competition between schools so as to improve their efficiency and educational standards (Matear, 2007). Private state-subsidised schools, under different providers (both profit and non-profit), were paid vouchers based on the number of enrolled students (Anand et al., 2009). There is broad consensus that the system implemented by Pinochet's government made no impact on improving school quality or student achievement (Carnoy, 1998; Delannoy, 2000). Instead, it undermined state schools and their ability to attract highly trained teachers, reinforced socioeconomic segregation, and created a market-oriented mentality towards education among families.

The other consequence was a major upheaval to school choice. Unprecedented numbers of students switched from municipal to state-subsidised private schools owing to the lack of caps on enrolment or restrictions through catchment areas. Education providers in effect sold their establishments as market products to the general public – who in turn were converted into clients – transforming school choice into a branding enterprise (Espinola, 1993). In truth, there was only school "choice" for those families in a strong position within the market. Likewise, private school administrators were able to screen students according to past achievement and financial capacity. The result, simply put, was an increasingly polarised education system negatively and disproportionately affecting the poorest and most geographically marginalised families (Elacqua, Schneider, & Buckley, 2006; Matear, 2006). One repercussion affecting Mapuche territories was the mass establishment of state-subsidised private schools in remote rural areas. While this "resolved" an issue of access that Frei's government had sought to address decades earlier, their lack of regulation had devastating consequences on educational outcomes, whilst benefiting their founders who profited from student enrolments (Espinola, 1993).

On 10 March 1990, the day before Pinochet's rule ended, his government introduced the Constitutional Organic Law of Education 18.962 (*Ley Orgánica Constitucional de Enseñanza*; henceforth LOCE). This constitutional law prevented the recently elected democratic coalition government from altering the neoliberal educational reforms enacted during the military regime. Despite this anti-democratic move, an unexpected consequence of the LOCE was that it provided a platform of possibility for IBE. By emphasising universal rights to education and the constitutional freedom of teaching (*principio constitucional de libertad de enseñanza*) in each community and municipality, new curricula could be designed and implemented. Initiatives led by NGOs (most notably the German Agency for Technical Cooperation), international development agencies, and the Catholic Church began to incorporate Mapuche knowledges as part of these new allowances (Ortiz, 2009). *Fundacion del Magisterio de la Araucanía*, a branch of the Catholic Church, was among the first to create a more systematic IBE system in Chile, which in 1985 implemented *mapuzungún* as a school subject in 14 primary schools in the Araucanía Region. Some 20 Mapuche teachers were employed at the schools since the organisation recognised that this task was impossible whilst white Chilean teachers remained the focal point of remedial education initiatives (Loncón, Martinez, & Breveglieri, 1997). However, for the vast majority of indigenous students, schooling under the military regime meant the suppression of alternate cultures at the expense of a singular nationalising discourse (Crow, 2006).

Post-Dictatorship Period

A new wave of optimism surrounded the end of authoritarian rule and a return to democratic politics under Aylwin's government (1990–1994). However, since the LOCE was a constitutional matter, this and subsequent coalition governments were forced to manoeuvre within the confines of the previously established policies (Matear, 2007). Public spending on education increased, but the private and subsidised structure of the education system remained in place. The solution for Aylwin's government was to initiate a number of remedial programmes such as the P-900 programme which ran from 1990 to 2000, focused on the most-at-risk schools in rural and urban areas. First to fourth grades were targeted with reading and mathematics initiatives under a slogan of "quality education for all." A number of the schools included in the programme were rural schools in the Araucanía with large Mapuche enrolments. Simultaneously, a MECE programme (Programa de Mejoramiento de la Calidad y Equidad de la educación), co-funded by the World Bank and the Chilean government, was launched to improve teaching resources in classrooms (Matear, 2007). Another programme, ENLACES, brought improvements to Information Technology capabilities (computers and later internet connections) to rural schools and eventually was extended to all Chilean schools.

Other initiatives were made to correct previous misrepresentations of indigenous Peoples in school textbooks. Crow (2006) notes that notions of mestizaje as a national problem to be overcome through whitening – between the 1930s to 1970s – were rewritten in textbooks upon the return to democracy, now looking to promote mestizaje as a cultural cornerstone of the Chilean national landscape. In particular, the author notes the key role of the History and Social Sciences textbook, given that Social Sciences had been banned as a school subject during the military regime. To date, this remains the textbook where the most focused "inclusion" of indigenous Peoples can be found in the national curriculum.

The most significant development was the introduction of a new Indigenous Law, 19.253, brought into effect from 1993. This replaced the 17.729 law which had only partially been implemented before Allende's presidency was cut short. In December 1989, presidential candidate Patricio Aylwin and indigenous organisations had signed an agreement in the town of Nueva Imperial in the Araucanía Region (*Acuerdo de Imperial*) promising a reworking of the former law (Bello, 1999; Cañulef, 1998; OEI, 2009). On 17 May 1990, the Special Commission of Indigenous Peoples (*Comision Especial de Pueblos Indigenas* – CEPI) was created to begin drafting the new legislation, which was then presented to indigenous communities in local assemblies and provincial meetings for approval (Cañulef, 1998). This process culminated in a congress (*Congeso Nacional de Pueblos Indigenas*) in Temuco and upon its conclusion the document was sent to the President of the Republic. The law was passed, though not according to all the terms proposed by the CEPI. The most notable absence was a proposal to change the national constitution so as to include the mention of "indigenous Peoples" and their rights to indigenous lands. Nonetheless, it represented an important step forward in legislative terms.

Optimism surrounding the Indigenous Law 19.253 raised hopes that it might represent a watershed in state-indigenous relations and new political cooperation (Cañulef, 1998). The Indigenous Law granted the creation of a state institution to replace the discontinued DASI from 1972, called the National Corporation of Indigenous Development (*Corporación Nacional de Desarrollo Indígena*, henceforth CONADI). Indigenous Peoples would be consulted on all administrative and legislative issues affecting their communities, and indigenous representatives would work on indigenous policies and programmes designed to recognise, respect, and promote indigenous cultures (OEI, 2009). The organism was overseen by the then named Ministry of Planning, and although the national director of CONADI was to be named by the president, crucially, eight indigenous representatives (Mapuche, Aymara, and Atacameño) were chosen from their communities to sit on the council.

Within the broader range of rights introduced by the Indigenous Law, articles 7, 28, and 32 were education-specific, stipulating that CONADI together with the corresponding state organisms would be responsible for designing, developing, and implementing Intercultural Bilingual Education, and for protecting indigenous culture and language. These initial activities were overseen by CONADI's subdivision of Culture and Education led by Alejandro Supanta, Eliseo Cañulef, and Jose Cañulef. Initially, a pilot scheme was established across seven regions of the country, each supported by a university in that region (MINEDUC, 2011). In the Araucanía Region (IX), Temuco's Catholic University was responsible for the pilot scheme carried out in Lumaco with three primary schools: one teaching *mapuzungún* as a first language, the second as a second language, and the third experimented with interculturality (Williamson, 1998, p. 14). During the same years (1996–1999/2000) CONADI supported eight schools with previous experience in developing innovative curricula related to bilingualism and interculturalism (two nurseries, one secondary school, and five primary schools) with a view to expanding and deepening this experience (Cañulef, 1998). Some experimental *mapuzungún* literacy programmes were also implemented in rural schools with high concentrations of Mapuche enrolment (Mariman, 1997, p. 181). Later CONADI would develop its own separate activities and policy recommendations for IBE under the auspices of MIDEPLAN. Part of the breakdown in organisation between the Ministry of Education and CONADI was due to leadership issues and a lack of clarity regarding the responsibility that each organism held in this process.

Under Eduardo Frei Ruiz-Tagle's term as president (1994–2000), more general educational reforms were undertaken through the National Commission on the Modernisation of Education. The MECE programme was extended to secondary level, and primary schooling switched from a part-time to a full-time model (*Jornada Escolar Completa*). The most significant change affecting indigenous populations was the establishment of article 5 of Decree 40 (*Decreto Supremo de Educación*) in 1996. Decree 40 set down the fundamental objectives and minimum core content of the national curriculum. However, article 5 made allowances for individual establishments to create their own educational plans and programmes (*planes y programas propias*), provided all the nationally stipulated curricular content was also covered (*contenido mínimo obligatorio*). This paved ways for establishments to formally become IBE-implementing schools.

This was a burgeoning period for private initiatives of intercultural education. In 1995, an association of Mapuche professionals (*Asociacion de Profesionales y tecnicos Mapuche*; APROTEMA) and a foundation responsible for transmitting rural radio (*Fundacion Radio Escuela para el Desarrollo Rural* FREDER) held meetings in Santiago and the Southern regions with a view to channelling and organising the Mapuche discourse regarding IBE in Chile (Marimán, 1997, p. 170). Proposals were made for greater community participation in IBE, particularly via classroom monitors who could assist with the teaching of *mapuzungún*. This would later become a crucial element of the Ministry of Education's IBE programme.

Quite rightly, there was a great deal of optimism surrounding these advancements. Key indigenous actors were involved in the planning and implementation of these pilot projects, and they were backed by state funds. However, it should also be noted that the 1990s were also a tense period for Mapuche-state relations. There is certain scepticism within scholarship about the intentions of the state regarding these initiatives, and whether they rather represent symbolic or tokenistic efforts to appease indigenous demands from more radical sectors of Mapuche society, and thus avert attention away from more long-lasting inequalities exacerbated by the continued neoliberal market logics (Richards, 2013). Also, supposedly empowering institutions such as CONADI – intended to act on behalf of, and from, indigenous interests – underwent a number of political interventions from the Chilean government that undermined its autonomy and effectiveness, especially over multimillion-dollar development contracts for hydroelectric power facilities affecting indigenous territories (Carruthers & Rodriguez, 2009).

The Twenty-First Century

Under the Lagos presidency (2000–2006), the third consecutive *Concertación* coalition government, the minimum number of years for compulsory education was raised from 8 years to12, whilst the MECE programme completed its interventions at university level (Matear, 2007). The year 2000 was a milestone for IBE, with the government announcing the launch of the official programme in place of the prior isolated and experimental projects (MINEDUC, 2011; OEI, 2009). From this time on, the main policies developed by MINEDUC in reference to the Mapuche were a) the incorporation of bilingual texts containing an intercultural pedagogy, b) the distribution of computer software regarding indigenous cultures and languages in Chile, c) bilingual teacher training, d) programmes of study which contextualise the cultural and linguistic reality of its students, e) educative projects with community participation, f) the participation of indigenous authorities in the schools, and g) the generation of new technologies in the schools (MINEDUC, 2011, p. 7).

A question mark hanging over the IBE programme was the government's commitment to its funding. The budget assigned to IBE was insufficient to make any headway and instead *Programa Origines* would prove to be a key factor in its expansion. A loan of US$79,000,000 by the Inter-American Development Bank (IDB) was secured to initiate a US$133,000,000 investment in economic and social development in 44 municipal districts (*comunas*) and 645 indigenous communities in Chile. *Origines* was designed to improve state relations with indigenous Peoples and to fulfil one of the Indigenous Law's central facets: "to respect, protect and promote indigenous development, their cultures, families and communities, adopting the appropriate means to these ends" (MINEDUC, 2011, p. 8).

Origines funded the implementation of IBE in 162 rural schools, at a cost of over $3,000,000,000 Chilean pesos, for teacher training, the creation of intercultural texts, assisting with the creation of Educational plans for IBE schools, and the distribution of additional student grants. Many of the schools selected were already participating in other MINEDUC programmes at the time, such as the P-900 and *Enlaces* (OEI, 2009). In the first phase of *Origines* (2002–2006), 900 teachers received specialised training in IBE and one of the most important advances was the introduction of indigenous educators – selected by the community – into the classroom.

Despite the financial support offered by *Origines*, there were questions raised over its effectiveness. A study published by MINEDUC evaluating the implementation of PEIB-ORIGINES recognised the following weaknesses during its first phase: the vagueness of its objectives (failure to produce a consistency in regard to interculturality or bilingualism); the absence of a systemised IBE model which could be used as a reference for the schools involved in, or wishing to work under, the programme; and the absence of any evaluations to assess the programme's success in terms of raising student achievements (MINEDUC, 2017, p. 11).

The second phase of *Programa Origines* was carried over to Michelle Bachelet's presidency (2006–2010). It introduced IBE curricula for 1st and 2nd grades and continued working at those established in the first phase (3rd–6th grades). In total, 192 schools participated in the IBE programme, though the results of phase II state that 274 primary schools had developed their own plans and study programmes. Upon *Origines'* conclusion in 2010, the Ministry of Education continued to fund the development of IBE in each of the schools. Three other key events also took place during Bachelet's final year of her first presidential period: Decree 280, the ratification of the ILO 169, and an educational reform called General Law of Education (*Ley General de Educación; LGE*), which includes specific references to the core values of interculturality and the implementation of IBE as key components of a more equal education system (articles 3 and 23).

Decree 280 was introduced with a view to establishing the norms under which IBE would be taught in schools following the national curriculum. It stipulates the number of hours to be dedicated to indigenous language teaching, and the establishments that would be obliged to *offer* IBE to its community. Initially, only schools with 50% or more indigenous student enrolments were to commit to IBE, which was reduced to 20% from 2013. Even so, IBE remained an optional subject for families and individual students (MINEDUC, 2009). The same year was momentous for the furtherance of indigenous rights because, after a long standoff, the ILO 169 convention was passed in Chile. It was one of the last Latin American countries to do so after years of campaigning by indigenous movements and NGOs (Richards, 2013). The ILO 169 further strengthened indigenous people's rights to a culturally appropriate education.

This period of Chilean education was marked by state discourses of recognition and inclusivity, both in regard to indigenous politics in general and education specifically. The LGE, introduced in 2009 to repeal the LOCE, is indicative of this stance. As I demonstrate below, the LGE is a reactionary law implemented in the face of civil disobedience and mass protests that forced the government's hand. The General Law of Education emphasises the core values of inclusion, diversity, human dignity, interculturality, and an integral education (social, moral, physical, spiritual, aesthetic) for Chilean society. Simultaneously, however, it allows the structural segregation caused by the school choice model, and the poor quality of education, to go unchecked. In the same way, interculturality during this period continued to be a developmentalist initiative for "closing the gaps," between the indigenous and non-indigenous, but without lending serious credence to intercultural relations on an equal footing. Hence, whilst the rhetoric of twentieth-century educational reform seems to tick the appropriate boxes, this has enabled new racism to go unchecked. The Chilean state can point to its financial and bureaucratic commitment to interculturality and greater educational access for indigenous youth. However, the responsibility is pushed, under the neoliberal education system, onto individual schools that are ill-equipped to carry it out.

Student Revolts

It would be difficult to overstate the role that the student population has played in bringing about reform to Chilean education. The LGE, as mentioned above, is a direct response to student protests and nationwide strikes initiated against the inequalities and educational segregation that have been ongoing since the 1980s. A first wave of protests began in 2001 when students mobilised over the rising costs of student passes for public transport (*Pase Escolar*). These protests were relatively minor in scale (in the low thousands) and limited to the capital. However, these escalated in 2006, just a month into Bachelet's first presidential term, when secondary school students began nationwide strikes, shutting down around 400 schools with barricades and sit-ins. Most were publicly funded schools with poor infrastructure and students expressed concerns over the inequalities of decentralised municipal funding. Additionally, the introduction of examination fees for university selection (*Prueba de Selección Universitaria*, PSU) led to further concerns that higher education was intended only for the economically privileged. This movement, known as the Penguin Revolution (on account of the black and white school uniforms of the protestors), successfully forced Bachelet's hand to create a Presidential Advisory Commission on the Quality of Education responsible for discussing reforms to the LOCE. Student representatives were included on its board, and although the student movement lost momentum and internal cohesion, it laid the foundations for General Law of Education (Donoso, 2013).

The LGE's focus on making state-subsidised private schools free of charge, increasing student participation in schools, and a strong emphasis on human rights, dignity, and inclusivity did little to alter the system's adherence to a neoliberal market dynamic. In 2011, the Chilean Student Confederation (CONFECH) led even larger mobilisations, labelled by the press as the "Chilean Winter" following the "Arab Spring" in the Middle East some months earlier. Students gained widespread support from the teachers' union and Chilean citizens during a seven-month period of protests, demanding free higher education (especially for lower income groups) and an end to for-profit education providers funded by public subsidies (Bellei, Cabalín, & Orellana, 2014).

In both the 2006 and 2011 student movements, Mapuche organisations rallied to obtain culturally relevant changes to the educational inequalities they face. In 2006, *Meli Newen*, a group composed of secondary school students, held meetings with the education minister, Yasna Provoste. Their demands included the contextualisation of region- (and territory) specific education for indigenous peoples, assurances of efforts to improve respect towards, and the recovery of, indigenous knowledges and languages in educational curricular, and the ratification of the OIT 169. By 2011, some of the members of *Meli Newen* were studying in higher education and were again active in the Federation of Mapuche Students (FEMAE) which participated within the CONFECH, demanding a free state-run intercultural university, more student grants, and better infrastructure in Mapuche residencies (*hogares*) for urban students.

Much like the young Mapuche intellectuals of the early- and mid-twentieth century, who played vital roles in negotiating with the Chilean state and promoting indigenous rights (Bello, 1999), the current generation have been protagonists of contemporary developments. However, cycles of state violence also repeat themselves through Chilean history, and some have paid the price with their lives. Heavy-handed responses to Mapuche activism and territorial demands have resulted in the tragic shootings of Mapuche youth activists by the police force, including 24-year-old Camilo Catrillanca in 2018, 22-year-old university student Matías Catrileo Quezada in 2008, and Alex Lumún, a 17-year-old secondary school student, in 2002. These cases give credence to Haughney's assertion that, "under the present ideological hegemony, the principal parties no longer serve as vehicles of reform, but rather as agents to diffuse societal conflict" (2007, p. 154).

On 18 October 2019, student evasion of metro fare increments gave rise to a series of nationwide protests on unprecedented scales known as the "social explosion" (*estallido social*) or the social crisis. Unlike prior movements, there were no singular political objectives, alliances, or spokespeople to give voice to specific demands; instead, public outpourings of frustration and anger were vented at ongoing structural inequalities across all spheres of Chilean society. Although the initial protests shared certain similarities to the 2001 demands for lower transport costs, they were merely the tipping point for expressing the lack of human dignity among the middle- and lower-income groups in matters as diverse as education, health, pensions and transport, low working wages, privatisation of water, and sexual harassment. In short, the excesses of the neoliberal political and economic models were finally met head-on by the citizenry's call for social well-being. During all the protests and marches, Mapuche flags were a prominent feature among the masses, and – although not specifically directed towards indigenous rights issues – there have been strong calls for quotas to be reserved for indigenous representatives to be involved in formulating the new constitution after the recent national referendum.

Progress in Indigenous Educational Equity?

This brief overview of the historical events in Chilean education affecting indigenous Peoples indicates some encouraging signs regarding educational access and achievement. Contemporary indigenous students in Chile might feel they have good reasons to be optimistic compared to former generations. According to the 2002 National Census, the cohort of school and university-age indigenous youth (between 16 and 29) have an average of 9.9 years of schooling, compared to 4.6 years among indigenous adults aged over 50. A nationally representative study from 2013 suggests that school attendance at primary levels is now equitable for indigenous and non-indigenous children, albeit that this figure drops off for each subsequent education level (CASEN, 2013).

However, access to quality education continues to be an issue. At primary level, indigenous and non-indigenous schoolchildren are distributed relatively evenly between public and state-subsidised private schools, with 50% of indigenous children attending primary public schools and 48.5% a state-subsidised private school, compared to 41.1% and 52.7% respectively of non-indigenous children. The vast difference lies in access to private education; 0.9% of indigenous students in Chile attend private primary/elementary schools compared to 5.8% of non-indigenous. As students advance through their educational trajectory, these differences become marginally more pronounced: 45.8% indigenous students attend a public secondary school, 48.3% a state-subsidised private school, and 0.9% attend private secondary schools, compared to non-indigenous students of whom 38.6% attend a public secondary school, 48.7% a state-subsidised private school, and 6.2% a private establishment, as seen in Figure 2.1.

Despite some educational advances, there are ongoing concerns among scholars and public organisations that the politicised rhetoric of recognition and inclusivity during the last two decades have failed to translate into systematic reform. This forms the crux of the new racism issue to be discussed in the remaining chapters. While the number

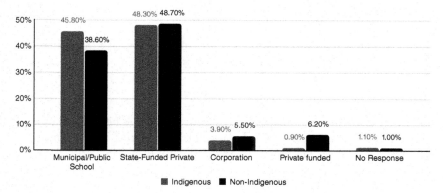

Figure 2.1 Indigenous and non-indigenous secondary school attendance by establishment type

of indigenous grants allocated by JUNAEB have continued to rise, and IBE textbooks are available for all levels of primary education (up to 8th grade), progress in IBE has also stalled over the past decade. As in other Latin American countries, IBE has come to represent a new governmental strategy of appeasing minimal multicultural demands for recognition, without challenging the status quo of a hegemonic, European-centred, and market-oriented neoliberal education system (Richards, 2013). Twenty years after the IBE programme commenced, there is a dearth of information about how effective it has been, either for indigenous (and non-indigenous) students' well-being or on their educational outcomes. To date I am only aware of two (publicly available) evaluations. One of these, a study conducted by the Organisation of IberoAmerican states for education, Science and Culture (OEI, 2009) on behalf of MINEDUC and MIDEPLAN (now MINDES, Ministry of Social Development and Families), finds that the implementation and practice of IBE in the Araucania Region is conceptualised in such limited terms that, "IBE is reduced to the incorporation of some exclusive artisanal practices, or something similar, in schools. What's more, IBE is often understood as a specific and definitive content, like a course or material, and not as a perspective or focus" (OEI, 2009, p. 135).

Since education is decentralised in Chile, the main onus of IBE's bureaucratic demands fall on school directors/heads (*directores*). Incorporating IBE therefore means breaking from the routine administrative duties of each school and requires a certain level of training and competency in order to comply with these criteria. Unless there is a specific demand for IBE to be implemented in a particular community, or a particular commitment on behalf of the school directive itself, those establishments which fall outside of the current policies of Decree 280 (schools with

20% or more indigenous enrolments) are unlikely to implement IBE. A study by the CIAE (*Centro de Investigación Avanzada en Educación*) also found that the Departments of Education in the respective municipalities did little to urge IBE in schools (MINEDUC, 2011).

Interculturality and Critical Narratives

In short, IBE cannot – under its current format – be the answer to existing (and long-standing) educational inequalities that indigenous youth in Chile face. That is to say that IBE should not be conflated with culturally sensitive or critical pedagogy, or decolonial and anti-racist education. Firstly because it is optional to those families who wish to partake in it, and secondly because there are no guidelines for training staff to ensure that there is a consistent approach and shared perspective about its importance in each school. In 2011 there were 352 educational establishments teaching indigenous language as a subject, and by 2016 there were 1,391 (MINEDUC, 2017). However, there is very little accountability about how this is taught or coordination between indigenous communities and schools. Instead, based on observations of IBE classes, all the onus is often placed on indigenous educators to provide IBE, while the rest of the school continues its monocultural socialisation. Hence, although three-quarters of the schools involved in the research have sufficient indigenous compositions to qualify for intercultural programmes, the manner in which each incorporates Mapuche culture and language range between what I would describe as segmented to peripheral. That is, in just two of the schools there is a direct effort, alongside the national curriculum, to incorporate indigenous knowledges into different subjects in more systematic fashion (Raimilla and Lihuén schools). In others, there is a *mapuzungún* class or workshop, usually once a week or twice a month, in which these issues are addressed as a separate and subordinate subject matter (Linterna, Tres Montes, Clorinda, Campaña, Quelentaro). In the remaining schools, there are no specific IBE efforts made, and the schools follow the national curriculum. All the schools promote normative discourses of equality and universal treatment, but the discourse of inclusion is part of a new racism era, and for this reason care needs to be taken to avoid promoting IBE as panacea since there is enormous diversity between and even within IBE schools.

In the final part of this chapter, I cite some young participants from the two schools implementing more segmented IBE programmes that were included in the research. I focus specifically on those practices that create a more critical stance towards structural racism, the construction of the Mapuche as *other*, and the exclusion of indigenous knowledges. A critical perspective allows us to ask how racial projects can be challenged, rather than focusing exclusively on the success of particular programmes or policies. A central aspect of this is how young people react to, and understand, their place in these institutional settings. These stand in stark contrast to some of the issues addressed in the following chapters, including some youth from these schools, so I do not present these schools as model solutions.[1]

Perhaps the issue that was reiterated the most in the Lihuén school was that students were taught about colonial history and the symbolic violence associated with *mestizaje*, which gave them a more critical perspective on the denial of racism and spurious ideas about racial purity:

HEBER: "[One of the things we've been taught is] there was a violent mixing (*mestizaje*); it was pretty bad and the truth is that the Chileans don't want to recognise it, that they are descendants of the Mapuche. They say they are just *criollos*, that they are children of the Spaniards and nothing else, but they don't recognise indigenous peoples. They're scared of doing that, they are ashamed, and that's pretty racist." (11th grade, Lihuén School)

Some students claimed that this had awoken them to the cultural value of being Mapuche:

JOHANNA: "The Mapuche culture was just like any other in my eyes. But then I came here and they [teachers] taught me what it meant, what its origins are, and then I began to appreciate it more and more. Now I'm proud to be Mapuche." (9th grade, Lihuén School)

LUCAS: "In the school I used to go to, they never actually, never incorporated those [Mapuche customs]. In fact some said it was a side issue; it was like 'no, we're Chilean', [so] nobody was Mapuche. Now that's changed here." (12th grade, Raimilla School)

Other students acknowledged the importance of national and local histories as a means of transforming their identities, and subverting implicit racism in standardised curricula content:

TRINI: "I'm learning more things, like in History I didn't know about the Mapuche heroes who lived before us, like Lautaro and how much I could learn from his life." (10th grade, Raimilla School)

EDITH: "In history classes the teacher is always defending the Mapuche race, and he uses it to teach us about our rights." (10th grade, Raimilla School)

HENRY: "The History teacher shows us a different point of view, different historians and authors. He doesn't just teach us from the textbook which sometimes presents false information. But the people writing those texts weren't there and they show it in a different way, like a discriminatory way. They present [the Mapuche] as bad people." (12th grade, Lihuén School)

As Crow (2006) details in her analysis of Chilean textbooks, the portrayal of indigenous Peoples has mostly conformed to a whitened hegemony. History and geography textbooks for many decades portrayed the Mapuche as "primitive," or as belonging to the past, while omitting the atrocities committed by the Chilean army when dispossessing Mapuche territories in the nineteenth century (see also Pinto, 2000). Whilst explicit forms of racism have been removed from these textbooks in recent years, Henry's words suggest that racialising discourses continue to be present. Exposure to alternate authors and sources as part of an IBE curriculum suggests avenues for developing more critical consciousness in students.

Another important practice is developing positive school climates and intercultural relationships premised on mutual understanding and dialogue. Some students-related incidents that they had experienced in other schools prior to switching to an IBE-focused establishment, and felt issues of discrimination were better dealt with under an intercultural vision:

NELLY: "Mapuche education should be for everyone, because since we all have some Mapuche or indigenous in us, we should all be interested in it." (12th grade, Raimilla School)

LUCIANO: "Here in the school we are allowed to express ourselves according to our culture and they emphasize that we are all from different places, with different cultures, so it allows us all to be who we are and that's a good thing." (10th grade, Lihuén School)

VERÓNICA: "[At other schools] they [non-Mapuche] make these sick jokes, they don't understand the other [Mapuche] students, so then no one feels comfortable participating in [cultural] activities because everyone's making fun of one another." (11th grade, Raimilla School)

RUBÉN: "In other schools the majority laugh at the Mapuche culture.... one classmate played the *kultrún* (Mapuche musical and spiritual drum) and then they all started making fun and bullying him, so after that they didn't have any more Mapuche celebrations.... but here the vast majority know about respect. They are all involved in culture." (11th grade, Lihuén School)

Students also narrated the benefits that indigenous knowledges had brought to their understanding of health and gastronomy – two of the technical-vocational specialities available:

NELLY: "I came here to study nursing and started in 11th grade. I started to learn about both types of illnesses and cures; Mapuche and common techniques. I saw that there was more than just traditional medicine." (12th grade, Raimilla School)

DANIELA: "I've been with my grandmother to the local health centre and she doesn't speak very good Spanish, and they discriminate her quite a bit there ... so I think it's good to have technician nurses or doctors who know how to speak in Mapzungún, so that all these elderly people can be looked after properly." (11th grade, Raimilla School)

LUCHO: "[Intercultural gastronomy] helps bring culture forward because there are many typical dishes that so many people have no idea about, and this course rescues these knowledges that are being lost, so it's more than just about learning to cook; it's about rescuing culture." (12th grade, Lihuén School)

The benefits of these practices are encouraging. The young people here are attentive to different forms of discrimination, emerging in different social contexts, and have pragmatic solutions about how to address these from their professional (indigenous) knowledges acquired in the programme. We also see the role that critical teachers can play in providing the young people with politicised knowledge resources that avoid essentialising and oversimplified histories, linking the subject matter to contemporary rights and personally lived experiences. The participants also note the importance of interculturality for all Chileans, rather than restricting it to an education *for* the Mapuche.

Overcoming New Racism Requires More Than IBE

Throughout this chapter, I have addressed the Chilean state's different political dispositions and actions towards developing a national education system. Over time there are clear instances of progress that have enabled greater access to mass education, the reduction of explicit forms of discrimination and cultural exclusion, and the partial inclusion of indigenous knowledges in specific geographic zones and schools through an intercultural and "bilingual" programme (though there is consensus that bilingualism is not a viable goal of these programmes).

I have discussed the double-edged nature of the decentralised neoliberal reforms to Chilean education introduced during the 1980s. On the one hand, the voucher system paved the way for state-subsidised private schools to implement their own curricular modifications, allowing for IBE content. On the other hand, although demands for autonomous education systems came from indigenous actors, IBE has, for the most part, been implemented as a top-down state initiative. This has meant indigenous knowledges have mostly been introduced as peripheral aspects of a mainstream curriculum that do not consolidate interculturality – by this we mean a mutual dialogue and learning between cultures. It is likely that, when implemented correctly, IBE has the potential to critically engage with structural racism, but this depends on each school's capacity to implement such measures.

IBE in Latin America has been interpreted as a political goal of appeasing lesser indigenous demands at the expense of more fundamental issues such as territorial and water rights, political representation, and autonomous governance (Richards, 2013). However, the students' comments suggest that cultural value can be salvaged even from state-led IBE programmes. The "freedom" provided by decree 280 for schools to develop their own educational plans and programmes has enabled individual actors and establishments to provide IBE programmes that are not completely restricted to following textbooks. However, this also means that each school is burdened with the task of developing their own ideas and initiatives within the financial restrictions that each establishment faces.

In an era of new racism, where practices of corporal punishment for speaking in *mapuzungún* (Poblete, 2003; Vergara & Mellado, 2018), or presenting indigenous peoples as primitive or backwards in textbooks have been superseded, IBE programmes operate under a new order of implicit racism. IBE stands as a constant symbol of *doing something* towards equality, even when nothing much is being done. Its limited scope means indigenous knowledges are subaltern or othered, always operating according to a diglossia logic in a peripheral and asymmetrical relationship to hegemonic, rational-positivist, whitened knowledges. *Mapuzungún* operates within a hierarchy of idioms, marginalised as a folkloric below the global language of English and the national language of Spanish. Yet the general gloss of IBE as an ongoing and present initiative from the state – inscribed in educational decrees, departments, and archives – gives the general appearance of being in favour of equality, cultural diversity, and individual rights. Perhaps most importantly of all, it prevents us from seeing the need for anti-racist education in all Chilean schools, capable of opening up spaces for critical and open discussions that confront these ideologies and practices. This is not within the remit of IBE, and even if it were, this would still be too restrictive given its formulaic implementation.

It is well documented that Chile has, over time, gradually shifted from an assimilationist discourse and practice towards one defined as neoliberal multiculturalism (Richards, 2013). There are clear signs of moving from a monolithic nation that is ethnically and culturally exclusive, towards one that acknowledges diversity, and proclaims inclusivity, without administering any radical changes to its organisation. Opposition to, and disassociation from, racism is the logical outcome of any political rhetoric in the modern era, but the conspicuous absence of any active mechanisms to overhaul systemic or institutional inequalities means they effectively comply with the reproduction of the same inequalities. Indeed, the freedom afforded to schools means a number of those included in the research, despite having indigenous compositions above the stipulated 20%, do very little to implement anything beyond the symbolic inclusion of indigenous students and knowledges. Even IBE schools do not address issues of discrimination or structural racism from critical and educationally enriching perspectives. Instances of peer harassment are dealt with as isolated instances (see Chapter 3), rather than as opportunities to create transformative climates in which students learn about inter-ethnic relations, inequalities, and cooperation.

New racism, I propose, enables us to view how young people today inhabit spaces that operate under ongoing racial projects that are refined and shift in their content and vocabulary, but which maintain specific ideological and material inequalities. Lived experiences in schools shape indigenous youth identities along racial lines as they are exposed to particular forms of knowledge, institutional values and norms, and school relationships (Pollock, 2005). However, as seen above, certain practices can challenge systems of racial inequality. Teachers can use alternate materials to teach an anti-racist curriculum to go beyond the exclusion or passive recognition of indigenous knowledges, both historical and contemporary. IBE schools offer no guarantees that all forms of new racism will be eliminated. In fact, they may even allow new racism to continue unopposed since they are held up as comparatively favourable advancements on formerly explicitly racist forms of schooling. In the chapters that follow I will demonstrate some of the ways schools either relegate Mapuche culture and language to the periphery of school life or subordinate it altogether. The conspicuous absence of knowledges relevant to Mapuche identity in schools with high indigenous compositions, I will argue, have detrimental effects on the young people's sense of belonging. To this end, I propose that solutions be sought beyond IBE initiatives, towards critically anti-racist education and culturally sensitive pedagogies that can interrogate the subtler forms of new racism that are entrenched in many Chilean schools, including some with IBE status.

Note

1 Some of the data was previously cited in Webb (2015) and Webb and Radcliffe (2013).

References

Anand, P., Mizala, A., & Repetto, A. (2009). Using school scholarships to estimate the effect of private education on the academic achievement of low-income students in Chile. *Economics of Education Review, 28*, 370–381.

Augostinos, M., Tuffin, K., & Every, D. (2005). New racism, meritocracy and individualism: Constraining affirmative action in education. *Discourse and Society, 16*(3), 315–340.

Bellei, C., Cabalín, C., & Orellana, V. (2014). The 2011 Chilean student movement against neoliberal educational policies. *Studies in Higher Education, 39*(3), 426–440.

Bello, A. (1999). *Intelectuales indígenas y universidad en Chile: Conocimiento, diferencia y poder* (Working Paper). Universidad ARCIS, Santiago de Chile.

Bengoa, J. (1985). *Historia del pueblo mapuche (siglo XIX y XX)*. Santiago: Ediciones Sur.

Boccara, G. (1999). Etnogénesis mapuche: Resistencia y restructuración entre los indígenas del centro-sur de Chile (siglos XVI–XVIII). *Hispanic American Historical Review, 79*, 425–461.

Canales Tapia, P. (1998). Escuelas chilenas en contextos mapuche. integración y resistencia, 1860–1950. *Última Década, 9* [online], 1–9.

Cañulef, E. (1998). *Introduccion a la Educación Intercultural Bilingue.* Temuco: Instituto de Estudios Indígenas Universidad de La Frontera.

Carnoy, M. (1998). National Voucher Plans in Chile and Sweden: Did privatization reforms make for better education? *Comparative Education Review, 42*(3), 309–337.

Carruthers, D., & Rodriguez, P. (2009). Mapuche protest, environmental conflict and social movement linkage in Chile. *Third World Quarterly, 30*(4), 743–760.

CASEN. (2013). *Encuesta de caracterización socioeconómica Chile.* Santiago: Gobierno de Chile.

Course, M. (2011). *Becoming Mapuche: Person and ritual in indigenous Chile.* Urbana, IL: University of Illinois Press.

Crow, J. (2006). *Rethinking national identities: Representations of the Mapuche and dominant discourses of nationhood in twentieth century Chile.* PhD Thesis, University of London.

Crow, J. (2010). Negotiating inclusion in the nation: Mapuche intellectuals and the Chilean state. *Latin American and Caribbean Ethnic Studies, 5*(2), 131–152.

Delannoy, F. (2000). Education reforms in Chile, 1980–98: A lesson in pragmatism. *Country Studies Education Reform and Management Publication Series, 1*, 1–80.

Donoso, S. (2013). Dynamics of change in Chile: Explaining the emergence of the 2006 'Pingüino' movement. *Journal of Latin American Studies, 45*(1), 1–29.

Egaña, M. (2000). *La educación primaria popular en el siglo XIX en Chile: Una práctica de política estatal.* Santiago: LOM.

Elacqua, G., Schneider, M., & Buckley, J. (2006). School choice in Chile: Is it class or the classroom? *Journal of Policy Analysis and Management, 25*(3), 577–601.

Espinola, V. (1993). *The educational reform of the military regime in Chile: The system's response to competition, choice, and market relations.* PhD Dissertation in Education, University of Wales.

Foerster, R. (1993). *Introducción a la religiosidad Mapuche.* Santiago: Editorial Universitaria.

Foerster, R. (1996). *Jesuitas y mapuches: 1593–1767.* Santiago: Editorial Universitaria.

Foerster, R., & Montecino, S. (1988). *Organizaciones, líderes y contiendas mapuches 1900–1970.* Santiago: Arancibia Hnos.

Haughney, D. (2007). Neoliberal policies, logging companies, and Mapuche struggle for autonomy in Chile. *Latin American and Caribbean Ethnic Studies, 2*(2), 141–160.

Loncón, E., Martinez, C., & Breveglieri, S. (1997). *Construyendo Una Educación Intercultural Bilingüe Mapuche* [Constructing a Mapuche Bilingual Intercultural Education]. Temuco: Conadi-Siedes.

Mallon, F. (2005). *Courage tastes of blood: The Mapuche community of Nicolás Ailío and the Chilean state, 1906–2001.* London: Duke University Press.

Marimán, P. (1997). Demanda por Educación en el Movimimiento Mapuche en Chile, 1910–1995. In A. Bello, P. Marimán, & A. Wilson (Eds.), *Pueblos indígenas: Educación y desarrollo*. Santiago-Temuco: Centro de Estudios para el Desarrollo de la Mujer-Instituto de Estudios Indígenas.

Matear, A. (2006). Barriers to equitable access: Higher education policy and practice in Chile since 1990. *Higher Education Policy, 19*, 31–49.

Matear, A. (2007). Equity in education in Chile: The tensions between policy and practice. *International Journal of Educational Development, 27*(1), 101–113.

Ministry of Education (MINEDUC). (2009). *Decreto de Educación 280*. Santiago de Chile: Government of Chile.

Ministry of Education (MINEDUC). (2011). *Estudio sobre la implementación de la educación intercultural bilingüe*. Santiago de Chile: Government of Chile.

Ministry of Education (MINEDUC). (2017). *Programa de Educación Intercultural Bilingüe 2010–2016*. Santiago: Ministerio de Educación.

Noggler, A. (1972). *Cuatrocientos años De misión Entre Los Araucanos*. Temuco, Chile: San Francisco.

Omi, M., & Winant, H. (1994). *Racial formation in the United States*. New York, NY: Routledge.

Organización de Estados Iberoamericanos (OEI). (2009). *Sistematización de los distintos ámbitos de intervención en los establecimientos educacionales del programa Orígenes*. Santiago de Chile: Valente.

Ortiz, P. (2009). *Indigenous knowledge, education and ethnic identity: An ethnography of an intercultural bilingual education program in a Mapuche School in Chile*. Ann Arbor: VDM Verlag.

Pinto, J. (2000). *La formación del estado y la nación, y el pueblo Mapuche: De la inclusión a la exclusión*. Santiago: Universidad de Santiago.

Poblete, M.P. (2003). Discriminación Étnica en Relatos de la Experiencia Escolar Mapuche en Panguipulli. *Estudios Pedagógicos, 29*, 55–64.

Pollock, M. (2005). *Colormute: Race talk dilemmas in an American school*. Princeton, NJ: Princeton University Press.

Richards, P. (2013). *Race and the Chilean miracle: Neoliberalism, democracy and indigenous rights*. Pittsburgh, PA: Pittsburgh University Press.

Samaniego, A., & Ruiz, C. (2007). *Mentalidades y políticas wingka: Pueblo mapuche, entre golpe y golpe (de Ibáñez a Pinochet)*. Madrid: CSIC.

Serrano, S. (1995). De escuelas indígenas sin pueblos a pueblos sin escuelas indígenas: La educación en la Araucanía en el siglo XIX. *Revista Historia, 29*, 423–474.

Serrano, S., Ponce de León, M., & Rengifo, F. (2018). *Historia de la educación en Chile, 1810–2010* (2nd ed.). Santiago de Chile: Taurus.

Stuchlik, M. (1979). Chilean native policies and the image of the Mapuche Indians. *The Queens University Papers in Social Anthropology, 3*, 33–54.

Vergara, J., & Mellado, H. (2018). La violencia política estatal contra el pueblo nación mapuche durante la conquista tardía de La Araucanía y el proceso de radicación (Chile, 1850–1929). *Dialogo Andino, 55*, 5–17.

Vergara, J.I., Foerster, R., & Gundermann, H. (2005). Instituciones Mediadoras, Legislación Y Movimiento indígena De DASIN a CONADI (1953–1994). *Atenea, 491*, 71–85.

Webb, A. (2015). Indigenous schooling grants in Chile: The impacts of an integrationist affirmative action policy among Mapuche pupils. *Race, Ethnicity and Education, 18*(3), 419–441.

Webb, A., & Radcliffe, S. (2013). Mapuche demands during educational reform, the penguin revolution and the Chilean winter of discontent. *Studies in Ethnicity and Nationalism, 13*(3), 320–341.

Williamson, G. (1998). Políticas de educación intercultural bilingüe y reforma educativa. In *Actas Seminario El Enfoque de educación intercultural bilingüe en la enseñanza media.* Temuco: Chile.

3 Mapuche Youth Identities in Chilean Schools

Based on the previous chapter, most would agree that educational experiences and opportunities for indigenous students have advanced positively since the colonial period in Chile. Access to schools is far wider, explicit forms of discrimination have been eradicated, and a number of social programmes have been implemented during the last decades favouring more democratic and inclusive practices. All schools reject the *isms* that have historically affected different social groupings, whether classism, sexism, racism, ableism, or others. However, in accordance with the theories reviewed at the beginning of the book, this progress does not equate to the eradication of systemic racism. This chapter brings into focus the ways schools continue to form, influence, and change young people's perceptions of what it means to be indigenous. I examine narratives about students' reasons for choosing their schools, their relationships with teachers and peers, and their academic aspirations. I do so with a view to presenting the ways Mapuche youth engage with the racially and class-inflected hierarchies of inequality present in the Chilean education system and how this affects their everyday negotiated meanings of indigeneity.

Above all else I wish to emphasise the ambivalence of this process. This is best captured by addressing the constraining effects of educational spaces in their capacity to mould and delimit young people into particular ways of seeing the world on the one hand, while paying due attention to the pathways and possibilities that the young people find to express their indigenous identities on the other hand. Structural racism exerts a pressure on its subjects to become accustomed to structural inequalities and symbolic violence as an everyday part of lived reality and I present a number of examples that represent the majority opinion of accepting a politics of omission and exclusion. In this way, young people must navigate within the racialising categories imposed by institutions that operate according to new racism logics. However, I also give space to those who see through these practices and exercise some agency to resist them. The mere fact that

DOI: 10.4324/9781003090700-4

this racialising pressure exists in schools does not mean individuals' identities are entirely determined because other spheres of life also influence how young people define their sense of self and place.

School socialisation is vital to understanding individual identity formation. In the early stages of life, social identity is developed from within the ethnic boundary (Wimmer, 2013) by significant others, such as family members, and, in most cases, proves relatively unproblematic. However, upon entering school life, the legitimation of why things are as they are is required. By entering a world of specialised and compartmentalised roles, with fragmented relations with generalised others, the individual's concept of reality during secondary socialisation requires more conscious decisions regarding how to present him/herself (Berger & Luckman, 1967). In short, schools represent life at the identity boundary, where conflicting narratives are presented and contested (Cohen, 1985). It is also worth noting that a number of the young people interviewed reside at their schools during the week due to the lack of educational provision around their rural homes. Extended periods of time spent in these spaces mean prolonged exposure to these socialising forces. As Edensor notes, these are spaces in which an interweaving process between action and structure occurs in individual identity formation:

> Institutionalization can be understood ... as the organisation of everyday life, and the solidification of everyday practical knowledge and value. In both cases, predictability is installed and bodies, things and spaces become subject to ordering processes ... the persistence of such common patterns over time underpins a common sense that this is how things are and this is how we do things. There is thus an interweaving of conscious and unreflexive thought which typifies everyday practice and communication. Most actions are habitually (re)enacted without reflection.
>
> (Edensor, 2002, p. 19)

There are clear overlaps here with the existing theory developed by Bourdieu and Passeron on the work of schooling. Institutions have the power – through the drudgery and monotony of daily life – to impose particular ideas about the legitimacy of identities and their choices. On the other hand, individuals are not helpless when confronted with this normative tide and can exercise their own forms of resilience or resistance by drawing on different resources or capital. Given this tension between structure and agency, I propose that new racism literature can benefit from a Bourdieusian framework. That is, it provides more scope for considering the ways racialised structures become ingrained into social actors' common-sense structures, exerting symbolic violence upon them. Below I consider the contribution of Bourdieu's concepts of educational field, habitus, and capital to new racism.

Moving Forwards with New Racism: A Bourdieusian Perspective

It may not be immediately apparent why Bourdieu would be a good fit for analyses of new racism, given that he is widely believed to have overlooked issues relating to ethnicity. Such accusations are erroneous, especially given that his earliest work on the Algerians demonstrated these sensibilities (Wallace, 2017), while his later texts (notably The Weight of the World [1999] and Pascalian Meditations [2000]) also acknowledge intersectional issues between class, race, and gender. It is true that during the middle period of his career – when his most influential and theoretically profound concepts were developed – Bourdieu focused on socioeconomic inequalities, but these have been usefully applied and adapted to understand racialising and discriminatory processes in educational settings (Ball et al., 2003; Lewis, 2003; Reay et al., 2007; Rollock, 2007).

In *Reproduction in Education, Society and Culture* (1990) Bourdieu and Passeron present a theory for understanding the symbolic violence enacted by education. This violence entails the reproduction of cultural norms misrecognised (or misunderstood) as natural, neutral, and legitimate to all those who participate in education, resulting in the perpetuation of existing power relations in the educational field and broader society. The importance of this theory to the current book is to consider why racialisation might be a pervading force in schools without entirely stripping individuals of the capacity to resist. That is, why people, on the whole adhere to structural rules in common-sense naturalised ways, but equally why social rules are not set in stone and can – occasionally – be modified. Bourdieu's work avoids the pitfalls of presenting social actors as *either* sole agents of their own futures *or* overdetermined by macrostructures (Jenkins, 1992). Instead, by offering a *both/and* scenario we can ask why, for example, racism is not more self-evident in schools, why there aren't more institutional efforts to reorganise anti-racist curricula, or why teacher expectations so often conform to discriminatory stereotypes. At the same time, we can ask how certain teachers disrupt existing racial categorisations, and how ethnic minority students survive in schools, react creatively to racist schooling, and maintain their identities.

There can be little doubt, from Bourdieu's perspective, that structural factors guide individual behaviour most of the time. The logic behind decisions made at school-levels, according to Bourdieu and Passeron, obey existing power relationships and the imperative to keep the education system functioning around the criteria deemed by dominant groups to be most prestigious or virtuous. In this way, the content of what the authors call *pedagogic action* always reflects the interests of dominant groups and is therefore arbitrary. That is, there is no inherent superiority about one group's cultural tastes and values than another's. However, this action ultimately comes to be accepted as *the* legitimate culture over time through *pedagogic work*, which refers to those aspects of schooling that are enacted over long periods of time, training students into particular dispositions and ways of behaving according to the principles of a cultural arbitrary:

> In any given social formation, the dominant education system is able to set up the dominant pedagogic work as the work of schooling without either those who exercise it or those who undergo it ever ceasing to misrecognise its dependence on the power relations making up the social formation in which it is carried on.
>
> (1990, p. 67)

These are generally accepted by students because of the *pedagogic authority* of the teachers carrying out daily *pedagogic action* in schools. As noted previously, teachers are not necessarily any more aware of this symbolic violence than students. This is because their training, and the standardised conditions that they have to work under (standardised testing, for example) also comply with this cultural arbitrary. Bourdieu explicitly links pedagogic work to a concept from his broader work: *habitus*. In the education field, all social actors' expectations and dispositions are delimited or inculcated into what is thinkable, through the exclusion of what becomes unconceivable, thus reproducing a particular cultural order. The authors call the institutionalised regulations imposed on all pedagogic work, the work of schooling (1990, p. 57), claiming that, "one of the least noticed effects of compulsory schooling is that it succeeds in obtaining from the dominated classes a recognition of legitimate knowledge and know-how" (1990, p. 42). Hence the majority of what goes on in schools is delimiting, maintaining an orthodoxy (or doxa) surrounding the culture it is designed to reproduce.

Related to this, success in the education field depends on having the cultural capital valued by dominant groups at one's disposal. According to Bourdieu, these forms of capital are seen as legitimate by all and misrecognised as merit or talent, including those whose family cultural heredity (inherited cultural capital) differs from that of the school. A school's pedagogic action requires students to conform to the dominant cultural capital that is selected to mirror broader social structures, and sanctions family pedagogic action that does not match its own as being non-academic and unbefitting. This ultimately results in a "subjective expectation of objective probability," meaning people's expectations of, and outcomes in, education are normatively understood as their own doing – their own achievement or lack of it – despite adhering to the existing structure of capital distribution in society (Jenkins, 1992, p. 71). Hence exclusion becomes a matter of personal responsibility, masking the unequal distribution of capital in society.

Bourdieu's class-centred analysis is readily applicable to the equally important issue of racism (among various social identities) (Reay et al., 2007). Racialisation, as discussed in the introduction, is not an automatic process; it occurs daily through certain structures, naturalising ideas about race, and maintaining the racial status quo (Cross & Naidoo, 2012; McKnight & Chandler, 2012). Racial meanings and categories are entirely compatible with Bourdieu and Passeron's definition of a cultural arbitrary, since they are symbolic impositions without any inherent or intrinsic justification other than the exercise of a particular form of power. That is, certain cultural aspects are made to seem natural and of value – particularly when attributed to physiological or phenotypical traits – within a field when in fact they are historic reproductions of symbolic violence that enable certain positions and structures of power to be maintained. The most obvious of these would be Western rationality, criticised by scholars working on intercultural knowledges as the globally predominant and legitimated mode of thinking that governs schools (Mignolo, 2000; Quilaqueo, 2012).

Cui (2017) extends Bourdieu's concept of habitus to its racialised significance, where durable dispositions are formed and socialised around dominant (white-) national ideals and cultural values, while marginalising otherness. According to Cui, an embodied habitus is particularly relevant in multi-ethnic schools because the school composition itself is a continual visible reminder of the colour/racial lines upon which the school is founded, and the subordination of minorities an expected or "natural" outcome of the field. Similar conclusions have also been reached by authors working on collective teacher beliefs and expectations (who use the term institutional habitus). They argue latent or implicit racism can be shared by staff creating a school culture that is more permissive or accepting of discrimination (Diamond, Randolph, & Spillane, 2004; Rubie-Davies, 2007). In a very real sense, this pedagogic authority will hold important sway over students' identities in their schools. Racial ideas are therefore hard to dislodge because they are historically inscribed into the contemporary cultural structure of society (McKnight & Chandler, 2012). These inscriptions create subjective expectations and bodily dispositions.

Up to this point, Bourdieu's ideas seem only to convince us of why subjective individuality almost invariably complies with the existing structure, rather than to exercise any agency within it. However, while Bourdieu placed greater emphasis on the structural aspects of habitus, he also acknowledged its agentic nature in so far as strategies and abilities can be used to acquire a broader array of capital (Reay, 2004). Another key text, *The Inheritors*, acknowledges that adaptive practices among students from lower social classes make it possible to survive in higher education (1979, p. 8). Edgerton and Roberts (2014) confirm that people's behavioural patterns and repertoires can adapt to new fields, particularly when they draw on capital from outside sources.

Bourdieu has often been accused of expressing a certain elitism in his work, especially in regard to cultural capital (Sullivan, 2002). That is, the structural implications of not having the "correct" type of capital to succeed in the education system takes us perilously close to deficit theories; that disadvantaged students will only get ahead when they acquire the standard culture they are lacking. However, as Lewis (2003) observes, Bourdieu's work can be usefully applied to understanding racial disparities due to different types of capital among students. Scholars have taken Bourdieu's work forwards by offering a counterproposal that stresses the importance of alternate forms of capital (including a more generic "ethnic capital" [Modood, 2004; Rollock, 2007]). From this perspective, alternative resources from home or community environments enable students to progress with their education without adopting the privileged culture of dominant groups. Yosso (2005), for example, states that students of colour draw on "community cultural wealth" to provide alternate knowledge and to resist inequalities from the margins of education. Similarly, Stanton-Salazar (2011) has drawn out the importance of social capital among ethnic minority populations for getting ahead in education; embodied in peers and transformative adult agents in schools. Overall these scholars demonstrate that Bourdieu's work on education can usefully be combined with critical race theories to understand the nuanced and complex ways that contemporary forms of racism – in particular those implicit and cultural-based assumptions – operate, and are resisted, in schools.

In short, Bourdieu's work provides a persuasive and impressive logic for why structural aspects of schooling ensure that racial meanings endure in pedagogic work, and although these dispositions are prevalent and powerful, they do not exclude the possibility of resistance or transformation in these fields. I now demonstrate these tensions through young people's narratives that can be divided into four broad issues: 1) (mis)recognising the education field, referring to structural issues of the neoliberal education system, 2) the subjective internalisation of educational chances or aspirations about school success and future prospects, 3) racialised habitus, which focuses on everyday teacher–student and peer relationships and attitudes towards discrimination, and finally 4) narratives of resistance that suggest how the work of schooling is countered by students who perceive the omission of indigeneity in daily school life.

Educational Field: (Mis)Recognising Institutional Inequalities

All the students involved in the research partake in a hierarchically asymmetrical educational field. In Chile this adheres to whitened, urban, progressive/modern ideals contained within an economically driven neoliberal model of educational competition. Schools associated with the rural countryside, technical-vocational education, and indigeneity fall outside this model. That is, these schools are socioeconomically and racially ascribed as inferior or deficient within this educational market-place. This applies to all ten establishments discussed in this chapter, since four are state schools and five private state-subsidised non-profit schools. Eight are located in rural or semirural areas of the Araucanía Region (two are in Temuco, the largest city in the region), and all have indigenous enrolments above the national average, ranging between 18% (Castaña School) and 88% (Lihuén School).

I directed general questions to the students about whether they thought they attended a high-status school, and the reasons for their answer.[1] Two students responded by referring directly to the school's Mapuche name and reputation, and how their standing in this hierarchy was affected:

DAVID: "[Others]see this school as just being for Mapuche. [As] a Mapuche school in the countryside which, in other words, means it is a lesser school."

ELENA: [Pupils from other schools] "see us like that because they go to [name removed] school, so they look down on us, all cool. They ask 'where do you study?', then say 'we trample all over you'" [the meaning here is 'we're so much better than you']

DAVID: "They have always thought of us as being the least/worst (*los menores*) and the poorest." (Focus group, 12th grade, Raimilla School)

Another student articulated a similar idea, but this time linking indigenous compositions to economic capital as determining their place within the educational field:

RENÉ: "In the school where I went before there was a lot of discrimination toward Mapuche kids from the countryside; the other kids thought they had more money and looked down on us."

INTERVIEWER: "So it was a money issue?"

RENÉ: "Money, where one was from, and if one was Mapuche or not." (10th grade, Raimilla School)

These were some of the few students who acknowledged the ways that their school fit into a broader status hierarchy. A majority were more prone to answer my question by criticising a lack of adequate infrastructure in their school. This is understandable from the students' perspectives, since they are the most pressing issues that affect them most directly. The moment one enters these establishments, a number of material concerns are immediately apparent. Most classrooms are poorly equipped, with crumbling and sparsely decorated walls, some had windows boarded up for months at a time awaiting repair, and in winter are often cold. When I asked students to specify why they weren't happy with the school, many indicated the following kinds of issues:

EVA: "No question, I'd change the bathrooms and the classrooms which are run-down and dirty." (8th grade, Acevedo School)

FERNANDA: "I like the library because there is internet there and it's the most enclosed and warmest space [in the school] ... It would be nice if all the classrooms were like that but they can't be because there are broken windows." (12th grade, Lago Profundo School)

ALEX: "Every year in winter it's the same, we are cold, we have to put our outdoor jackets on indoors. Sometimes we complain about the lack of firewood for the classrooms, but they [school staff] hardly take any notice." (9th grade, Campos Verdes School)

JUAN: "I don't like the lack of supplies here, especially as I'm studying intercultural nursing but they don't have the things we need to properly learn the course." (12th grade, Raimilla School)

However, the real issue here is how the inadequate facilities in these schools cause certain colour-blindness, reducing systemic inequalities – affecting the overly represented indigenous students in these establishments – to individual school problems. That is, they draw attention away from why the neoliberal education system produces low quality state-funded private schools catering to indigenous and poor families in the Araucanía Region. It deflects scrutiny from the educational field towards an individually focused problem of being a poor rural school and that this is framed as a naturally occurring phenomenon. In this way, racial and class-inflected issues are left aside, thus failing to call to accountability the educational market dynamics, or to query who benefits from the power relations governing this hierarchical arrangement.

The quality of education and unequal school choice are huge political concerns in Chile. Few students directly criticised aspects of the national education structure and equality of opportunity, but most attend these schools due to a lack of better options. According to Elacqua (2012), school choice in Chile is a market-oriented discourse that provides the illusion of autonomous choice, but which reinforces existing social stratification. Those likely to be disproportionately concentrated in public and private state-subsidised, low-quality, technical-vocational schools are low-income families and those from indigenous homes. Unlike private schools that are empowered to "cream skim" the highest performing students, private state-subsidised schools must compete in a mid- and low-range educational market that seeks enrolments from lower achieving students, in order to raise enough finances to keep the schools running.

When asked about how they came to study at the school, students gave different reasons, often repeating the concept of *choice*. The most common reasons were the technical-vocational curricular, proximity to their home, and the desire to go to school with students similar to themselves. Some answers are provided below, and as becomes apparent, these outcomes do not equate to "choices," given their limited range of options:

JULIO: "It was partly my parents choice and partly mine. I wanted to go to Temuco, but I didn't get in to the school I wanted, so I came here." (12th grade, Lago Profundo School)

ANGELA: "Where I live there aren't any secondary schools, so I chose to come here." (12th grade, Campos Verdes School)

ENZO: "I chose to come here because of the profession it could offer me." (11th grade, Campos Verdes School)

GREGORIO: "My parents sent me here because they thought I was mixing with the wrong crowds in my other school, and they thought because it's a small town the other kids would be better, so they chose this one." (11th grade, Lihuén School)

Although none of the students mentioned financial hardship (possibly a sensitive and private issue), head teachers working at two of the schools with boarding facilities mentioned that some families sent their children to the school because they didn't have enough to feed all the family members (Campos Verdes and Lago Profundo).

Following McKnight and Chandler (2012), I suggest Bourdieu's notion of field can be applied to racialised educational contexts in which valued resources are unequally distributed. As Bourdieu noted, the "field presupposes, and generates by its very functioning, the belief in the value of the stakes it offers" (Wacquant, 1989, p. 39). Bourdieu clarified that fields are monopolised by agents with capital, located within the "structure of the distribution of species of power (or capital) whose possession commands access to the specific profits that are at stake in the field" (Ibid.). Parents and students "choose" these schools, but largely because of a lack of access to other options with a better mix of students, educational opportunities, or positive school climates. The education field becomes an accepted social arrangement that determines who has access to which types of school. School choice legitimises this process by creating false expectations of new possibilities and opportunities for Mapuche parents and students who struggle for limited resources, but without access to the higher stakes of educational status or prestige. In this supposedly level playing field, establishments operating in this social arena become valued for providing boarding, food, good school climate, and professional certificates/credentials. In this sense, school choice is suggestive of agency and empowerment, but actually just normalises the existence of market-oriented hierarchies of schools. Only those with elite economic and cultural capital are able to access the profits to be derived from this process.

In other cases, students explicitly named the benefits of attending a school with high indigenous composition as providing a safe haven from external prejudice:

LIDIA: "There's no need to discriminate here but it's different at other schools. Where I went [before] for example I was discriminated against because I was Mapuche and the rest weren't [...] but here I feel welcomed (*acogida*) because we are all the same." (12th grade, Lago Profundo School)

EDUARDO: "Here in the school they all respect me because I respect them [...] but outside [the school] I'm not respected because they [the public] are more racist. I lived on a road and everyone there was racist and called us countrysiders [derogatory term associated with rural poverty] and Indians." (12th grade, Lihuén School)

School segregation has been shown to be detrimental to equal education opportunities (Orfield & Lee, 2007). Isolating disadvantaged (including ethnic minority) students from peers from other socioeconomic backgrounds can have detrimental effects on educational performance and outcomes (Elacqua, 2012). Spatial segregation in Chile cannot be understood outside the context of ongoing racial discourses and power hierarchies that create normalised expectations of disadvantage for Mapuche youth attending these types of establishments. Following Bonilla-Silva (2006), I would argue that these inequalities – stemming from deeply segregated education are explained away by a naturalised framing of the social world, as "just how things are" in these rural areas of the Araucanía. Teachers also assume (as I demonstrate in Chapter 4) that high indigenous compositions in the poorest schools are merely owing to parental choices who gravitate towards others who are similar to them. This allows the unequal educational field to continue unopposed.

The power of the education field, McKnight and Chandler note, is to "take oppressive social actions," without them being recognised as such (2012, p. 88). In this subsection I have noted three narratives that denote a misrecognition of the current educational field: individual school deficiencies, school choice, and indigenous "safety in numbers." These overlook and divert attention away from the pernicious effects of racialising logics in the field that cause indigenous peoples to be overrepresented, even segregated, into underfunded low-quality schools (Treviño et al., 2017). People thus normalise, and become accustomed to, white elite Chileans having access to the best educational stakes, leaving working class and indigenous students to "choose" from the inferior public and private state-funded schools available. The fact that this is usually reduced to a solely socioeconomic issue is part of the new racism era (Bonilla-Silva, 2006).

Internalisation of Educational Chances

Closely related to the difficulties of recognising the structural inequalities of the Chilean educational field, are young people's internalised aspirations about their educational chances. Bourdieu directly addressed educational expectations in *Distinction* (1984), stating that they are caught in a tension between individuals' and families' agentic habitus and capital accumulation, and the rules of the education system:

> Through the mediation of the disposition towards the future, which is itself determined by the group's objective chances of reproduction, these strategies depend, first, on the volume and composition of the capital to be reproduced; and secondly, on the state on the instruments of reproduction (inheritance law and custom, the labour market, the educational system, etc.), which itself depends on the state of the power relations between the classes.
>
> (cited in Jenkins, 1992, pp. 90–91)

That is, individuals form subjective expectations about the objective possibilities of success in education based on their own economic and cultural capital, but also based on their understanding of the "fairness" of educational opportunity. In what follows, I demonstrate how young Mapuche compare their families' economic capital and educational opportunities to those of the past, and therefore reach very favourable subjective expectations about their educational and labour possibilities. However, this internalised and historic comparison may be blind to the reproduction of privileges available to elite (white) Chileans in the contemporary neoliberal education market. This leads to misrecognition of educational opportunity. In *Reproduction*, Bourdieu and Passeron state that this consists of false pretences about objective possibilities:

> It follows that working class children pay the price of their access to secondary education by relegation into institutions and school careers which entice them with false pretences of apparent homogeneity only to ensnare them in a truncated educational destiny.
>
> (1990, p. 158)

If we extend this to a continuing racial project in Chile, we must ask how young Mapuche legitimate their trajectories through some of the lowest quality, technical-vocational educational establishments in the country. How does the goal of finishing 12th grade translate into positive outcomes for these young people? In this subsection, I argue that it is legitimated through expectations of educational credentials that were previously unavailable to their parents.

Across all the schools in my conversations with the young people I heard one word repeated time and again; *surgir*. Translated literally this means progress or emergence and was used by the participants to refer to their future social mobility. They carry the weight of expectation to exceed their parents' education levels (mostly incomplete secondary), whilst also recognising the need to contribute to family income without accumulating higher education debts. However, these aspirations also become a burden as they have internalised family narratives of the extreme poverty and difficulty their parents faced, so as to exacerbate their own feelings of privilege:

NATY: "Our parents say that we mustn't be like them, we must be our own person."

DENISSE: "Yes, our parents are right because they know about life in the countryside – they've lived longer in the country."

NATY: "They couldn't finish their studies because there wasn't enough money, they are giving us the opportunity to study, so we might have a job and live well. Now we can get ahead [*surgir*]."

JAVIER: "So we don't go hungry."

NATY: "It's about not staying down at the bottom, begging, like they had to, well, not begging but so that it's not difficult for us to find work, so we might have a job and hopefully one that lasts, depending on the [technical vocational] subject we study." (Focus group, 10th grade, Nacional School)

IGNACIO: "[My parents] always tell me off, saying, 'it wasn't the same for us as it is for you'. Because we have everything; but it wasn't like that for them. Now parents are involved in giving [children the chance to] study but they didn't have that chance. So now someone in the family can progress (*surgir*)."

FLORENCIA: "They tell me that I must study in order to be somebody better than they were, because they didn't get that chance, because they didn't study and didn't finish school. So I have to." (Focus group, 10th grade, Lago Profundo School)

HEBER: "We don't want to end up like our parents, because for other people our parents are nobodies." (11th grade, Lihuén School)

In all these narratives, there is a strong message of obligation and imperatives to succeed, placing a high degree of personal responsibility on themselves. This is highly commendable, under conditions that favour the rewarding of this effort. Comparisons with their parents cause students to conclude "we have everything," even though the conditions of this privilege are only true next to the extreme poverty that families in rural Araucanía homesteads experienced during the 1970s and 1980s. Most of the young people involved in the study come from households in the lowest two socioeconomic quintiles and they do not participate in a privileged education sector; average standardised test scores for these schools are below the regional and national mean. Mitigating this pressure to "succeed," is the hope of supporting the family. However, this also means moving away from the rural economy where most of their families live and work:

JULIA: "In the countryside it's like, empty, it's not like it was before when there were more young people, more people, but not any more. Apart from that, there are no more schools and no universities. And I think us youngsters are aiming higher ... at least I'm not thinking of finishing school and leaving it at that, but rather to keep studying. If I go [back] to the countryside, I'm not going to go there to study picking potatoes." (11th grade, Campos Verdes School)

ELENA: "Young people aren't very interested in continuing to live [in the countryside]. There are few who remain there because they prefer to go and study and leave home ... They [parents] want us to be more than simple bricklayers or farm workers. They prefer us to go to the city and work there, because there is more stable work than in the countryside where you practically can't get paid work." (12th grade, Raimilla School)

The young Mapuche students, then, are caught in structurally defined preferences, all of which require sacrificing some aspect of their future. Urban migration may mean (for those from rural homesteads) success in terms of social mobility and opportunities, but simultaneously may involve moving away from family territories.

In addition to the pressures of the past, and the anticipated sacrifices that social mobility will bring, there is another issue that structures the young people's expectations; the supposed opportunities available to them as Mapuche in an era of "affirmative action." Some participants expressed a belief that historic forms of discrimination are now a thing of the past, since state grants are given to the indigenous to support their studies and based on the idea that the Mapuche are now socially mobile. Of course, there are elements of truth to both these beliefs. As Fine notes (1993) half-truths allow systemic inequalities to continue unabated. For Alejandro and Pablo, both studying at the Campos Verdes School, it is only a matter of obtaining the education that the Mapuche used to lack:

ALEJANDRO: "A long time ago the Mapuche were always slaves or workers. But today, it's not like that. Nowadays, Mapuche are architects, police officers, soldiers, so there are many more opportunities than there used to be." (12th grade, Campos Verdes)

PABLO: "The Mapuche want to become middle class. But without an education you can't do anything. It's the same for someone who is completely Chilean – if they don't have an education, they will be street sweepers ... So I think the Mapuche are fighting for that." (11th grade, Campos Verdes School)

These participants see education as the "great equaliser;" something that was historically lacking for former generations of Mapuche. What is missed (or misrecognised), is that the school credentials provided by these establishments will not necessarily lead to the high-status job markets named by Alejandro. Contrasting their parent's and grandparent's upbringing leads the young people to assume their social mobility will be upward, but this overlooks existing inequalities in the labour market and the types of cultural capital rewarded. For Bourdieu, class position (which overlaps with a racial hierarchy) is maintained through the unequal assignment of educational credentials (institutionalised cultural capital), which give the appearance of meritocratic opportunity. Following Lewis (2003), I argue that whilst merit and effort are key aspects of educational success, not all students are given the same encouragement, support, or funding to reward that effort. One example of this more negative outcome, discussed by Simón, shows how schools' lack of information capital provision (guidance or knowledge) about higher education led many of his peers to seeking employment and remaining at home:

SIMÓN: "You can't do anything just with a school diploma. Because in my case, I know a number of young people ... who reach secondary school and afterwards don't know what to study. So they just drop out or some reach their final year, finish and stay at home." (11th grade, Lihuén School)

Besides these inequalities, the young people must also navigate, and resist, stereotypes directed towards them about the Mapuche being low achievers. Some young people were critical of these labelling effects:

LUCAS: "You hear people say ´no they're Mapuche, they won't make it' and like put us down so that you're tempted to say 'they're right, better give up now if they say I can't'. So it's easy to get discouraged, and to get bogged down and you wonder why they don't continue studying; it's because they feel they can't do it." (12th grade, Raimilla School)

NELLY: "I have a lot of reasons for wanting to continue studying [and one] is because of how they've treated me and my family ... so my objective is to return home and say I've found work, I have my certificate, and that in the countryside that shuts up the mouth of all those people who said we wouldn't amount to anything." (12th grade, Raimilla School)

PÍA: "For a long time there's been this idea that the Mapuche aren't as quick as the Chileans, or that they don't like studying, that they are the poor little ones [*pobrecitos*], and that the Mapuche ladies end up as nannies in the rich neighbourhoods." (12th grade, Campos Verdes School)

All this amounts to a heavy burden placed on the young people as they must negotiate poorly equipped schools, limited family resources, incomplete information about higher education, and pressures to succeed. This is especially the case for those holding beliefs about equality of opportunity for the Mapuche in the labour market. Failure to meet these expectations occasionally resulted in students blaming themselves.

MATEO: "They [my parents] didn't go to school because they had to look after the pigs."

TRINIDAD: "And now we have all these comforts."

AMANDA: "They had to walk to school."

JOSÉ: "Through all the mud. Imagine, we're so lazy in comparison." (Focus group, 10th grade, Lago Profundo School)

ANDRÉS: "I've really got to make the most of the opportunities I've been given. We have so many things in our favour to get ahead, like us students, today we have the chance to finish school and get a professional certificate, which before you couldn't get; it was only for middle class but now the working class are valuing that too and now there are more professionals than 20 years ago. Now the universities help those from rural areas, and the state are also helping those with few economic possibilities to get ahead." (12th grade, Campos Verdes School)

In accordance with a neoliberal education ideology, the participants frequently said a lack of educational success was their own fault; whether owing to age-related factors, or their own lack of motivation. In two exchanges, students proposed their hypotheses for why they or their classmates had low grades:

INTERVIEWER: "Why do you think the grades are low then?"

JOSEFA: "He fell in love."

PEDRO: "Yep, fell in love."

EMILIA: "He definitely fell in love."

JOSEFA: "The change in age, I guess."

FRANCISCO: "Puberty."

EMILIA: "the dopey age." (a Chilean expression *la edad del pavo*)

PEDRO: "Good point, it might be an age thing." (Focus group 8th grade, Linterna School)

ENRIQUE: "It's obvious isn't it? I don't concentrate, I mess around a lot with my phone."

DAVID: "The teachers are talking but I don't listen enough, or I forget to study."

BELTRÁN: "Sometimes I don't understand the task that we have to do, but when I do I make sure I do it."

INTERVIEWER: "And what about you girls?"

FLORENCIA: "Sometimes we just don't study, it's so dull." (8th grade, Quelentaro School)

Edgerton and Roberts (2014) discuss the importance of the alignment between subjective expectations and the reality of the educational field (habitus-field congruence). Whenever students who value the goal-oriented nature of the school (obtaining credentials) do not obtain grades that reflect these values, their habitus will require an adjustment, such as interpreting this incongruence as one's own failure. The vital issue at stake here is that schools do very little (or nothing) to address these inequalities. Schooling is about preparing students for technical-vocational professions or for high stakes testing. There is very little educational content directed towards addressing these structural inequalities; critically engaging Mapuche youth about what it means to grow up in the rural Araucanía Region or confronting external prejudices and stereotypes. As I demonstrate below, these are offset in preference of treating "all students alike," thus consigning Mapuche students to work out, identify, and manage these inequalities by themselves.

Ideas about the quality of education depend, then, on the point of reference around which students have been socialised and conditioned. Wherever students deem completing school to be a privilege, and a way into a simplified concept of social mobility and opportunity, there will be more tendency to understand failure as an individual problem. That is, there will be less inclination to see the field as failing to provide the necessary skills and competencies (capital) for success. The crucial issue here is not that students have deficient aspirations, but that those aspirations are socially produced in unequal structures of preference (Wacquant, 1989). There is a tension between new horizons of possibility, and the negative experiences of significant others.

What struck me most was that almost every student I spoke to agreed that the teachers in their school are concerned with their welfare, and always help to explain what students don't understand in class. I rarely heard complaints about the quality of teaching staff in schools. Likewise, confirming the general thesis of this book, it was hard to find any students who felt discriminated against by teachers. Typical complaints were made about certain teachers' pedagogical styles – usually disciplinarian – but they very rarely blame teachers, their schools, or the educational marketplace for their own grades or the school's averages. Instead, they associate their own success or failure as pertaining exclusively to their own merits and efforts (or lack of). Whilst I cannot confirm how much of what the young people say is accurate regarding their study habits, I can piece together a broader picture of how these young people's habitualised aspirations fit into the inequalities of the schools that – at the very least – contribute to lower academic performances.

Racialised Habitus and (Non) Peer Discrimination

This misrecognition is achieved and maintained, according to Bourdieu, through daily pedagogic work (cumulatively *the work of schooling*), transforming these inequalities into normative expectations. Many of the students are caught in an ambivalent space of accepting this persistent pedagogic work and its messages, incorporating them into a shared racialised habitus (McKnight & Chandler, 2012). One example is that of school discourse about equality; the idea that discrimination has been minimised (Bonilla-Silva, 2006). As will be seen in the next chapter, teachers frequently draw on this colour-blind framework to describe their non-prejudiced outlook. Chileanness is persistently established in classrooms as the normative category of belonging against which all else is measured. A number of the Mapuche youth echoed similar phraseology throughout the different research projects. These messages are replicated from other social spheres, but crucially schooling does little to abate or alter these perceptions; instead, reproducing them. Given the prevalence of this message in the young people's narratives, I cite a number of different schools and students:

FERNANDO: "They treat us normal [at the school]."
LIDIA: "Yes, like Chileans." (11th grade, Lago Profundo School)
LEO: "We don't feel any different to Chileans. It's where we're from." (8th grade, Tres Montes School)
CONSUELO: "I couldn't say I'm not Chilean, having been born and raised here. Maybe my surname is different but nobody treats me as any different." (10th grade, Campaña School)
JUDITH: "We're the same as Chilean, there's no real difference."
SIMÓN: "That's right, we're the same." (Focus group, 9th grade, Campos Verdes School)
ALEX: "I think we're all the same, and we have the same [material] things, the same feelings, there's no difference, we're all the same." (10th grade, Lihuén School)
VALÉRIA: "Some might feel different because they speak Mapuche or dress in their traditional clothes, but not me, I don't see myself as any different." (10th grade, Lago Profundo School)

Following Bourdieu's concept of *doxa*, when talking about categories of belonging, people express something of taken for grantedness about why things are the way they are. Talking about categories of belonging reveals something of our feel for the socially imposed game, and the inevitability of our position within it. Many of the young people are mestizo, so it is not unusual that the young people should express national pride. However, the subtle ways in which this reproduces hierarchical racial taxonomies of normality is certainly more striking. Under these terms, being Mapuche means being *othered*, and choices for expressing Chileanness may become preferred categories for most contexts. According to Moreno Figueroa (2010) racial politics in Latin American countries (she uses Mexico as a case study) draw on racelessness in which, "people are not recognized as racialized subjects but live through the consequences and everyday presence of racism and its distributed intensity" (2010, p. 391). Some of the young people live under this sense of racelessness in terms of believing in an increasing equality for all, but only through the negation of legitimate difference. Misrecognising sameness as a form of equality is part of new racism, by which the absence of explicit discrimination is taken to mean everyone is valued the same (Denis, 2015).

Many of the young people framed these ideas in relation to temporal distinctions between the past and the present. For many, being Mapuche was once a distinct category of belonging, encapsulated in knowing how to speak *mapuzungún* and participating in cultural practices. The young people see this mode of being as pertaining to their grandparents' generation, and expressed concern that their own lack of involvement in these traditions will result in this way of life being lost. Again, I emphasise that these narratives refer to issues that extend beyond the school gates, so while these establishments are by no means culpable of these issues, they do little to challenge the status quo. Put simply, they are not culprits, but they are accomplices:

VALÉRIA: "[the Mapuche] before knew about Mapuche culture, now the traditions are being lost, because now we Mapuche are together with Chileans, we're like the same because we live the same [way]."

INTERVIEWER: "So what has happened in society that those traditions are being lost?"

STEPHANNIE: "Because the young people don't care, it's all the same to them."

CRISTÓBAL: "They're ashamed."

STEPHANNIE: "There aren't too many Mapuche left either."

VALÉRIA: "Many don't speak Mapuche [*mapuzungún*]." (Focus group, 10th grade, Lago Profundo)

INTERVIEWER: "How does it make you feel that the traditions are being lost?"

EDUARDO: "Guilty really, because we don't stick our necks out and say to the rest that we are Mapuche. Sometimes we feel ashamed because of discrimination." (11th grade, Tres Montes School)

EVA: "I feel kind of guilty about the fact that my family traditions are dying out." (10th grade, Campaña School)

It is significant, following Bonilla-Silva's notion of colour-blind racism, that the young people have internalised a personalised guilt about failing to maintain indigenous traditions, language, and customs. Few students recognise institutional racism, or ask questions about why schools are not teaching them anything to the contrary. It will also become apparent in the next chapter that the students are replicating the same narratives as those voiced by teachers in their schools.

It should also be noted that not all students shared this sense of guilt or shame. For some, concerns about the loss of Mapuche identity were voiced in connection to the loss of certain benefits from social policies and affirmative action:

INTERVIEWER: "How do you feel about the Mapuche losing those traditions."
ROBERTO: "It's all the same to me."
DIEGO: "Me too."
MAX: "Well, not all the same really, because they give us lots of benefits."
    (Focus group 12th grade, Campaña School)
INTERVIEWER: "What is it that makes you proud to be Mapuche?"
EVELYN: "Mostly the access to studies – the grants, things like that."
NATALIA: "Now, like, there has been more pride [among Mapuche pupils] because there are people …. I have a sister in law who is not Mapuche and she says that the Mapuche have so many opportunities now, and that she would like to be Mapuche for that reason, and that's how it is for us."
PEDRO: "Yes that's it, the grants."
FLO: "So at least now the young people are taking it seriously, saying I am Mapuche, that's good, but yes it's mostly out of self interest than anything else. [various participants nod and say yes]."
BASTIÁN: "Yes. Grants are the most important thing." (Focus group 9th grade, Campos Verdes School)

These young people recognise the capital associated with indigenous status, and understand its strategic importance in order to get on in their education. Strategic ethnic identity has on occasion been associated with the negative connotations of abandoning more "authentic" cultural selves, or acculturation (St. Denis, 2007; Weaver, 1991). However, narratives like these are responses to a racialising system that reduces the value of indigeneity to a disadvantaged condition worthy only of compensatory policies. If these young people express "thin" identities (Cornell & Hartmann, 2007), I believe it is because they are forced to navigate within these inequalities. These broader social issues tie in with a lack of school proactiveness in regard to challenging monocultural norms and educating on the value of cultural diversity.

Part of this racialised habitus is the normalised expectations about schooling and experiences of inclusion. For many students, the perceived norm is when no distinctions are made between Mapuche and Chilean. On the few occasions when intercultural celebrations or ceremonies are enacted at the non-IBE schools, these became instances that forced the young people to take a position regarding their own belonging. Participants referred to feelings of shame or of losing face with other peers:

INTERVIEWER: "And how's the atmosphere among your classmates when they hold the *we tripantu* here?"
SERENA: "Hardly anyone comes."
TATIANA: "No-one participates."
SERENA: "And those that do are scared to because the rest make fun of them." (10th grade, Lago Profundo School)

INTERVIEWER: "Where have you experienced the most discrimination?"
EDUARDO: "At school."
INTERVIEWER: "And is that with Mapuche, or non-Mapuche peers?"
EDUARDO: "With the non-Mapuche, they treat us like Indians." (9th grade, Campaña School)

Once again, schools may not be the main cause for these expressions of shame, but their annual celebrations of *we tripantu* in very reductive and folkloric formats certainly reinforce this sentiment. For the most part, the whitened status quo of daily school life remains uninterrupted. Students are not asked to "act Mapuche" or observe any cultural customs that might connect them to indigenous knowledges or practices at any other point in the school year. This pedagogic work of exclusion has clear consequences for developing a racialised habitus; that is, an identity that is accustomed to being marginalised or hidden.

When asked about the school climate, and in particular relations with peers, the students consistently denied that racism or racist bullying practices occur there. As mentioned above, the students we interviewed see "safety in numbers" as a good reason for attending these schools. This is, to some extent, a credible notion since the "social misfit theory" proposes that ethnic discrimination is more likely to occur in schools with lower ethnic compositions where individuals who are seen as different are singled out for harassment (Graham & Juvonen, 2002). However, other comments offered by students suggest that occasional low-key forms of ethnic discrimination still occur in these high-indigenous composition schools. This gets to the heart of the issue of "racism with a smile" as those aspects of everyday new racism that are not considered truly racist or offensive (Bonilla-Silva, 2006). *Joking around, having a laugh* and *fun and games* were just some of the terms used to describe the ways being Mapuche could be a subject of derision.

Perhaps the most surprising aspect of these peer dynamics is that some of the young people indicated that it was not always non-indigenous Chileans who discriminated against them; it also arises from indigenous peers. Numerous participants called out others, or even themselves, as occasionally crossing the boundary and using derogatory categories of ascription about the Mapuche. The clearest example of this was highlighted by one student in a focus group at Nacional School:

ESTEBAN: "But you discriminated yourself the other day."
CRISTOBAL: "Why?"
ESTEBAN: "Don't you remember? The other day behind the workshop, and as a joke you said, ok, let's throw stones at the Mapuche." [laughter from group] .... And you're Cayuqueo Catrileo." (11th grade, Nacional School)

The reference to the student's two Mapuche surnames draws attention to his "non-mestizo" status (however spurious this concept is), implying that he had all the more reason not to discriminate against himself; that is, his own people. As I noted in Chapter 1, different categories of "purity" are a cause for internal differentiation, and are occasionally drawn on to distinguish social status. Below I cite some more examples of this widespread dynamic:

TATIANA: "Some know how to speak [*mapuzungún* words] but others then bully them with jokes."

STEPHANNIE: "They laugh at them and all that."

INTERVIEWER: "Where does that usually happen?"

TATIANA: "When we're in class and they start bothering each other, they start making jokes like saying "yayayayaya" [a well-known traditional war cry called *afafan*], and that they are f*ing *machi*."

INTERVIEWER: "Is that non-Mapuche classmates who do that?"

IGNACIO: "Sometimes."

STEPHANNIE: "But almost everyone here is Mapuche, most of the class, and they all make fun of each other as well." (10th grade, Lago Profundo School)

INTERVIEWER: "Is there any discrimination of the Mapuche in your class or school in general?"

AMELIA: "We sometimes make fun of each other, we'd say like…"

GONZALO: "We make fun among ourselves."

ELENA: "But it's well-meaning."

AMELIA: "We'd say like 'you're an Indian' or 'you're a brute' (*un bruto*)."

ELENA: "but well-meaning"

AMELIA: "Though [pause] not always. It depends who it's said to."

GONZALO: "If it's among friends its okay." (12th grade, Campos Verdes School)

VENANCIO: "Sometimes the Mapuche themselves say things to others, even I've called others 'indian' and I'm half Chilean half Mapuche." (10th grade, Campos Verdes School)

LEO: "When you get a group of Mapuche and Winka together, sometimes one of the non-Mapuche kids will give a nickname to the Mapuche, they start to mock them. That really makes me mad. When my friends do something [like that] I get all riled." (8th grade, Tres Montes School)

ALEJANDRO: "You get used to those who make fun, or who hit. It just becomes part of school life. It's nothing serious, just mucking around and those who are bored, just part of being an adolescent." (7th grade, Mapocho School)

PABLO: "It's like everyone in a Chilean society, because we're so accustomed to discriminating, you get me, that you end up discriminating yourself."

GREGORIO: "It's crazy that"
PABLO: "And you don't realise it but you just end up discriminating yourself." (Focus group, 11th grade, Campos Verdes School)

Racialised jokes and name calling are often part of boundary maintenance, offering youth a rhetorical space in which to navigate the ambiguities of new racism (Roberts, Bell, & Murphy, 2008). This is significant to the extent that issues of inclusion and exclusion are not predetermined; it is not only a matter of how Chilean society categorises the Mapuche, but also of how these individuals identify or position themselves in relation to these categories. Mapuche youth, in the absence of any explicit or direct treatment of these issues in school spaces, are left to work out (new) racism among themselves. There is a general sense among these students that nobody "really means it" when they treat others in derogatory ways. Of course, ethnic discrimination is not the only form of harassment that occurs in these contexts. Alejandro expanded on his comment (cited above) by arguing that it is part of an age-related process of social status negotiation among adolescents:

> Well, we're always laughing about something negative in others, that's just part of our habits; we're always messing with everyone.
> (7th grade, Mapocho School)

During focus groups in Santiago, we asked about whether the schools tackled discrimination, or how the young people would resolve issues of racist harassment if it occurred, and the most common answer was to deal with it individually, or through mechanisms beyond the school hierarchy:

JAIME: "I think the kids who get picked on are from another country, or for being darker-skinned, or because they are weaker than other boys, but also because they don't know how to defend themselves."
INTERVIEWER: "So if you saw or experienced harrassment, what would you do?"
ELENA: "Well in the school there's not that much help."
TAMI: "If you say something and they get suspended, then they come back and go after you."
ABRAM: "yeah, or they come back and maybe give you the cold shoulder."
JOSEFINA: "I'd hit the person, defend myself."
ERIC: "I'd tell my parents, but it's never happened to me so I wouldn't know how it feels."
ABRAM: "I'd defend myself too ... a punch for a punch."
JAIME: "Yep, you've just got to fight, that's the way it is." (Focus group, 8th grade, Clorinda School)
BEATRIZ: "Making fun of someone usually starts with a nickname, then it becomes something established and they keep bothering them with it. But if it keeps going, it usually ends in a fight."

PATY: "I know someone in the school who threatened to hit another boy if he continued to bother him."

INTERVIEWER: "And what do you think they ought to do, or what would you do in their situation?"

BEATRIZ: "Speak to my parents."

PATY: "Try to not let it affect me but if it continued I'd tell my parents too." (Focus group, 8th grade, Mapocho School)

The fact that students did not expect school support to deal with racist discrimination, or harrasment in general, is indicative of the role that schooling plays in their everyday lives. Schools are not places where these young people expect to find a solution to this kind of treatment – no matter how underplayed it is – since the establishments do not emit a clear and consistent message about the value of Mapuche identity (see Chapter 4).

Schools tend to look to contain or resolve issues of school climate through sanctions or peacemaking, but rarely through transformative and transversal practices that look to educate on issues such as racism (Carbajal & Fierro, 2018). In view of this, racism – albeit in its "playful" formats that the young people describe – tends to be misrecognised as harmless or as part of normal school life. This acceptance, for a majority of students, means coming to terms with an identity that is on the periphery and different, requiring careful management if it is to be approved. Contesting these whitened identities requires a willingness to go against the normative grain. Individuals who do so are required to legitimise their choices of identification and contend with the categories imposed upon them by dominant groups or institutions. These categorisations, and the narratives that underlie them, carry force and authority because they are deeply ingrained and legitimised at institutional and national levels.

Being Left Aside: Narratives of Resistance

Thus far I have emphasised the ways exclusion and marginalisation are assimilated and accepted as normal by the young people. However, Bourdieu's notion of habitus opens up possibilities of agency and resistance (Reay, 2004). Despite the subtler aspects of new racism, a number of students in the research expressed critical and derisive comments about national schooling and its omission of the Mapuche, or indigenous Peoples more generally, signalling a struggle against colour-blind racism. These young people were able to draw on family or personal capital to discursively oppose the racialised symbolic violence that they perceived in their school. Yosso's (2005) concept of resistant capital is particularly relevant here in detailing how young indigenous people – whether discursively or in practice – are able to forge different responses to their schooling. Crucially, all the cases cited below occur in two schools that do not provide IBE classes, and are therefore acts of resistant agency that come from outside the school gates. This smaller proportion of students were alert to whitened normative practices and the conspicuous absence of cultural diversity in their schools:

GASPAR: "At my last school, where I went until 8th grade, there was a teacher who taught *mapuzungún* .... I got here but there wasn't anything, it was like we were left aside." (11th grade, Campos Verdes School)
CATALINA: "In this school they don't value the Mapuche, they leave them to one side."
INTERVIEWER: "Do you mean the teachers, or students, or who?"
CATALINA: "Some teachers."
VICENTE: "Some, not all. But some speak with like innuendo [about the Mapuche] so that…"
RENATA: "So that you can't complain." (10th grade, Lago Profundo School)
ANDRÉS: "Have you realised about the school anthem? It's got nothing to do with the Mapuche, absolutely nothing, and an anthem is part of your identity, where you are educated, but nothing, nothing at all, it's a foreign anthem." (12th grade, Campos Verdes School)
ANA: "I was expecting something Mapuche at this school, I mean, the state schools are supposed to promote Mapuche culture but there's nothing here." (12th grade, Lago Profundo School)

Responding to the comments made by the students at the Lago Profundo school, I asked how that could be the case given that the school had built a *Ruka* (traditional Mapuche house) in an open space at the school. I assumed that such inclusive measures must have translated into some form of intercultural dialogue – perhaps even classes in a more culturally responsive environment. However, the response I received was emphatic:

RENATA: "But they never open it."
INTERVIEWER: "So can anyone tell me why it's there, and what they use it for?"
JOSÉ: "They only use it for the *we tripantu*."
CATALINA: "Only for that, and they don't open it at any other time."
RENATA: "after the *we tripantu* it's just there to look pretty."
JOSÉ: "I think they made it just to copy others, to look like a Mapuche school."
RENATA: "To resolve the lack of enrolments." (10th Grade, Lago Profundo School)

According to the logic of the educational marketplace, these private state-subsidised schools must compete for "customers" since state funding is allocated according to pupil enrolments. Shallow celebrations of multiculturalism in schools are commonplace in this context, as schools attempt to offer niche products. During my time in the schools, I saw on their websites, on posters, and on pamphlets, mission statements that included images of indigenous symbols (such as the *kultrún* – a *Machi* shaman's drum used for rituals – or pictures of children in traditional indigenous clothing), all suggesting deeper connections with indigenous culture. Folkloric recognition of difference does not demand changes to culturally normative school curricula. Instead, it favours a liberal discourse of inclusion, but only insofar as "other" students (ethnic minority in this case) learn to behave according to the standards of a national "us" (Ríos-Rojas, 2014) (Figure 3.1).

At the Campos Verdes School, some students were also critical of the school's exclusion of indigenous knowledges, and were especially condescending of sporadic and essentially folkloric attempts to signal intercultural sensibilities. Decades earlier the school had implemented a number of IBE practices, but after funding ran out, these aspects were left in ruin and demise. A *ruka* after falling into disrepair was eventually dismantled, faded school signs written in *mapuzungún* were left hanging at various points around the school without care, and a *rewe* (Mapuche altar for religious ceremonies) was left abandoned on the premises. Referring to the latter, Alex provided a scathing summary of the school's attitude towards sacred Mapuche symbolism, but then acknowledged that this same disrespect was replicated by the students:

Figure 3.1 The unused *ruka*

ALEX: "It's just there to look pretty [...] they should put the *rewe* somewhere where it can be respected [...] even though it's not used, it
should be in a sacred place. But even we use it as a goal post and we
kick it." (9th grade, Campos Verdes School)

The schools' decisions to allow these cultural elements to be discarded
or fall into disrepair offers a window onto the everyday ways that indigeneity is construed as something belonging to the past, or at best, as
something exceptional and inferior to the normative spaces, times, and
content of Chilean schooling. It is, in the words of Van Ingen and Halas,
indicative of how, "schools are landscapes shaped by colonial encounters,
including the obvious legacy of Indian Residential schools where white
superiority was violently asserted" (2006, p. 381) (Figure 3.2).

These power relations and cultural meanings are inscribed onto the
very fabric of school architecture and the demise of interculturality.
Fading murals and signs depicting Mapuche culture, and the elimination of the *kultrún* from the school emblem were all symbolic of
a present-day dilapidation. The curriculum also adheres to similarly
unchallenged monocultural dominance, as two young people at the
Lago Profundo School narrated:

Figure 3.2 A ***rewe*** returned by students to the playing field

ANA: "It's the Ministry who write the textbooks, they couldn't care less [about Mapuche perspectives] and that's why they only put in the World War and stuff like that." (12th grade, Lago Profundo School)

SERENA: "They were supposed to teach Mapuche here. In the enrolments it said they taught Mapuche here." (10th grade, Lago Profundo School)

Other students claimed to be dissatisfied with their knowledge of Mapuche history, and because of the lack of input from the schools, decided to study it by themselves. What is interesting to note, from the examples given below, is that despite being left aside by the school, students resist these assimilatory and asymmetrical forms of schooling:

SEBA: "I learnt all the same, because that's not taught here in the school, the cultural stuff and all that, the Mapuche history isn't taught much, sometimes in second year, in the history of Chile, but that's not much, two or three classes, nothing more, and they are all rubbish summaries."

MARTIN: "So we just investigate it ourselves." (Focus group, 10th grade, Campos Verdes School)

Students were also critical of the lack of politicisation in the teaching of history. Certain students recognised that this was not a neutral history, but one told from the Chilean perspective of a Republic seeking a unified nation. Although many students did not possess detailed knowledge of the historical-political aspects of their People's past, some held clear beliefs about the character and nobility of the Mapuche cause. This extended to opinions about Chilean society in general and a politics of exclusion. Some students (including some from the more "segmented" IBE schools) were quick to identify examples of stereotypes transmitted in the media, government, and the general public about the Mapuche – topics which they said had not been discussed at school:

JULIA: "What the government does is make the [general public] see what they want them to see and not the reality. So they start to say 'yes, we give them something and they just start terrorist activity that they are doing this and threatening with that'. [Chileans] don't realise that [activists] asked for something and haven't been given it yet. It's like they want to cover up the requests made by emphasising the supposed disorder caused. So it's their [Chilean government] fault, but they want to give the impression that they're in the right." (10th grade, Raimilla School)

BERNARDO: "Do you see what happens with the news, how the Mapuche are made to look? That they are terrorists, plotting, and all that." (11th grade, Campaña School)

DAISY: "On the news, the state shows what it suits them to show."
INTERVIEWER: "And why do you think it suits them to show the Mapuche in this way?"
JAVIER: "Because they make themselves the victims."
DAISY: "Because that way they can create the idea that the Mapuche are terrorists and they want to cover up the fact that they are wrong or behave wrongly." (11th grade, Tres Montes School)

Others were able to extend this critique to aspects of supposed affirmative action, and reformed policies designed to improve equality. These narratives serve as a direct point of contrast to statements made earlier by other peers about accepting indigenous grants as being the most important aspect of Mapuche identity:

MANUEL: "My view is that [the government] treats us like fools ... Because by giving us [grants], it's like saying 'Oh, those poor things! Let's give them something so they don't feel so bad.'" (12th grade, Raimilla School)
GASTÓN: "There's never been that respect, because Chileans don't want to acknowledge our worth as a People, as a nation, they don't want to see that; there's no respect."
EDGAR: "They always see us as an ethnic group, not as a People."
MATEO: "Yes, the schools should show us as a People. Our grandparents, for example, have that knowledge, and schools need to show it more." (Focus group, 10th grade, Nacional School)
LUCIA: "They [schools] are taking away the opportunity from many students to continue developing their culture within secondary education. [...] so even if they want to, they can't and that's why afterwards it [Mapuche culture] is being lost." (11th grade, Lihuén School)

Although only a minority among the whole sample of participants, these young people provide a critical voice among this generation, opposing racialising discourses and penetrating its marginalising practices. As Manuel and Lucia (cited above) identify, the affirmative action of indigenous grants is premised on an ideology of helping the deficient to assimilate more fully into a monocultural curriculum. They provide a glimpse into the possibilities of what a critical, anti-racist, and culturally sensitive education could achieve among its students were real change to be implemented in Chilean classrooms. The work of schooling, in Bourdieu's terms, has the potential to transform students' socialised habitus and offer possibilities of resistance against new racism.

Finding a Place for Mapuche Identity in Schools

The conversations presented in this chapter provide evidence of a subtle form of symbolic violence exercised in schools with high indigenous enrolments. Based on these compositions, one might think that these establishments would be those most likely to contribute to the young people's identity development. For the most part, the students attending these schools are resigned to an unequal educational field; accepting the secondary benefits of attending a high indigenous composition school in terms of fitting in and avoiding discrimination. Although some participants articulated how economic capital determines the school hierarchy, many students discuss their school's status in relation to individual deficiencies in infrastructure.

Regarding the internalised aspirations of the young Mapuche students, these mostly adhere to what Bonilla-Silva (2006) calls the abstract liberalism framework. That is, they see their educational outcomes as individualised pathways that rely solely on hard work and meritocracy in order to get ahead (*surgir*). The young people are socialised to reproduce a key ideology of schooling; that everything is in place to support them and that if they apply themselves enough then success is the most likely or only outcome. Social location is not deemed to be determining, and whatever disadvantages they do face are deemed minimal compared to those of their parents. Schooling, then, teaches that the only identities of worth in these contexts are those that adhere to neoliberal and capitalist values of social mobility and economic success, leaving indigenous worldviews aside.

There seem to be few instances of physical violence or egregious and sustained bullying in these schools, but mundane everyday forms and expressions of "mucking around" often involve denigrating indigenous status – whether by making fun of surnames or references to being *Indian* – often from fellow indigenous peers. I have argued that this constitutes part of a racialised habitus that disposes young Mapuche to these kinds of practices and a certain acceptance of new racism. Whilst there is a general consensus among the young people that this is not serious, schools do little to encourage their students to find reasons for taking pride in diverse cultural expressions or produce critically transformative ideas about their interactions in this regard.

I dare suggest this is one of the drawbacks of a new racism era, in which indigenous students are accepted and welcomed, provided with grants, and whose *we tripantu* celebrations are commemorated each school year. As the young people commented, there is little desire among them to participate in such out-of-place activities. Indigenous identities, in these settings become depreciated inasmuch they are encouraged to remain hidden, even though there are no guarantees that this will happen. One consequence is that certain young people adopt colour-blind positions of normality or sameness; the notion that it is better to just be a regular Chilean, or someone who is not singled out. If they are treated this way for the rest of the school calendar, they are unlikely to want to change for one event. Being a "normal" student, the same as the rest, means fitting into a whitened taxonomy premised on liberal ideas about individual equality, but which triggers a sense of shame to those who are sporadically asked to acknowledge their differences.

In the final part of the chapter, I provided some reasons for more optimism surrounding some young people's critical and resistant narratives that are alert to how schools exclude and disparage their identities. These perspectives overlap those offered by students attending schools with segmented IBE practices, seen in the previous chapter. However, these young people receive no such help from their establishments, and their resistant capital is most likely from home or community experiences. That being the case, perhaps the most striking thing about the students' comments from Lago Profundo and Campos Verdes schools is that both establishments exhibited explicitly contradictory approaches to Mapuche identities. Their school logos, pamphlets, and even architectural constructions allude to inclusion of the Mapuche, while their practices omit them.

It is possible that such blatant contradictions are what sparked or aided the students' critical perceptions. In schools where omissions are absolute, perhaps new racism becomes even harder to identify. Both sets of narratives contrast the majority of the young Mapuche cited in this chapter. This is not akin to a blame game or a deficit theory. The point, rather, is that schools reproduce such subtle forms of racial projects that one would not expect many students to see through the whitened cultural arbitrary transmitted to its subjects. Young people are forced to inhabit and navigate these racialising categories in everyday life in schools, affecting how they self-identify and relate to other indigenous peers. In these spaces, schools should certainly be held accountable for failing to interrupt broader racial stereotypes and exclusion, and for the lack of input into forming positive indigenous identities. Central to this, I propose, lies in the normalising effects of teacher expectations and perspectives; an issue to which I now turn.

Note

1 Some of the data was previously presented in Webb (2014) and Webb and Radcliffe (2015).

References

Ball, S., Reay, D., & David, M. (2003). 'Ethnic choosing': Minority ethnic students, social class and higher education choice. *Race Ethnicity and Education*, 5(4), 333–357.

Berger, P., & Luckman, T. (1967). *The social construction of reality: A treatise in the sociology of knowledge*. London: Allen Lane.

Bonilla-Silva, E. (2006). *Racism without racists: Color-blind racism and the persistence of racial inequality in the United States* (2nd ed.). Oxford: Rowman & Littlefield Publishers.

Bourdieu, P. (1984). *Distinction: A social critique of the judgment of taste.* Cambridge, MA: Harvard University Press.

Bourdieu, P. (2000). *Pascalian meditations.* Stanford, CA: Stanford University Press.

Bourdieu, P., & Ferguson, P.P. (1999). *The weight of the world: Social suffering in contemporary society.* Stanford, CA: Stanford University Press.

Bourdieu, P., & Passeron, J. (1979). *The Inheritors: French students and their relation to culture.* Chicago: University of Chicago Press.

Bourdieu, P., & Passeron, J. [1977] (1990). *Reproduction in education, society and culture.* Beverly Hills, CA: SAGE.

Carbajal, P., & Fierro, C. (2018). *Diez Premisas sobre la convivencia escolar y su evaluación.* México: Instituto Nacional para la Evaluación de la Educación.

Cohen, A.P. (1985). *The symbolic construction of community.* Chichester: E. Horwood.

Cornell, S.E., & Hartmann, D. (2007). *Ethnicity and race: Making identities in a changing world.* Thousand Oaks, CA: Pine Forge Press.

Cross, M., & Naidoo, D. (2012). Race, diversity pedagogy: Mediated learning experience for transforming racist habitus and predispositions. *Review of Education, Pedagogy, and Cultural Studies, 34*(5), 227–244.

Cui, D. (2017). Teachers' racialised habitus in school knowledge construction: A Bourdieusian analysis of social inequality beyond class. *Journal of Youth Studies, 18*(9), 1154–1169.

Denis, J. (2015). Contact theory in a SmallTown settler-colonial context: The reproduction of laissez-faire racism in indigenous-White Canadian relations. *American Sociological Association, 80*(1), 218–242.

Diamond, J., Randolph, A., & Spillane, J. (2004). Teachers' expectations and sense of responsibility for student learning: The importance of race, class, and organisational habitus. *Anthropology & Education Quarterly, 35*(1), 75–98.

Edensor, T. (2002). *National identity, popular culture and everyday life.* Oxford: Berg.

Edgerton, J., & Roberts, L. (2014). Cultural capital or habitus? Bourdieu and beyond in the explanation of enduring educational inequality. *Theory and Research in Education, 12*(2), 193–220.

Elacqua, G. (2012). The impact of school choice and public policy on segregation: Evidence from Chile. *International Journal of Educational Development, 32*(3), 444–453.

Fine, M. (1993). *Framing dropouts: Notes on the politics of an Urban public high school.* New York, NY: State University of New York Press.

Graham, S., & Juvonen, J. (2002). Ethnicity, peer harassment, and adjustment in middle school: An exploratory study. *The Journal of Early Adolescence, 22*(2), 173–199.

Jenkins, R. (1992). *Pierre Bourdieu.* London: Routledge.

Lewis, A. (2003). *Race in the schoolyard: Negotiating the color line in classrooms and communities.* Piscataway, NJ: Rutgers.

McKnight, D., & Chandler, P. (2012). The complicated conversation of class and race in social and curricular analysis: An examination of Pierre Bourdieu's interpretive framework in relation to race. *Educational Philosophy and Theory, 44*(1), 74–97.

Mignolo, W. (2000). *Local histories/global designs: Coloniality, subaltern knowledges and border thinking.* New Jersey: Princeton University Press.

Modood, T. (2004). Capitals, ethnic identity and educational qualifications. *Cultural Trends, 13*(50), 87–105.

Moreno Figueroa, M.G. (2010). Distributed intensities: Whiteness, mestizaje and the logics of Mexican racism. *Ethnicities, 10*(3), 387–401.

Orfield, G., & Lee, C. (2007). *Historic reversals, accelerating Resegregation, and the need for new integration strategies.* Los Angeles: The Civil Rights Project, University of California.

Quilaqueo, D. (2012). Saberes educativos mapuches: Racionalidad apoyada en la memoria social de los Kimches. *Revista Atenea, 505*, 79–102.

Reay, D. (2004). 'It's all becoming a habitus': Beyond the habitual use of habitus in educational research. *British Journal of Sociology of Education, 25*(4), 431–444.

Reay, D., Hollingworth, S., Williams, K., et al. (2007). 'A darker shade of pale?' Whiteness, the middle classes and multi-ethnic inner city schooling. *Sociology, 41*(6), 1041–1060.

Ríos-Rojas, A. (2014). Managing and disciplining diversity: The politics of conditional belonging in a Catolinan Institut. *Anthropology & Education Quarterly, 45*(1), 2–21.

Roberts, R.A., Bell, L.A., & Murphy, B. (2008). Flipping the script: Analyzing youth talk about race and racism. *Anthropology & Education Quarterly, 39*, 334–354.

Rollock, N. (2007). Legitimizing black academic failure: Deconstructing staff discourses on academic success, appearance and behaviour. *International Studies in Sociology of Education, 17*(3), 275–287.

Rubie-Davies, C.M. (2007). Classroom interactions: Exploring the practices of high- and low-expectation teachers. *British Journal of Educational Psychology, 77*, 289–306.

St. Denis, V. (2007). Aboriginal education and anti-racist education: Building alliances across cultural and racial identity. *Canadian Journal of Education / Revue canadienne de l'éducation, 30*(4), 1068–1092.

Stanton-Salazar, R. (2011). A social capital framework for the study of institutional agents and their role in the empowerment of low-status students and youth. *Youth & Society, 43*(3), 1066–1109.

Sullivan, A. (2002). Cultural capital and educational attainment. *Sociology, 35*(4), 893–912.

Treviño, E., Valenzuela, J., & Villalobos, C. (2017). Segregación de estudiantes indígenas en el sistema escolar chileno. In E. Treviño, L. Morawietz, C. Villalobos, & E. Villalobos (Eds.), *Educación Intercultural en Chile. Experiencias, Pueblos y Territorios.* Santiago: Ediciones UC.

Van Ingen, C., & Halas, J. (2006). Claiming space: Aboriginal students within school landscapes. *Children's Geographies, 4*(3), 379–398.

Wacquant, L. (1989). Towards a reflexive sociology. A workshop with Pierre Bourdieu. *Sociological Theory, 7*, 26–63.

Wallace, D. (2017). Reading 'race' in Bourdieu? Examining black cultural capital among black Caribbean youth in South London. *Sociology, 58*(3), 24–50.

Weaver, H. (1991). Indigenous identity: What is it, and who really has it? *American Indian Quarterly, 25*(2), 240–255.

Webb, A. (2014). Re-working everyday concepts of civic virtue and ethnic belonging among indigenous youth in Chile. *Journal of Youth Studies, 17*(6), 717–732.

Webb, A., & Radcliffe, S. (2015). Whitened geographies and education inequalities in southern Chile. *Journal of Intercultural Studies, 36*(2), 129–148.

Wimmer, A. (2013). *Ethnic boundary making: Institutions, power, networks.* New York, NY: Oxford University Press.

Yosso, T. (2005). Whose culture has capital? A critical race theory discussion of community cultural wealth. *Race Ethnicity and Education, 8*(1), 69–91.

4 Staff Perspectives and Implicit Racism

Teachers, for the most part, enter into their profession looking to make a difference to society by helping young people learn and acquire new skills for adult life. From this perspective, the good intentions, and the vital role that their profession holds in preparing young people for adult life, civic society, and labour market participation are not in question. It would also be true to say, however, that teachers are formed within the ethos of training institutes that replicate the values and norms of the society in which they are located. This means that no matter how good teachers' intentions may be, no pedagogy is ever value-neutral since both the teacher and their style of teaching are subjective iterations of broader power relations. Hence whether consciously or unconsciously, teachers participate in the reproduction of a cultural arbitrary (Bourdieu & Passeron, 1990).

There is a vast amount of research on teacher's expectations and attitudes towards underprivileged students and minority social groupings in their classrooms. The broad consensus is that negative stereotyping by teachers and deficit theories about their students' abilities will affect both cognitive and non-cognitive outcomes. These include less teacher–student interactions in the classroom, low student self-esteem, lower educational achievements, pejorative ideas about student motivation, and an increased likelihood that students will be labelled by teachers as having behavioural problems (Thys & van Houtte, 2016). In this regard, teacher expectations constitute a vital component in reproducing social inequalities in schools. These outcomes particularly apply in multi-ethnic and impoverished school contexts where teachers' perceptual biases lead to "misinterpretation or inaccurate evaluation of student behaviour, achievement, attitude, or other outcomes" (Brault et al., 2014, p. 149).

Teaching in contexts of ethnic diversity is an enormous challenge, and one that is largely ignored in teacher training institutions. Scholarly work demonstrates the pervasiveness of whitened privilege among pre-service and in-service teachers, and the mixed results of multicultural training initiatives (Da Costa, 2014 on Brazil; Solomona et al., 2005 on Canada). Generally, this research argues that teachers adopt colour-blind attitudes

DOI: 10.4324/9781003090700-5

in their classroom practices, overlooking power differentials and privileging a specific worldview within curricular content (de Freitas and McAuley, 2008; Picower, 2009; Van Ingen & Halas, 2006). Furthermore, it has been demonstrated that education outcomes depend on teachers' abilities to challenge their own implicit intolerance and racist attitudes, and to be open to alternate values, practices, and the worldviews of ethnic minority students in their classrooms (Banks, 2009; McAllister & Irvine, 2000; Villegas & Lucas, 2002; Walters, Garii, & Walters, 2009). A lack of adequate training is likely to culminate in insufficient critical self-awareness among teachers and ethnocentric responses to ethnically diverse students' behaviours so as to privilege dominant national-majority norms (Gay & Howard, 2000). One of the difficulties surrounding this matter is that most teachers see themselves as anti-racist (Cobb, 2017).

In the field of education, Christine Sleeter (2004) emphasises that teachers must avoid seeing racism as an individual issue of prejudice to be rectified by changing student attitudes, ideas, and stereotypes. This she claims constitutes a psychological approach to racism, and instead urges that they acknowledge and teach racism as a structural arrangement that determines access to power and privilege. Other scholars confirm that colour-mute practices exist in ethnically mixed schools. Castagno, for example, details the ways teachers use "racially coded language" and silence students from using race talk or from discussing racism, despite persistent and systemic inequalities affecting minority students' educational outcomes (Castagno, 2008, p. 321). This silencing is an act of power that abdicates teaching staffs' responsibility to question the grey areas between tolerance and discrimination, political correctness and explicitly derogatory terminology, culture, and nature (Gillborn, 2008).

One of the dangers of celebrating "anti-discriminatory" or "anti-racist" pedagogies is that some facile versions tend to comply with this goal simply by avoiding all forms of discriminatory language, rather than developing critical discourses or political commitments among their students. Pollock (2005) captures this well: "Knowing silences ... are themselves actions with racializing consequences: actively deleting race words from everyday talk can serve to increase the perceived relevance of race as much as to actively ignore race's relevance" (2005, p. 174). Racial issues are rarely acknowledged or directly addressed, but are always latent issues in classrooms, schools, and their surrounding communities.

Other authors demonstrate that white teachers are particularly prone to colour-blind racism because they fail to acknowledge the culture of power operating in schools and often insist they only see children, rather than race, in their classrooms (Dickar, 2008). The lack of cultural understanding between teachers and students of different ethnic origins affects mutual empathy and expectations in the classroom, as well as the possibilities of developing culturally relevant pedagogies. Another important aspect of colour-blindness in schools is the under-representation of co-ethnic teachers (Thijs, Westhof, & Koomen, 2012). One rarely enquires about the cultural background of the staff working in a school, or the compositional effects of having a majority of white staff working in super-diverse schools. However, evidence suggests that staff contribute towards creating specific school cultures that vary in how permissive or accepting they are of discrimination (Diamond, Randolph, & Spillane, 2004; Demanet & Van Houtte, 2012; Rubie-Davies et al., 2012). In contexts where there are few ethnic minority teachers – such as the schools involved in this research – it is unlikely that culturally sensitive teaching will be promoted among the school staff. That is, a lack of sociocultural fit between teachers and students in schools affects academic expectations, the appropriateness of teaching styles and cultural sensitivity, as well as the quality of interaction and school climate (Dickar, 2008; Nieto, 1996; Rist, 1970; Thapa et al., 2013). Accordingly, any stereotypes that teachers have about certain groupings of students – whether conscious or unconscious – are likely to result in differential treatment. Dickar (2008) makes the case that schools will continue to reproduce cultures of whitened privilege as long as ethnic minority teachers are underrepresented.

Deficit theories of indigenous students' abilities are also widely documented in countries such as Australia, Canada, and the US; whether it be through the language of closing indigenous test score gaps, health and nutrition, language abilities, or literacy skills (Hare & Pidgeon, 2011; Vass, 2017). These adhere to colour-blind principles precisely because they are usually framed in terms of family socialisation, cultural difference, or socioeconomic limitations that avoid addressing systemic and enduring inequalities that indigenous peoples face on account of the selection and curricular design that match non-indigenous middle-class values, pedagogic styles, and knowledges. Instead of addressing these inequalities, compensatory forms of education only incorporate partial acknowledgement of other worldviews and languages, and always as something separate from mainstream curricular knowledge. These policies and programmes legitimise ongoing visions of indigenous peoples as vulnerable; as those susceptible to harm and lacking the necessary abilities to get ahead by themselves. Partial inclusion looks to provide compensatory solutions that overlook the accumulative disadvantages created by structural barriers that young indigenous people face prior to, during, and after their educational trajectories.

Of course, teachers do not act alone in schools, and cannot shoulder the entire responsibility for these issues. Hackman (2005) has demonstrated the role that communities, schools, and students also need to play in eradicating racism. However, even if communities and school administrators decide to implement culturally sensitive pedagogies, everything hinges upon the dedication and commitment of teachers. The problem, she suggests, is wherever these topics are avoided on account of believing situations to be hopeless, or impossible to change. Pollock et al. (2010)

and Fine (1993) also report on the ways teachers often voice frustration at their impotency to change or challenge broad-reaching social issues such as racism. These authors find that teachers usually opt for the avoidance of controversial or politically contestable issues as the best and most comfortable tactic, through the, "purposeful silencing of race words" (Pollock, 2005, p. 3) or the "fear to name" (Fine, 1993).

As I discuss later in the chapter, Chilean schools are currently beset by a bureaucratic web of protocols and legal requirements within anti-discriminatory frameworks. Michelle Fine calls this type of proceduralism "administrative craft" (1993, p. 35). She demonstrates how educational institutions are absolved of blame for unequal educational outcomes by turning them into managerial or organisational matters. The fact that youth from particular social classes and ethnic groups experience disproportionate and intersecting barriers compared to peers from other social identities is overlooked by reducing disparities to individual cases to be bureaucratically resolved.

In instances where limited efforts are made to counteract racism, Geneva Gay (2010) warns that pedagogies and compensatory programmes must avoid a focus on student deficits (such as educational outcomes or test scores), since these fail to take racial inequalities into account. Tokenistic efforts can be as damaging as altogether avoidance of racism. Instead, Gay argues that pedagogies need to draw on the cultural competencies and skills that students from different backgrounds bring to the classroom. As I demonstrate in this chapter, regardless of whether IBE programmes exist or not, school staff are not well-prepared for teaching in these sociocultural contexts.

Rubie-Davies (2006) have investigated the role that teacher expectations play in ethnically diverse classrooms in New Zealand, arguing that their input and attitudes have effects on student outcomes – as self-fulfilling prophecies – but also on issues of self-esteem and academic motivation. In both cases, teacher influence impedes student progress in their education. Motives for lowering expectations are, of course, diverse, and range from broad social categories such as gender, ethnicity, and social class, to more personal, subjective, and emotional perceptions about physical attractiveness, language or accent, personality, age, or social abilities. Rubie-Davies and colleagues' empirical work shows teachers have lower expectations for Maori students in their primary classrooms.

Finally, there is also evidence that the ethnic composition of schools may make teachers more inclined to biased perceptions of the student body (Agirdag et al., 2013). That is, where low income and minority students are clustered together in large numbers, teachers are more likely to lower their expectations of academic performance, while peer relationships are anticipated (by teachers) to be more violent (Brault et al., 2014; Dumay & Dupriez, 2008; Thrupp et al., 2002). This is hypothesised to be so because the high visibility of ethnic groups in the schools create shared assumptions among teachers. This results in a general school culture of group-level teacher expectations, rather than individual teacher expectations which might vary more towards a specific student (Van Houtte, 2005). In these cases, entire school staff may develop differential treatment towards ethnic students or lower their expectations of the whole school populations' academic abilities (Brault et al., 2014). This is relevant to the Chilean case in which most of the schools have indigenous compositions above the national mean.

Continuing with Bourdieu

Once more, Bourdieu's work can provide additional conceptual sophistication to the analysis of new racism among teachers. In addition to the contributions addressed in the previous chapter, *pedagogic action* and *pedagogic authority* are especially important in transmitting specific cultural messages through schooling. Bourdieu and Passeron (1990) note that this arbitrary power is rarely recognised as being culturally specific; that is, as symbolic violence. Instead, pedagogic authority is taken to be legitimate and neutral by both students and teachers. Although Bourdieu's analysis focuses on social class, his insistence that the model can refer to "any social formation" (1990, p. 5) means the applicability to ethnically oriented cultural presuppositions and biases are clear.

Bourdieu and Passeron assert that pedagogic action will always indirectly reproduce the dominant material and symbolic interests of any given social formation, which in this case refers to intersecting interests of dominant white, Chilean, middle-class values. Again, the fact that the meanings transmitted through pedagogic actions are attributed a superior value is entirely arbitrary since it does not adhere to any universal principle of nature, but instead has its reason in the social conditions by which it came to be established. There is no biological reason, following Bourdieu and Passeron's argument, why Mapuche pedagogy and knowledge are not valued; only cultural reasons insofar as they serve to reproduce the power relations, cultural capital, and dominant interests of the Chilean society that has excluded them.

What responsibility, then, can be attributed to teachers in this process? Bourdieu and Passeron argue that pedagogic authority is a necessity, since any attempt to expose pedagogic action for what it truly is – an act of symbolic violence – would risk undermining a teacher's own vocation by acknowledging that the entire system upon which they exercise authority over their students is arbitrary and lacks legitimacy. My reading of the text is that teachers have little choice but to transmit some kind of cultural arbitrary. Schools have relative autonomy to modify their pedagogic communications, but will still reproduce the dominant pedagogic action, since the broader fields of power determine what is valuable knowledge. Teachers, then, continue to reward those dispositions and tastes that adhere to the dominant capital of the economic and cultural elite. This relegates all other types of knowledge and capital to a subordinate status, turning culturally sensitive pedagogies into compensatory mechanisms which do little to challenge the status quo.

Scholars have proposed that teachers can challenge and disrupt racialised habitus in their classrooms. Cross and Naidoo (2012) draw on critical and anti-racist pedagogies to argue that deeply held beliefs about other social groupings and ingrained dispositions towards racist structures can be unlearned precisely because the boundaries of racial categories are never fixed. In this case, they propose that changes to the educational field, starting from the classroom, have the potential to make students feel "like a fish out of water" in Bourdieu and Wacquant's famous phrase. The authors propose that by disrupting student habitus, and directly addressing issues of power, justice, and subtle forms of racism, the status quo of the social structure can be challenged from within the educational field. They propose that educators who give more space to mutual learning from the lived experiences of students will promote positive interethnic/racial interactions and challenge racist habitus and worldviews (2012). However, in order to do so, teachers must be alert to their own prejudices and implicit role in reproducing racial projects.

From this perspective, Bourdieu's work on cultural reproduction in schools provides a vantage point from which to understand teachers' implicit support for new racism in Chilean schools and especially those where racial and socioeconomic inequalities operate simultaneously.

Teacher Assumptions and Bias in Chile

Scholarly research in Chile has shown tendencies among teaching staff to maintain monocultural outlooks, to isolate or silence students from different ethnic backgrounds, and to hold higher expectations of non-indigenous Chilean students' academic abilities (Gonzaléz et al., 2003; Poblete, 2003; Quilaqueo, 2012; Valoyes-Chávez & Martin, 2016). The inadequacies of teacher training for multicultural contexts have been further evidenced in Chile by the recent arrival of Latin American migrants (which have been ongoing for a number of decades but have increased in intensity during the last 10 years). The OECD's report on Chilean Education recently suggested that,

> Ensuring that classrooms with a larger share of indigenous and immigrant students are places where the best possible pedagogy is pursued is crucial to enhancing the educational opportunities of these students. It is also vital that teachers are highly skilled in formative assessment, and that they regularly adjust their approaches in response to indigenous and immigrant student needs.
>
> (2017, p.105)

The report concludes that whilst measures have been implemented to address gender equity, considerably less has been done to ensure indigenous or migrant students are provided with opportunities to achieve on an equal footing. Teachers are generally not equipped to integrate culturally relevant teaching into their classrooms (Quintriqueo et al., 2016). Recognising normative whiteness is not an easy task, as most teachers believe their pedagogic practices adhere to non-racial criteria, thus denying any racially constructed power differentials in the classroom (Marx, 2004). Other research in Chilean classrooms with Mapuche populations has demonstrated that teachers tend to use disciplinarian and traditional teaching styles (Mellado & Chaucono, 2015), and teaching–learning methodologies that contradict the Mapuche worldview (*cosmovisión*) (see Luna, 2015; Luna, Telechea, & Caniguan, 2018). Becerra's (2011) interviews with 52 teachers in secondary schools in the Araucanía Region found that teacher stereotyping of Mapuche students tended to view them as intellectually inferior to non-indigenous and devalued their traditional culture. Crucially, the author notes that teachers were generally unaware of their own prejudices since they emphasised the universal worth of all students.

In this chapter, I address the role that staff perceptions play in contributing to new racism in schools. Results are taken from research projects conducted in the Araucanía Region and from the country's capital, Santiago. I demonstrate the unwillingness of a majority of administrative and teaching staff to recognise specific forms of institutional inequality or racism in schools with high and medium density indigenous compositions. These findings confirm those of previous studies, but I extend the analysis to new racism literature and Bourdieusian concepts. I demonstrate how the Chilean education system reproduces a fear of talk among teachers working in these areas, which obscures unequal social structures and opportunities for specific (class, gender, ethnic) groups in school contexts. Most teachers are non-indigenous and believe that, compared with historic forms of explicit discrimination against indigenous students, contemporary schooling has moved beyond this to offer a more equitable education.

I also show how the arrival of Latin American migrant children in Chilean classrooms (especially in Santiago) tends to further invisibilise new racism's negative effects on indigenous youth. As noted earlier, intercultural bilingual education has gone some way to countering a monocultural syllabus, but many teachers – even in schools where these programmes are implemented – may not share the same vision or cultural openness. In this way, it is possible for schools to transmit contradictory messages from teacher to teacher about valuing and dialoguing between cultures.

Perceptions of Inclusivity, School Climate, and Discrimination

Schools are social contexts in which values and attitudes are shared and socialised among staff. Teachers do not work in isolation; they are part of staff meetings, they usually have to accept a school's identity and educational mission to be employed there, and must abide by institutional norms and values, as well as national education policies and laws. Here I address the ways these organisational aspects of daily school life influence staff narratives about victimisation and ethnic discrimination in their establishments.[1]

This is especially relevant to formal discourse about school inclusiveness, as part of national and international education policies promoting the elimination and disciplining of all forms of harassment and victimisation. The benefits of positive school climates are well established, in terms of improving mental and physical health, student self-esteem and motivation to learn, mitigating the negative effects of the socioeconomic context, decreasing school dropout rates, and diminishing conflictive relationships (Thapa et al., 2013). Rather than question these benefits, I assess how confidence in, and concerns to be seen abiding by, these institutional mechanisms and discourses conceal deeper issues of exclusion or homogenising forms of inclusion. A vital aspect of this is the concern to be seen to be abiding by anti-discrimination laws and promoting diversity in their school communities.

It is worth repeating that I see schools as reproducing broader sociohistoric structures of inequality, or racial projects, to borrow Omi and Winant's concept once more. These maintain the same ideological and material hierarchies in society across time, whilst being open to modifications in their format and expression. The same, then, can be said of protocols and discourses about discrimination in schools. According to Pérez Huber and Solorzano (2015), racial microaggressions are everyday occurrences in schools that operate to keep marginalised people in their place. The authors emphasise that although these microaggressions can take physical and verbal form, they are often non-verbal, and operate through references to layered identities and characteristics such as phenotype, surname, accent, sexuality, gender, or class. This perspective problematises merely formulaic or legal approaches to understanding harassment, which is the dominant model in contemporary Chilean schooling.

Since 2011, Chilean schools have been heavily regulated by three laws designed to regulate discrimination (20.609), school violence (20.536), and school inclusion (20.845). In particular, they have required schools to form school climate committees (*comité de convivencia escolar*) responsible for developing protocols to deal with instances of (peer) harassment. As a result of these sanctioning frameworks, staff are acutely aware of the need to tread carefully when discussing inclusivity. Staff were generally very positive about the climate at their school and were equally emphatic about their own efforts to be inclusive. Discrimination was spoken of as something abnormal in their establishments, and which, when manifested is quickly controlled:

NICOLÁS: "We don't have problems, just situations. There are situations like children arriving consistently late, situations with parents, absenteeism, situations between students, but we don't have problems. We want to eliminate that concept through a systematic way of working." (Head of school climate committee, Imperial School)

CATALINA: "Here [in the school] there is a lot of emphasis placed on diversity, and we've had training days about school climate." (Teacher, Acevedo School)

MATÍAS: "In our school climate committee we're able to contain the [main issues] especially among the younger students. Because we have a lot of children with diagnosed conditions, like attention deficits, those who oppose or look to defy, and we can keep them under control. We've learnt to deal with those contentions, help them regulate themselves, get rid of their anger." (Head of school climate, San Pablo School)

When recognising the challenges of diverse school communities, most focused on issues relating to psychological and personality disorders, or issues related to gender, rather than ethnic criteria. In some cases, staff went as far to say that ethnic discrimination did not occur in their establishments:

PRISCILLA: "I think, on the teachers part, there's been a lot of work on inclusion lately in different schools. We work on the fact that everyone is equal, we all have the same rights. We work on issues to do with inclusivity into the school calendar; days to celebrate with certain activities so as to include foreign students, or those with indigenous ancestry. We do this so that all children are included and are treated as an equal." (Teacher, San Pablo School)

HEBER: "We've not had any difficulties with this, it's so, so rare to find cases like "Eh, go back to your country", I've heard it twice during my time here at the school, and I've never heard anything said to Mapuche, nothing about their ethnicity; quite the contrary." (Head-Teacher, Apertura School)

ANDRÉS: "There are behavioural problems in school climate, like in all educational experiences, but they don't have racial connotations, because of their origin. No, nothing like that. So that's why we've not focused on any kind of intervention, because there's no need." (Head-Teacher, Cerro Bajo School)

GEORGINA: "Maybe it's because we are in the region where the Mapuche are most [numerous], maybe if it were Valdivia or, wherever, Santiago, where the Mapuche are less of an issue, where they stand out more (*llama más la atención*), because here they are all so well integrated." (Teacher Acevedo School)

One of the reasons for why teachers believe that ethnic discrimination has mostly been eliminated in their school is by referring to the past. Like the students cited in the previous chapter, staff members (especially in the schools implementing intercultural bilingual programmes) recalled the treatment and stereotyping of Mapuche children two generations before, and how indigenous culture was seen at that time:

LORENA: "If you'd have thought back then that someone could come into a classroom and teach about Mapuche culture; it would have just been impossible. They used to think it was a culture that was good for nothing, that it didn't have any value, and nobody cared about it. Mapuche were just thought of as lazy or conflictive." (Teacher, Raimilla School)

To briefly reiterate the point made in the previous chapter, this allows for the minimisation of racism (Bonilla-Silva, 2006). That is, by framing inequalities as an enduring but continually improving process, this removes the need for proactive changes to be implemented in the immediate present. Racism becomes something that will simply taper off by itself through proper management.

A different justification, offered by two other staff members, was due to a change in the demographics of the student population and the consequential power dynamics and relationships between peers. In multi-ethnic school contexts in Santiago, staff narrated that indigenous discrimination had been displaced by peer harassment of migrants:

BARBARA: "There used to be a lot more bullying toward the Mapuche [indigenous group]; it was terrible, but not anymore. That issue disappeared when the foreigners started arriving at the school, it just dissolved. It's mostly the Haitians that are now the focus of bullying." (School Monitor, Apertura School)
CARLOS: "There haven't been any accusations or complaints from the indigenous students, no, not one, and it must be because there are so many foreigners now in the country and in the school." (School Psychologist, Neblina School)

Indeed, theories about group dominance in school climate literature advocate changing dynamics whenever newer outsiders arrive, especially when they grow in numbers and threaten the status quo of power relations (Thapa et al., 2013). Nonetheless, the issue at stake here is the tendency to assume an "all or nothing" mentality about indigenous discrimination and thereby invisibilise or dismiss this issue as one needing to be addressed.

A third explanation is the attention that schools have given to intercultural events and activities. Many of the staff expressed confidence in positive social relations and inclusivity on account of these school-organised events. As noted in the previous chapters, intercultural activities have the potential to be simultaneously inclusive and exclusionary, in so far as students claimed the exceptionality of interculturalism led to further ostracisation among peers when they opted to participate. Hence, on the one hand staff may misinterpret the purported benefits of these events, but on the other – and perhaps even more significantly – their descriptions of these proceedings indicate assimilatory tendencies:

IGNACIO: "We have been working a lot on the themes of our ethnic groups, our origins, because we have the objective of knowing more about native peoples (*pueblos originarios*) among which the few that are left are the Mapuche. We've done a lot of work, it has been greatly valued so we don't have many complications with this group [of students]." (Teacher, Mapocho School)

GERARDO: "Something really important that we've told our students is that a Mapuche isn't someone who has indigenous blood, but whoever lives on the land. So one doesn't have to have an indigenous surname to be Mapuche. We are all Mapuche. We appropriate that language, and so if we are all Mapuche you can't discriminate. Now we have foreign students who say they are Mapuche, if you ask them they'll say 'because I played Palín (Mapuche sporting and political activity), I speak *mapuzungún*, ... because I was in the *we tripantu*.'" (Teacher, Clorinda School)

Whether it be a post-colonial appropriation of indigenous peoples as "*our*" ethnic groups or "*our*" origins, or the reduction of indigenous identities to geographical residence, both narratives indicate severely delimiting notions of indigeneity under the celebratory guise of recognition or cultural valuation. These are indications of how a critical approach is needed when examining staff perceptions of inclusivity, particularly where broad-strokes assertions are made that ethnic discrimination and exclusion have ceased to be issues.

It is worth noting that all the staff who we interviewed are keenly aware of the institutional norms and national laws that govern school life. Many made explicit reference to the anti-discrimination law, and the need for specific training to ensure everyone working at the schools is open to diversity. Some conceded that not all staff members in their school were receptive of these values, especially those who held on to more traditional ideas about cultural homogeneity in the classroom:

ENRIQUE: "[Discrimination in the school] is somewhat complex because it's not an open issue. Everyone has their own ideas [about others] but now with the new anti-racism laws, everyone is careful. So no, openly there is nothing – the teachers are careful here. Sometimes a certain comment may insinuate [something discriminatory] but it's never something open." (Teacher, Lago Profundo School)

HERALDO: "I always say to the teachers, I always encourage them, but some are somewhat unwilling to avoid being discriminatory and to understand the pupils. I try to convey the importance of our Mapuche culture in education, because there are so many pupils from Mapuche families. Some [teachers] don't pay much attention." (Teacher, Lago Profundo School)

ANDREA: "The Physical Education teacher has certain beliefs, it's been difficult for me to convince him that we might have a transsexual student, or to break down that chauvinism because of his age. All these barriers need to be broken down, for example with foreigners, which I think is easier. What I'm saying is we need to work at it, but some teachers have been here 33 years and I'm sure some of them might resist. Some of them think they [migrants] are here [in Chile] to take people's jobs." (Curriculum Planner, Imperial School)

Identifying and responding to victimisation in schools depends on how discrimination is defined. The general consensus about improvements in school climate does not equate to the absence of discrimination, but the potential to overlook its more implicit forms. The supposed absence of discrimination necessarily entails a subjective process of excluding certain microaggressions as falling short of violence or harassment. Typically, for example, name-calling is dismissed to playful bantering or teasing rather than discrimination (Mishna et al., 2005).

Below I provide one example in regard to xeno-racism (Sivanandan & Fekete, 2001) that was redefined as more neutral name-calling. Andrea (also cited above) argued that advances had been made in becoming more inclusive. However, upon closer inspection, it was clear that her frame of reference for inclusivity was to take Chilean as the normative category of reference:

ANDREA: "We've had a debate, a respectful one, with students who say 'it's not like that in my country', and also we've had discussions where, for example one student said 'Miss, this person shouted Peruvian at me', so ok I asked who it was but I added 'but look, are you or aren't you Peruvian? You are, so come on, don't be so offended. If that person said it in an inappropriate way I will speak to that person, but don't be offended, because you are Peruvian'. If someone were to say to me 'Chilean', I'd say 'yes, and very proud to be so'." (Curriculum Planner, Imperial School)

In this instance, the teacher ignores the contextual significance of being called out as different – in this case as Peruvian – recognising only that her status as Chilean is a source of pride (in the national context of Chile). Likewise the general denial of discrimination among staff also conflicts with the reports provided by the young Mapuche we spoke to (see Chapter 3).

What seems more certain is that explicit forms of racism appear scarce in these school environments. However, the confidence that teachers exude regarding positive school climate and the lack of discriminatory practices should be read in the context of their narratives about ethnic differences – discussed in the next section – and educational expectations of the types of students who attend these schools – discussed in the final section of this chapter. Both reveal complex and naturalising discourses that, while avoiding explicit racial connotations, provide coded versions of static cultural difference in clearly demarcated taxonomies or categories.

Staff Perspectives on Ethnic Exclusion

One of the most significant results to emerge from the research was the unwillingness of staff to talk about, and confront, ethnic exclusion. The general consensus among teachers is that all children are treated equally (universal individualism), and that this equates to all cultures being equally valued, or granted equal status. As in Pollock's (2005) work, there is a narrative that focuses on "all" which can actually work against efforts to create equal education opportunities. As Parekh (1998) observes, those aspects of equality which are deemed relevant are always a cultural arrangement, since every society has existing cultural structures that it seeks to preserve. As I detail below, there is a tendency among the adults in the schools to conflate individual rights with community-based or group-based rights.

A crucial difference should be drawn, then, between an unwillingness to talk about ethnic exclusion, and tendencies to reproduce these inequalities through their pedagogic actions. Their focus on individual-based equality does not prevent staff from drawing on racialised ideas that carry naturalising assumptions about certain student profiles and their expected behaviour. For example, many teachers in Santiago referred to a national taxonomy that holds Venezuelans and Peruvians above Chileans in terms of educational and linguistic capital, and Haitians, Bolivians, and Colombians as being below the rest. Equally significant is that indigenous children are seen as analogous or synonymous with Chileans in regard to these categorisations:

DIANA: "Here [at the school] the indigenous children are just like Chileans, I don't see them needing any other type of recognition. For us, the foreigners are different, but we [including indigenous] are all just Chileans." (School Monitor, Cerro Bajo School)

ELENA: "The Chileans use more monosyllables, less vocabulary, even their body language is less expressive. The Colombians are more like salsa, the Cubans more exaggerated, so the Chileans seem more timid, quieter. Foreign children stand out more." (Curriculum Planner, Neblina School)

Notably, staff perceptions of difference – including academic abilities as I discuss below – are pitted against a Chilean norm. Students are judged on how alike, or how far they diverge from this status quo. Despite numerous teachers acknowledging the positive cultural contribution of Latin American migrant students, such as good manners, *standing out* is a comparison that positions the *other* outside culturally regulated parameters. In some cases, students from other countries were even encouraged to tone down their cultural differences in order to better fit in:

CAROLINA: "The Peruvians are very good students, they stand out as the most respectful, and don't have aggressive vocabulary and it's always a joy to talk with them. Us Chileans are very poor in that regard and the Peruvians put us to shame … The Venezuelans are more extroverted, and we've sometimes had to put the brakes on them a bit, otherwise they end up showing off." (School Monitor, Imperial School)

This underscores the role of cultural capital reproduction in schools through teachers' pedagogic actions (Bourdieu & Passeron, 1990). Teachers are responsible, in exchanges like these, for establishing a hierarchical distinction that elevates certain cultural traits as desirable. Although teachers appreciate Venezuelan children as exercising academically desirable linguistic capital, they are nonetheless held back on account of not complying with other nationally constructed (Chilean-centred) cultural arbitraries also valued by the school such as "not standing out" (Figure 4.1).

Figure 4.1 Break time at Mapocho School

However, when it came to asking school staff to talk about inclusivity in the school, or the pedagogic methods that they employ in order to promote cultural diversity, most respondents indicated that they avoid making any differences between students; that is, they take a passive approach to accommodating new criteria of inclusion:

JOSEFINA: "We have Venezuelans, Colombians, Peruvians, Chileans, Mapuche, all cultures and there is no-one who will say 'I'm Colombian or I'm Venezuelan'; no, here everyone is equal, they are all students who identify with the school." (Head Teacher Mapocho School)

VIVIANA: "The teachers, who spend the most time in the classroom, are working on [the concept of] 'we are all equal'; we all have the same rights whether we are black, white, fat, thin, from another country or the same country." (Teacher, San Pablo School)

As the first citation suggests, students are expected to leave their cultural differences aside in order to fit into the school culture. What is not stated is that this normative environment is premised on Chilean curricular content and the cultural values that define regular behaviour and school relationships. Likewise, the silencing of multicultural origins is not equivalent to the removal of inequalities. In the Araucanía Region, although school compositions are less diverse, staff are equally keen to narrate their concerns to treat everyone universally. This was evident in the Acevedo School:

GEORGINA: "I think it's the same for all; all are equal, there is no difference because everyone studies the same, so you can't compare one group with another. There's no difference – they [Mapuche] are on a level footing with the others." (Teacher, Acevedo School)

FRANCISCA: "Here the issue of being Mapuche and non-Mapuche is not discussed; no differences are made because everyone is treated equally. I've never seen a school year where they single out the Mapuche student in the corner – no, never." (Teacher, Acevedo School)

A similar justification also exists for not being more proactively inclusive of different cultural practices. School staff deem this to be principally an issue connected to home life, and that families' *perceived* lack of interest in Mapuche culture justifies the school omitting indigenous knowledges:

ANDREA: "Indigeneity often isn't important in the home, and what's more it's been a denigrated issue for years, like "oh dear, the Mapuche" so I don't think they develop any sense of pride in belonging, especially not in Santiago. So how can you expect it at school?" (Curriculum Planner, Imperial School)

XAVIERA: "In the majority of schools I've worked in during 17 years, many [pupils] feel ashamed of being Mapuche ... very few know their origins and wouldn't you just know it, it's the parents who don't want to teach them, so how can we be expected to rescue the[ir] culture considering that we don't have bilingual speakers here? ... Some communities which are closed off have their own school with a bilingual teacher." (Teacher, Quelentaro School)

JAIME: "If a family wants to give different values to those of the school, they can, but as I say, here we don't emphasize culture, Mapuche culture." (Teacher, Castañeda School)

ERNESTO: "The only thing they'd like is not to be Mapuche ... they'd be happier being *winka*, they feel *winka*. I think it's because they associate being Mapuche with poverty and also a bit of discrimination." (Teacher, Lago Profundo School)

FREDERICO: "The Mapuche have become more modern and haven't kept their customs. Rather, they inserted themselves into all that's Western ... they didn't know how to respect their own traditions or knowledge." (Teacher, Campos Verdes School)

These narratives are a vital component of colour-blind racism; it is not merely that all groups are equal and require equal treatment, but that individually, Mapuche students would not *want* to be treated any differently. This two-pronged justification absolves staff from any responsibility to incorporate critical perspectives into their teaching. Jaime's comments can be interpreted from Bourdieu's work on the disconnect between family and school pedagogic actions (Bourdieu & Passeron, 1990). Jaime's words indicate a belief that if something is taught in the home, it remains separate from the school. However, this ignores the symbolic violence that schools enact. That is, the cultural arbitrary reproduced in schools is presented as value-neutral or only concerned with intellectual development. However, value-neutral socialisation is impossible, thus meaning that any curricular construct is culturally arbitrary, and which actively devalues and excludes pedagogic actions from the home that do not match those taught in the school.

A third, but related, narrative was introduced by another teacher, who suggested that acculturation is an inevitable social process, and on account of this, it would be counterproductive for schools to attempt to resist this, and should instead focus on mainstream curricular content:

PATRICIO: "Over time the Mapuche culture will disappear – it will be consumed by the culture into which they [the Mapuche] integrate. ... When the young people go out to get work [will it matter] if he/she knows how to speak Mapuche? No, they need to know how to speak good Spanish." (Teacher, Lago Profundo School)

Some of these teachers do not see the promotion of cultural diversity as part of their professional role. Instead, they treat all children in their classrooms in uniform fashion; that is, as though all were Chilean. This *racelessness* (Moreno Figueroa, 2010) allows all students to be counted as one essence, despite ongoing categorising practices that judge students against the Chilean norm. These colour-blind policies refer to a new form of abstract liberal racism that justifies a lack of attention to group-based rights, by focusing exclusively on treating everybody as essentially being the same (Bonilla-Silva, 2006; Cooper Stoll, 2014).

Treating all students *equally* under more culturally sensitive or group-based criteria would consider how to engage students through knowledges that apply to their lifeworld, and to promote explicitly anti-racist curricular content (Gay, 2010). McGee and Banks (1995) similarly argue that equitable pedagogy means creating classroom environments and teaching strategies that incorporate different viewpoints from diverse cultural and ethnic groups so as to enable all students to attain knowledge and skills that promote their participation in a more just society. As Gorski (2008) notes, any educational system that does not have this as its primary aim will be complicit in educational colonisation. That is, it will continue to reproduce the same cultural capital designed to maintain existing racial hierarchies. However, as noted in Ximena's words (cited above), schools are no longer thought of as places of innovation or transformation; they are institutions that "cannot be expected" to teach anything beyond the established status quo. These are expressions of fully socialised expectations about the role of schooling and a fully legitimated reproduction of a cultural arbitrary that are bound up in nationalised and class-based values and norms but expressed as pedagogic authority.

In short, equality is not achieved by ignoring difference, but by acknowledging its historical and political relevance. Along a similar line, Parekh (1998) argues that the denial of difference not only blocks off recognition, but also leads to assimilatory policies and practices. Following this author, I would argue that whilst teachers are not to blame – since they are not critical educators or sociologists – Chilean teacher training is clearly producing subjects who reproduce pedagogic actions and authority centred in cultural domination that denies racialising inequalities. Quintriqueo and Arias-Ortega (2019) argue that Chilean teacher training courses continue to operate according to western-scientific logics, and decontextualised local realities that invisibilise social and cultural diversity. I would agree with these authors, but I would add that this only occurs underneath a veneer of politically correct rhetoric about equality of opportunity.

Perceptions of Abilities and Educational Expectations

Given the absence of explicit forms of ethnic discrimination, in this final section I review some of the intersections and racially coded language used to describe educational achievement in the school, that further typify naturalised behaviour into fairly static cultural taxonomies. These are difficult to separate from issues of social class since indigenous peoples are overrepresented in the lowest socioeconomic quintiles in Chile. However, as critical race theories argue, a common error is to assume that social class is *the* central and defining criteria by which communities and groupings are stereotyped (Solorzano & Yosso, 2002). Instead, they propose that race is intercentric to other forms of subordination; that is, racism is intimately tied up with gendered and class-based criteria, but in such a way that its importance cannot be overlooked or undermined.

Colour-mute racism was by far the most common feature of school staff talk. From all the interviews conducted, I only heard one explicit reference to ethnic criteria being directly linked to low school achievement, which I cite here:

XAVIERA: "Language scores are low, low because of the low level among the families, and since there are a lot of Mapuche communities, vocabulary is limited, they speak incorrectly and write incorrectly. That's why it is low." (Teacher, Quelentaro School)

The remaining quotes come from much more subtle narratives about different achievement levels. Deficit theory proposes that neoliberal market-oriented educational systems frequently attribute failure to individual deficiencies, rather than identifying structural components that inhibit individuals from thriving. In multi-ethnic contexts, these ideas mirror a resurgence of colonial racial ideologies about populations' intellectual capacities (Gorski, 2008). This form of pathologising has shifted from biological explanations to cultural ones, that stereotype people into static patterns, values, or attributes. I am aware of the dangers of explaining away the difficulties that teachers face working in underfunded and understaffed schools, with students from diverse backgrounds, as merely deficit theory. I am concerned to capture, amid these structural barriers to teachers' vocational practices, how the implicit categorising of students legitimises why indigenous students are concentrated in these types of low-achieving school environments.

By far the most common complaint in regard to the difficulties of working in these school environments were the students' home backgrounds and socialisation. Again, the point is not to query staff members' authority on these matters, since they unquestionably understand the most common types of problems that the schools face. Rather, it is the way these systemic inequalities come to materialise individualised and *raceless* narratives, which avoid confronting uncomfortable questions about why families in these areas are disconnected from schools:

RAÚL: "Here we're not only the pupils' teachers, but we're also social workers [and] psychologists, because many pupils arrive with problems and deficiencies. ... We have a high percentage of pupils with, let's call it, high social deterioration." (Head teacher, Lago Profundo School)

JOSEFINA: "The children only come to school because the parents or grandparents say they must, not because they have a mission to fulfill, like going on to further study, but because they have to go to school, and that's the concept that the parents have at home." (Teacher, Lihuén School)

ERIC: "The students need more than a teacher, they need a father, a mother, a psychologist." (Teacher, Linterna School)

CATALINA: "You must understand that the world is so small for them [...] they can't see beyond that [world] [...]." (Teacher, Campos Verdes School)

Indigenous students were not singled out at any time in these narratives; references to "they" and "them" do not specify any particular subject. That is, it is a broad-sweeping generalisation about the types of students the schools receive and could easily be reduced to a class-based narrative. As noted in previous chapters, white-Mapuche distinctions are complex owing to continuous histories of racial mixture (more so than black–white binaries in the US, as Telles [2004] argues) making these general descriptions all the more ambiguous. Typologies about the rural uneducated poor extend to a more general mestizo population in these areas, but they are nonetheless impossible to separate from colonial histories of indigenous segregation and assimilatory schooling. These issues, however, go unmentioned.

The most common terminology for describing these inequalities – adopting technocratic educational jargon and measurements – is student vulnerability. The Department of Education distributes additional funds to schools that score highly on the "vulnerability index," so schools are well versed in these definitions. Such policies are commendable inasmuch as they provide affirmative action in terms of equalising opportunities for schools with students from less advantaged homes, but it also appears to have a pathologising effect in terms of seeing students as in some way deficient:

FLAVIO: "The truth is that we work with a very high number of students with vulnerable characteristics. In fact, according to what information the JUNAEB give us, 89.6% of those in primary and 94.6% in secondary, so I mean 90% of our students are from highly vulnerable backgrounds." (Head Teacher, Castañeda School)

VANESSA: "They belong to very vulnerable families, that don't have the conditions to get ahead ... the children have unmet emotional needs and it is very evident, for example, when they are working at their desks and you go up to them and touch them they jump." (Teacher, Quelentaro School)

ELSA: "It makes no sense to have regular curricular programmes here, if they aren't applicable to the type of learners we have here, 95.38% vulnerability." (Head Teacher, Lihuén School)

RAMÓN: "I spoke with a teacher the other day and he/she said, 'I'm trained to give lessons to normal pupils, I'm not trained to deal with those with learning problems, nor those with serious educational problems'." (Teacher, Castañeda School)

This amounts to assumptions about deficient or inadequate cultural and social capital for educational success. That is, they lack the required social skills or abilities, and the cultural knowledge to be "good" students. When vulnerability becomes standardised jargon – a "not having" or an absence of the desired conditions to "get ahead," as Vanessa puts it – it overlooks the accumulation of structural disadvantages throughout these young people's lives. That is, it becomes reductive of the ways intersecting inequalities operate so as to make their educational trajectories more disadvantageous than those of students from other backgrounds, and in increasing degrees as they accumulate throughout progressive life stages. Many of the young people spoke of the harshness of rural life (as well as its pleasures) and a lack of transport, but this is only one aspect affecting access to quality schooling. Socioeconomic factors also limit which schools are financially viable for their families, the school-related materials, and spaces available in the home, while agricultural lifestyles also limit the time parents are able to spend with their children on school homework and related matters.

If low teacher expectations and subtle forms of discrimination are added to these structural issues, then we can see a very different picture of what it means to be "vulnerable." Although a vulnerability index may help teachers to understand the difficulties that young people face in their day-to-day lives, and their susceptibility to educational harm, it cannot be reduced to the deficit or want of desirable academic characteristics. The ways I heard this term used in schools was akin to a fatalistic and predetermined future for the young people. This definition of vulnerability overlooks how individuals must manage this inferior social status (imposed upon them by external categories), combined with their exclusion from the benefits that others take for granted and utilise to their own advantage. Rather than just labelling these youth as vulnerable to harm, one needs to understand the intersubjective ways these students are exposed to structural inequalities and socioeconomic disadvantages that accumulate over time.

Not every teacher misrecognises the reproduction of group inequalities; especially in a society that emphasises social class as the main dividing line in Chile. Staff certainly acknowledged the difficulties of working in a low-status public school that struggles to "hold on" to its best students in the educational marketplace, and its inability to compete on account of material deprivations:

JAIME: "The good students have a different vision – many of our best students leave in sixth grade to study a science and humanities curriculum at St. Agustina ... Private schools get better results not just in SIMCE but also in PSU (university entrance exam) because they have more resources, and better social relations. Here by contrast the youngsters don't even go to the nearest cities, so their relationships are restricted." (Teacher, Castañeda School)

ERIC: "I don't want to detract from the school's efforts but if you do the simple calculation any given teacher working in a low achieving school might get their students to reach 230 points in SIMCE, and the following year in a private school the same teacher will get students to reach 300 points, even using the same methods. The answer is the family's socio-economic position. If you compare SIMCE by socio-economic group – something the municipality encourage us to do with other public schools in the region – we are comparatively competitive." (Teacher, Linterna School)

Yet by focusing on national standardised test scores and by restricting explanations for achievement to social class, teachers risk further invisibilising more complex intersectional (or intercentric) inequalities. LatCrit studies has articulated the ways classism, sexism, and racism combine, drawing on tropes such as language, accent, phenotype, and surname, to define ideal and privileged values and behaviours. Distinctions between desirable and undesirable tropes reinforce colour-blindness; they do not lead to a more critical questioning of why social relations, pedagogic strategies, or curricular content may not be culturally sensitive to the communities they serve. They also tend to overlook the cultural wealth that these communities bring to school life despite not coinciding with white middle-class capital (Yosso, 2005). Instead, socioeconomic factors remain the sole interpretation (and solution) for a more systematic response to inequalities.

Additionally, class inequalities become something that transpire in the neighbourhoods or rural spaces around the school rather than in the school. There is no critical analysis of how schools might reproduce middle-class white culture through valuing specific inherited criteria. Good test scores can reductively become the work of individual motivation and good teaching practice, while negative results owe to inadequate family environments, low income, and a lack of educational capital (Bourdieu & Passeron, 1979). This tends to absolve schools from any responsibility other than to offer all students the same conditions under which to work. More extreme perspectives were also offered to suggest that socioeconomic disadvantage should not be used as an excuse to absolve individuals from their responsibilities:

EMILIO: "We have seen instances where a child from a very humble family, with parents with little education, but a well-formed family – I don't mean others, I don't want to be accused of discrimination, rather I mean well-formed in the sense of having a supportive mother and father – and that child goes very far because of the family behind him/her." (Head Teacher, Acevedo School)

ANDRÉS: "I personally don't think that it [socio-economic status] affects anything – they are always talking about gaps and inequalities, but I myself was educated in a rural school and when a person wants to, they can achieve – it takes a lot of effort, but it can be done. That's what I try to communicate to the students but if we keep looking at our level within the national mean, of course we will always be talking about gaps and inequality." (Teacher, Quelentaro School)

However, these definitions of socioeconomic disadvantage oversimplify structural barriers that operate simultaneously. When pressed further to consider other possible factors that might be involved in structural educational inequalities, teachers were quick to dismiss ethnic school compositions as sounding too close to discriminatory rhetoric for comfort:

FLAVIO: "No, honestly I don't think so. Being Mapuche wouldn't make a kid more or less intelligent. I think it is more related to the economic side of things." (Head Teacher, Castañeda School)

ANDRÉS: "I think there are Mapuche students who are intelligent, just like other cultures. That's not related, no it's got nothing to do with that. I think it is a family issue, homes that are badly constituted, and I know a lot of cases. It's mainly that. There is a lot of alcoholism, at weekends, and those factors are negative influences." (Teacher, Quelentaro School)

DIANA: "No no, I don't think so, I don't think it's related [high ethnic composition and lower test scores], not at all, that would be like, er, completely discriminatory toward a student for having Mapuche ethnicity." (Teacher, Linterna School)

ROSITA: "No, ah now that I definitely don't think ethnicity influences ... it doesn't influence much, at all in fact. No, why would having a Mapuche origin or Chilean or German origin influence. The family environment has an influence, but their surname doesn't, nor their ancestry, no." (Teacher, Castañeda School)

The teachers correctly distance educational achievement from biological explanations of indigeneity, but are unwilling to consider whether collective or intersecting structural effects might operate in schools. As observed earlier, schools reject culturally intentioned curricular as something the students do not want. Simultaneously, the second teacher's narrative seems to equate the cultural characteristics of Mapuche homes, such as alcoholism and badly constituted relationships, as an enduring influence (see Van Ingen & Halas, 2006 for similar staff perspectives in Canada). The fact remains that most of the schools have at least one-third indigenous student compositions, and in some cases two-thirds, but there is little space given to more critical examinations of the sociopolitical implications of being indigenous in these spaces. These tend to be silenced, and in their place rurality, vulnerability, and family background become substitute terms – what Bonilla-Silva (2006) calls racial codes – for being poor and indigenous. These offer an appearance of neutrality, but replicate similar cultural explanations for low achievement, despite the non-naming of ethnic difference. These racial codes constitute the institutional talk that provide alternate meanings and explanations for regional inequalities, and how the normality of whiteness impacts upon class-based expectations.

Socioeconomic and indigenous status are a double bind of systemic inequality in the Araucanía Region, and require culturally sensitive understandings of how these overlapping taxonomies operate in daily life. The implicit white privileges contained within class-based criteria generally go unrecognised in these new forms of reference, enabling pervasive forms of inequality to go unchallenged. In high indigenous composition schools, disadvantages are reduced to family or individual deficits; whether a lack of funds, a lack of ambition, or as failing to take the meritocratic opportunities offered to them. My interpretation of these narratives, rather than apportioning blame to the teachers, is that they fail to address institutional racism.

Dysconsciousness and Fear to Name

To repeat once more, during the ten years conducting this research I have rarely met a teacher who could be described as racist. Instead, I have outlined the ways systemic and implicit forms of racism are replicated and are allowed to continue unchecked in high indigenous composition schools. Colour-blindness and colour-mutism are two forms by which racialising effects are left unchallenged and naturalised in institutional settings. Another term capturing this general tendency is dysconsciousness (King, 1990). It is perhaps questionable whether the avoidance of racial issues is as dangerous or harmful as the promotion of explicitly racist ideologies, but it is certainly complicit by leaving its structural consequences unchecked (Lewis, 2003). Fissures between indigenous identity and a normative Chilean identity, or between interculturality and monoculturality are apparent in many of the schools that took part in the research projects. Many of the young people voiced similar narratives to those of the teachers, and given that the latter hold pedagogic authority in the school space, it would not be unreasonable to conclude that at least some of this racialised habitus derives from collective teacher attitudes (Diamond, Randolph, & Spillane, 2004).

Many of the staffs' perceptions noted in this chapter have ostracising effects. The belief that students at these schools perform poorly due to the cultural backgrounds of the rural families, or the belief that all children are essentially the same (or equal), and by implication must fit into the monocultural norm, mirror varied forms of new racism. In all the schools, white staff are majorities (the most Mapuche teachers employed were at Lihuén School – approximately 20%), and the collective expectations reflect the maintenance of an education system that privileges monocultural values as its core standard by which all else is measured.

The examples cited in this chapter do not come from careless talk or throwaway comments. Unlike case study or ethnographic studies of schools using participant observation, such as those carried out by Lewis (2003) or Pollock (2005), I do not have evidence of private informal race talk. I only have the narratives formally registered through interviews. Inevitably, this meant less confidence between the interviewer (whether myself or a research assistant) and school staff, and consequently there was less likelihood of interviewees divulging more explicit racialising categories. Yet it is striking that in these interview contexts school staff offer up such clear instances of dysconscious new racism.

The fear or apprehension to name, on account of political correctness and anti-discrimination laws create a fine but relatively grey margin that prevent a discussion of cultural racism. Staff understand that biological links between indigenous students and school achievement are abhorrent and unwarranted, but feel comfortable describing the general characteristics surrounding their upbringing, lack of parental education, poverty, alcoholism, and geographical surroundings as explanations for their failings. It might be asked whether perhaps these criteria apply to non-Mapuche rural families, and consequently whether this is not just a further example of classism in the Chilean education system? It is possible that staff have in mind issues solely relating to the material conditions of student homes, but the crux of this matter is that they fail to see why those conditions structurally affect concentrations of indigenous families, and that by silencing these inequalities they inadvertently allow them to continue unimpeded. The intersecting nature of structural inequality in these geopolitical spaces adhere to symbolic expressions of whiteness, ideologically associated with the modern, progressive, urban, educated, and civically active. Mapuche are overrepresented outside these symbolically prestigious categories thereby leading us to consider how racial disparities are reproduced through a predominantly class-defined field.

As Augoustinos et al. (2005) argue, there is often a vagueness that surrounds new racism, expounding "good reasons" for expecting meritocratic education founded on individual effort and hard work as a means of achieving equality. "The rhetorical strength of vagueness," they state, "is that it lays open the possibility that the causes of disadvantage lie within the individual themselves, and by logical inference, Aboriginal people" (2005, p. 335). These discourses – which are moderate and free from crude discriminatory language – consistently overlook structural inequalities, and instead focus on the cultural deficits of individuals as an allegedly non-racial issue. According to Bonilla-Silva (2006) this is one of the central features of new racism; its elasticity, allowing for half-truths and avoiding absolutes. That is, obstacles to academic achievement do not apply solely to Mapuche, but they do seem to repeat in contexts where they happen to be concentrated. Mapuche youth, of course, have the right to consider themselves as Chileans, but not at the expense of being treated only as Chileans.

On the other hand, it is clear that these silences are intended to ensure no racist dialogue ensues. Numerous authors have noted the importance of dialogues that interrupt and query taken-for-granted and false notions about human difference and deficits, by discussing justice and conflict resolution, and by explicitly denouncing systemic and structural forms of inequality (Cooper Stoll, 2014; Lewis, 2003; Gorski, 2008; Pollock, 2005). It is clear from the student narratives reviewed in the previous chapter that even where intercultural programmes are implemented, the potential pitfalls and dangers of folklorising or reifying indigeneity as cultural fundamentalism (St. Denis, 2007), without a critical content capable of producing a decolonising or anti-racist effect, are very real in these schools.

I close by noting that eliminating new racism hinges on teacher attitudes. As Lewis notes, problems that are not seen cannot be fixed (2003, p. 85). As I have mentioned throughout this chapter, many of the attitudes and expectations voiced by teachers correspond to, or at least reflect onto, student values and normative ideas. Are teachers, then, equally susceptible to a racialised habitus, imposed by the educational field? Teacher training and schools (as collective cultures) certainly do little to change teachers' minds about what to expect from schooling, or how to go about it. Teachers may not be more culpable for these dispositions, but they do hold pedagogic authority in the classroom making their role particularly decisive for reproducing and legitimising a whitened elite cultural arbitrary. This takes nothing away from students and their agentic potential drawn from alternative capital (Yosso, 2005). Yet transformative pedagogies that resist endemic racism and other types of structural oppression require breaking away from the doxa of taken-for-granted schooling. That is, imagining another type of education that does not just take all children to be the same, to "only see students," or that can consider structural inequalities as part of everyday school life.

Critical teacher perspectives, as many scholars have pointed out, are essential in this process (Castagno, 2008; Cooper Stoll, 2014; Pollock, 2005; Sleeter, 2004). For those who do see this need in the classroom, feelings of isolation and personal disempowerment are additional detractors (Pollock et al., 2010). Yet resistance can occur through teachers' micro-practices, perhaps most importantly through opening the classroom to oppositional intellectual inquiry that can challenge the normative cultural arbitrary of schooling (Giroux, 1988). This means becoming an enabling force through pedagogic action – or perhaps more importantly through sustained pedagogic work – rather than through the imposition of pedagogic authority, so that students can explore these issues (McKnight & Chandler, 2012).

There can be no illusions about the difficulty of such transformations. IBE schools, in the current climate, seem best positioned to achieve this in some measure; though as I have emphasised, this status offers no guarantees. Instead, the "institutional habitus" or school culture of each establishment – and its willingness to interrupt racial inequality – is of equal weight in this matter (Diamond, Randolph, & Spillane, 2004). Though individual teachers may manage to interrupt new racism tendencies, only by changing the school culture through the combined actions of its staff, will students' lives be impacted.

Note

1 Some of the data was previously cited in Webb and Radcliffe (2016), Webb, Canales, and Becerra (2018), and Webb (2019).

References

Agirdag, O., Van Avermaet, P., & Van Houtte, M. (2013). School segregation and math achievement: A mixed-method study on the role of self-fulfilling prophecies. *Teachers College Record*, *115*, 1–50.

Augoustinos, M., Tuffin, K., & Every, D. (2005). New racism, meritocracy and individualism: Constraining affirmative action in education. *Discourse & Society*, *16*(3), 315–340.

Banks, J. (2009). Multicultural education: Dimensions and paradigms. In J. Banks (Ed.), *The Routledge international companion to multicultural education* (pp. 9–32). London: Routledge.

Becerra, S. (2011). Valores de equidad y aceptación en la convivencia de escuelas en contexto indígena: La situación del prejuicio étnico docente hacia los estudiantes mapuche en Chile. *Revista de Educación*, número extraordinario 2011, 163–181.

Bonilla-Silva, E. (2006). *Racism without racists: Color-blind racism and the persistence of racial inequality in the United States* (2nd ed.). Oxford: Rowman & Littlefield Publishers.

Bourdieu, P., & Passeron, J. (1979). *The Inheritors: French students and their relation to culture*. Chicago: University of Chicago Press.

Bourdieu, P., & Passeron, J. [1977] (1990). *Reproduction in education, society and culture*. Beverly Hills, CA: SAGE.

Brault, M.C., Janosz, M., & Archambault, I. (2014). Effects of school composition and school climate on teacher expectations of students: A multilevel analysis. *Teaching and Teacher Education*, *44*, 148–159.

Castagno, A. (2008). "I Don't want to hear that!": Legitimating whiteness through silence in schools. *Anthropology & Education Quarterly*, *39*(3), 314–333.

Cobb, J.S. (2017). Inequality frames: How teachers inhabit color-blind ideology. *Sociology of Education*, *90*(4), 315–332.

Cooper Stoll, L. (2014). Constructing the color-blind classroom: Teachers' perspectives on race and schooling. *Race Ethnicity and Education*, *17*(5), 688–705.

Cross, M., & Naidoo, D. (2012). Race, diversity pedagogy: Mediated learning experience for transforming racist habitus and predispositions. *Review of Education, Pedagogy, and Cultural Studies*, *34*(5), 227–244.

Da Costa, A.E. (2014). Training educators in anti-racism and Pluriculturalismo: Recent experiences from Brazil. *Race Ethnicity and Education, 19*(1), 23–45.

De Freitas, E., & McAuley, A. (2008). Teaching for diversity by troubling whiteness: Strategies for classrooms in isolated White communities. *Race Ethnicity and Education, 11*(4), 429–442.

Demanet, J., & Van Houtte, M. (2012). Teachers' attitudes and students' opposition. School misconduct as a reaction to teachers' diminished effort and affect. *Teaching and Teacher Education, 28*(6), 860–869.

Diamond, J., Randolph, A., & Spillane, J. (2004). Teachers' expectations and sense of responsibility for student learning: The importance of race, class, and organisational habitus. *Anthropology & Education Quarterly, 35*(1), 75–98.

Dickar, M. (2008). Hearing the silenced dialogue: An examination of the impact of teacher race on their experiences. *Race Ethnicity and Education, 11*(2), 115–132.

Dumay, X., & Dupriez, V. (2008). Does the school composition effect matter? Evidence from Belgian data. *British Journal of Educational Studies, 56*, 440–477.

Fine, M. (1993). *Framing dropouts: Notes on the politics of an Urban public high school*. New York, NY: State University of New York Press.

Gay, G. (2010). *Culturally responsive teaching: Theory, research, and practice*. New York, NY: Teachers College Press.

Gay, G., & Howard, T. (2000). Multicultural teacher education for the 21st century. *The Teacher Educator, 36*(1), 1–16.

Gillborn, D. (2008). *Racism and education: Coincidence or conspiracy?* London: Routledge.

Giroux, H. (1988). *Teachers as intellectuals: Toward a critical pedagogy of learning*. Westport, CT: Bergin & Garvey.

González, R., Manzi, J., Saiz, J.L., Brown, R., et al. (2003). *Prejuicios y actitudes intergrupales: La experiencia de estudiantes de origen mapuche y chilenos no indígenas en Temuco, Chile*. Presented in Simposium *Internacional Prejuicio y Discriminación: Aspectos Psicológicos, Culturales y Legales*, Pontificia Universidad Católica de Chile y British Council, Santiago, Chile.

Gorski, P. (2008). Good intentions are not enough: A decolonising intercultural education. *Intercultural Education, 19*(6), 515–525.

Hackman, H. (2005). Five essential components for social justice education. *Equity & Excellence in Education, 38*(2), 103–109.

Hare, J., & Pidgeon, M. (2011). The way of the warrior: Indigenous youth navigating the challenges of schooling. *Canadian Journal of Education / Revue canadienne de l'éducation, 34*(2), 93–111.

King, J. (1990). Dysconscious racism: Ideology, identity, and the Mis-education of teachers. *Journal of Negro Education, 60*, 133–146.

Lewis, A. (2003). *Race in the schoolyard: Negotiating the color line in classrooms and communities*. Piscataway, NJ: Rutgers.

Luna, L. (2015). Construyendo 'la identidad del excluido': Etnografía del aprendizaje situado de los niños en una escuela básica municipal de Chile. *Estudios Pedagógicos, 41* (especial), 97–113.

Luna, L., Telechea, C., & Caniguan, N. (2018). Mapuche education and situated learning in a community school in Chile. *Intercultural Education, 29*(2), 203–217.

Marx, S. (2004). Regarding whiteness: Exploring and intervening in the effects of White racism in teacher education. *Equity & Excellence in Education, 37,* 31–43.

McAllister, G., & Irvine, J. (2000). Cross cultural competency and multicultural teacher education. *Review of Educational Research, 70*(1), 3–24.

McGee, C., & Banks, J. (1995). Equity pedagogy: An essential component of multicultural education. *Theory into Practice, 34*(3), 152–158.

McKnight, D., & Chandler, P. (2012). The complicated conversation of class and race in social and curricular analysis: An examination of Pierre Bourdieu's interpretive framework in relation to race. *Educational Philosophy and Theory, 44*(1), 74–97.

Mellado, M.E., & Chaucono, J.C. (2015). Creencias Pedagógicas del Profesorado de una Escuela Rural en el Contexto Mapuche. *Actualidades Investigativas en Educación, 15*(3), 316–344.

Mishna, F., Scarcello, I., Pepler, D., & Wiener, J. (2005). Teachers' understanding of bullying. *Canadian Journal of Education / Revue canadienne de l'éducation, 28*(4), 718–738.

Moreno Figueroa, M.G. (2010). Distributed intensities: Whiteness, mestizaje and the logics of Mexican racism. *Ethnicities, 10*(3), 387–401.

Nieto, S. (1996). *Affirming diversity: The Sociopolitical context of education.* New York, NY: Longman.

Organisation for Economic Cooperation and Development (OECD). (2017). *Reviews of National Policies for education: Education in Chile.* Paris: OECD Publishing.

Parekh, B. (1998). Equality in a multicultural society. *Citizanship Studies, 2*(3), 397–411.

Pérez Huber, L., & Solorzano, D. (2015). Visualizing everyday racism: Critical race theory, visual microaggressions, and the historical image of Mexican banditry. *Qualitative Inquiry, 21*(3), 223–238.

Picower, B. (2009). The unexamined whiteness of teaching: How White teachers maintain and enact dominant racial ideologies. *Race Ethnicity and Education, 12*(2), 197–215.

Poblete, M.P. (2003). Discriminación Étnica en Relatos de la Experiencia Escolar Mapuche en Panguipulli. *Estudios Pedagógicos, 29,* 55–64.

Pollock, M. (2005). *Colormute: Race talk dilemmas in an American school.* Princeton, NJ: Princeton University Press.

Pollock, M., Deckman, S., Mira, M., & Shalaby, C. (2010). "But what can I do?": Three necessary tensions in teaching teachers about race. *Journal of Teacher Education, 61*(3), 211–224.

Quilaqueo, D. (2012). Saberes educativos mapuches: Racionalidad apoyada en la memoria social de los Kimches. *Revista Atenea, 505,* 79–102.

Quintriqueo, S., & Arias-Ortega, K. (2019). Educación intercultural articulada a la episteme indígena en latinoamérica. el caso mapuche en chile. *Dialogo Andino, 59,* 81–91.

Quintriqueo, S., Torres, H., Sanhueza, S., & Friz, M. (2016). Competencia comunicativa intercultural formación de profesores en el contexto poscolonial chileno. *Alpha: Revista de artes, letras y filosofía, 45,* 235–254.

Rist, R. (1970). Student social class and teacher expectations: The self-fulfilling prophecy in ghetto education. *Harvard Educational Review, 40,* 411–451.

Rubie-Davies, C.M. (2006). Teacher expectations and student self-perceptions: Exploring relationships. *Psychology in the Schools, 43*(5), 537–552.

Rubie-Davies, C.M., Flint, A., & McDonald, L. (2012). Teacher beliefs, teacher characteristics, and school contextual factors: What are the relationships? *British Journal of Educational Psychology, 82*(2), 270–288.

Sivanandan, A., & Fekete, L. (2001). *The emergence of Xeno-racism.* Institute of Race Relations.

Sleeter, C. (2004). How White teachers construct race. In G. Ladson-Billings, & D. Gillborn (Eds.), *The RoutledgeFalmer reader in multicultural education* (pp. 163–178). London: RoutledgeFalmer.

Solomona, R.P., Portelli, J., Beverly-Jean, D., & Campbell, A. (2005). The discourse of denial: How White teacher candidates construct race, racism and 'White privilege'. *Race Ethnicity and Education, 8*(2), 147–169.

Solorzano, D., & Yosso, T. (2002). A critical race Counterstory of race, racism, and affirmative action. *Equity & Excellence in Education, 35*(2), 155–168.

St. Denis, V. (2007). Aboriginal education and anti-racist education: Building alliances across cultural and racial identity. *Canadian Journal of Education / Revue canadienne de l'éducation, 30*(4), 1068–1092.

Telles, E. (2004). *Race in another America: The significance of skin color in Brazil.* Princeton, NJ: Princeton University Press.

Thapa, A., Cohen, J., Guffey, S., & Higgins-D'Alessandro, A. (2013). A review of school climate research. *Review of Educational Research, 83*(3), 357–385.

Thijs, J., Westhof, S., & Koomen, H. (2012). Ethnic incongruence and the student-teacher relationship: The perspective of ethnic majority teachers. *Journal of School Psychology, 50*(2), 257–273.

Thrupp, M., Lauder, H., & Robinson, T. (2002). School composition and peer effects. *International Journal of Educational Research, 37*, 483–504.

Thys, S., & Van Houtte, M. (2016). Ethnic composition of the primary school and educational choice: Does the culture of teacher expectations matter? *Teaching and Teacher Education, 59*, 383–391.

Valoyes-Chávez, L., & Martin, D. (2016). Exploring racism inside and outside the mathematics classroom in two different contexts: Colombia and USA. *Intercultural Education, 27*(4), 363–376.

Van Houtte, M. (2005). Climate or culture? A plea for conceptual clarity in school effectiveness research. *School Effectiveness and School Improvement, 16*, 71–89.

Van Ingen, C., & Halas, J. (2006). Claiming space: Aboriginal students within school landscapes. *Children's Geographies, 4*(3), 379–398.

Vass, G. (2017). Preparing for culturally responsive schooling: Initial teacher educators into the fray. *Journal of Teacher Education, 68*(5), 451–462.

Villegas, A.M., & Lucas, T. (2002). Preparing culturally responsive teachers. *Journal of Teacher Education, 53*(1), 20–32.

Walters, L., Garii, B., & Walters, T. (2009). Learning globally, teaching locally: Incorporating international exchange and intercultural learning into pre-service teacher training. *Intercultural Education, 20*(1), 151–158.

Webb, A. (2019). Staff perspectives on victimisation in multi-ethnic Chilean elementary schools. *International Journal of Inclusive Education.* doi:10.1080/1 3603116.2019.1620353

Webb, A., Canales, A., & Becerra, R. (2018). Denying systemic inequality in segregated Chilean schools: Race-neutral discourses among administrative and
teaching staff. *Race Ethnicity and Education, 21*(5), 701–719.

Webb, A., & Radcliffe, S. (2016). Unfulfilled promises of equity: Racism and
interculturalism in Chilean education. *Race Ethnicity and Education, 19*(6):,
1335–1350.

Yosso, T. (2005). Whose culture has capital? A critical race theory discussion of
community cultural wealth. *Race Ethnicity and Education, 8*(1), 69–91.

5 Staying on Course
Partial Success Stories from Mapuche Trajectories to Tertiary Education

Despite all the inequalities presented thus far, Mapuche youth still find ways to overcome structural barriers and inequalities to reach higher education. In the previous chapter I addressed staff expectations about student achievement in high indigenous composition schools. Some of those interviewed indicated that Mapuche youth have little or no desire to express indigenous identities and queried whether many would go on to further studies. In this chapter I turn to narratives that repudiate both these notions, including those of Mapuche students who have already reached post-secondary education, relating the ways they use these spaces to further indigenous issues. I ask what it means to aspire to tertiary education, what institutional barriers these establishments continue to present, and how Mapuche youth manage these challenges.

Chile currently offers multiple pathways into post-secondary education, with over 150 higher education institutions, of which only 60 are universities, and only 16 of those state-funded (Navarrate, Canadia, & Puchi, 2013). This heterogeneity has led to the massification of higher education in recent years; in 1990 245,408 students were enrolled at higher education institutions, just 15.6% of 18–25-year-olds, compared to 1,165,654 in 2015 (53.1%) (Espinoza, 2017). In a period of just eight years (2005–2013), the number of students in post-secondary education rose by 78.6%; the highest increase of any OECD country during this period (OECD, 2017, p. 177). In 2016, following prolonged student protests, higher education became tuition-free in most universities for students from the lowest income families. Despite these positive steps, access to elite higher education remains heavily skewed towards students from private education and upper-middle and elite social classes. Many of the students from working-class families and the public sector who gain admission to elite universities do so through special talent and inclusion programmes but remain heavily under-represented in these spaces (Santelices et al., 2019). The quality and regulation of the diverse number of technical post-secondary institutions and private universities have also come under scrutiny (Manzi, 2006). In short, attending a higher education establishment does not equate to increased prospects of social mobility given the current saturation of the credentials market.

DOI: 10.4324/9781003090700-6

Who is Higher Education for?

Although higher education is intended to be increasingly inclusive and equitable, authors have queried the extent to which the educational field is able to disrupt existing class, gendered, and racial hierarchies (Bathmaker, 2015; Maton, 2005; Smith, 2007). In particular, scholars have argued that elite courses and institutions remain particularly elusive to social groups with less capital at their disposal, whilst improved access to lower status institutions and professions give an impression of improving meritocracy (Reay, David, & Ball, 2005). Bourdieu and Passeron (1979) discussed at length the inequalities that female and working-class students face in universities, arguing that individuals work within "restricted choices" in what is believed normal or possible in regard to higher education. Even when this doxa is overcome, students must enter a culturally foreign environment, or what Reay and authors call an "out-of-habitus experience" (Reay et al., 2009, p. 1110). Bourdieu and Passeron were emphatic that reaching these prestigious establishments counts for little since their entire institutional setup will make students with these social origins feel "out of place" (1979, p. 13). Surviving elimination in these fields requires the capacity to transform cultural habits, dispositions, and self-assurance, and acculturate to the linguistic and symbolic capital of the elite.

Bourdieu and Passeron assert that the crucial difference between middle- and upper-class students and the working-class entering university is that the former are seen (misrecognised) as "gifted" and desire an education for its own sake (1979, p. 24). Instrumental attitudes towards higher education – solely looking towards the labour market – and values of hard work or sacrifice are shunned in favour of playing the game of becoming the intellectual class. The safety net of their inherited capital means higher education is treated as a rite of passage rather than occupational training. According to the authors, working-class students experience frustration at the lack of coherence between the university and the occupational world, and its apparent indifference towards this. This is because they have more invested in the social mobility potential of higher education, rather than the intellectual game.

A caveat is that Bourdieu and Passeron's analysis was focused on elite French universities, and does not necessarily apply to more vocationally oriented or less privileged institutions. As Reay et al. (2010) suggest, the institutional habitus of post-secondary education establishments varies greatly. That is, every institution has different ingrained dispositions about educational expectations, and the types of students it typically receives. In each of these spaces, the embodied cultural capital – such as language, dress, and attitudes – of students is likely to be distinct. However, the authors note that this also maintains a hierarchy between prestigious institutions and lower status ones, also delimiting which students have access to elite capital including institutional cultural capital like top-ranked university degree certificates which open more doors to employment.

That said, mobilising and activating capital is a crucial part of maintaining an advantageous position in the higher education field. For students from less privileged backgrounds, this usually requires explicit and calculated strategies, unlike those from upper middle class and elite families who tend to already possess and activate this capital unconsciously (Bathmaker et al., 2013). Reay et al. (2009) pose the question of whether this might have negative effects on working-class students' identities. That is, whether changing one's dispositions may mean a rejection of family and community culture, or emotions of insecurity, tension, and uncertainty about the authenticity of self. Some of the students they interviewed, however, developed, "a propensity for dealing with the discomfort of being a 'fish out of water'" (2009, p. 1107), indicating the vital role that resilience and coping mechanisms can play for remaining in higher education.

Lehmann (2009) also suggests that entering higher education can cause a "make or break" scenario, in which the habitus remains either dislocated and out of place, or is transformed. Crucially, though, Lehmann rejects the idea that low-status students only have one habitus, or that it necessarily implies switching wholly to a middle-class culture. An evolutionary process of adaptation need not equate uniquely to mimesis of, or acculturation to, the dominant culture. Following Ingram (2011), I would suggest that it is more beneficial to think of a conflicted or destabilised habitus, inasmuch as it is caught between two conflicting social fields. People can play multiple roles, and have compartmentalised identities, that enable them to cross over social worlds such as higher education institutions.

As I will demonstrate in this chapter, Mapuche youth learn to play by the rules of these academic establishments, but some do so by setting themselves different goals. Hence the evolutionary process of habitus adaptation does not necessarily delimit students to only acquiring the career and educational dispositions imposed by the education system. In this way, we can avoid inferences to discredited notions of *acting white*, or desires to simply become middle-class Chileans. Instead, Mapuche students can reorientate higher education to meet their own goals and values, whilst also playing according to the rules.

Racism and Resistance in Higher Education

Many of the studies cited above are based on research that emphasises the prevalence of class-based inequalities in higher education, affecting working-class students' access to and experience of university life. We also know that gendered and ethnic inequalities intersect with socioeconomic ones to affect "choices" about what course to study, which institution to attend, or even whether to continue with educational studies. Some of the inequalities that may intersect include raising finances for fees, poor academic preparation, lack of self-confidence, a lack of cultural representation on campus, everyday experiences of discrimination (racism, sexism, or classism), access to certain peer groups, and issues with transportation and commuting times – particularly in segregated cities (Ottmann, 2017).

Bonilla-Silva (2006) argues that white habitus is the outcome of the hyper-segregation of social networks and solidarity among whites that normalises cultural tastes and perceptions of racial matters. This is especially relevant to higher education, in which predominantly white universities become spaces in which ethnic minorities (especially those from working class backgrounds) are made to feel "out of place." As Yosso et al. (2009) note, reaching university is a bittersweet moment for minority students; having overcome previous structural barriers, and entering an institution promising new life skills, knowledge, and opportunities, they find that success is contingent on following specific racial and class-based cultural symbols. Reaching post-secondary education, then, is just half the challenge.

Part of the new racism discourse is driven through race equality policies and affirmative action grants in universities to tackle under-representation by promoting widening participation of ethnic minorities. These have generally contributed to a belief that inequalities in higher education have mostly been eradicated (Pilkington, 2013). A consequence of this is to dismiss disparities in access as deficit theories like "a failure to take advantage of the benefits provided" (Augostinos et al., 2005) or by cultural variants, such as ethnic preferences to follow traditional family professions, or to not be academically inclined (Boliver, 2016). In Australia, Hollinsworth et al. (2021) emphasise that indigenous student "failure" at universities is usually attributed to social, cultural, and economic issues, but rarely discussed in the context of institutional racism or the lack of culturally relevant pedagogies or curricular content.

Bourdieu's concepts of capital and habitus have been incorporated by some authors to demonstrate ethnic minority students' capacity for resistance and resilience against structural barriers in education. Stanton-Salazar (2011) notes that students from low-status backgrounds (including ethnic minority groups) are empowered to overcome institutional barriers via their social capital; especially through institutional agents and network relationships. In particular, the author details how *resource-full relationships* can help social development and well-being, as well as academic achievement, in educational spaces. Similarly, Zemblayas (2012) notes that the resources required to stay in higher education extend to emotional resistance in contexts where racism is present. The author emphasises how racism is an embodied experience that compels individuals to seek affective social support from their communities.

Yosso et al. (2009) detail how institutional microaggressions such as racial jokes and social isolation or marginalisation in higher education tend to lead to minority students dropping out. If instead they are to remain in education, these microaggressions need to be resisted using community building and critical navigation. That is, students must develop alternate counter-spaces and support from the margins of these establishments. Yosso (2005) emphasises that alternate forms of capital and cultural assets are vital to these resistance practices, and may include fostering or strengthening collective identities, or oppositional behaviour to the standard institutional norms. Similarly, Sabzalian (2019) – writing in the Canadian context – notes that, "Recognizing Native survivance means recognizing the various ways Indigenous peoples continue to chart for themselves meaningful futures for ourselves in spite of colonial violence" (2019, p. 2). A vital aspect of this survivance is the resilience required in the face of structural inequality.

In sum, ethnic minority narratives of marginalisation and racism in higher education, and their adaptive and resilient capacities to these unfamiliar and unequal fields are critical forms of disrupting whitened norms. One means of resisting these new racism discourses is through counter-storytelling. Scholars from critical race perspectives argue that personal narratives draw attention to forms of social injustice that usually go untold (Solórzano & Yosso, 2002). In doing so, the dominant discourses of new racism are offset. Power hierarchies are interrupted, the authors claim, through stories of resistance that draw on alternate forms of capital (Sleeter & Delgado, 2004). As I demonstrate below, while access to higher education is changing for indigenous youth in Chile, it is vital that we hear their stories about experiences of education and how they view their participation within it.

Indigenous Participation in Chilean Higher Education

Public data on the number of indigenous students enrolled in post-secondary education in Chile is limited. This notwithstanding, it is possible to piece together data from nationally representative CASEN surveys and OECD data. During the early 2000s, just 11.8% of non-indigenous and 7.7% of indigenous populations had completed studies at post-secondary levels (CASEN, 2003). One document cites the proportion of students aged between 18 and 24 in tertiary education registered with indigenous ancestry as having increased from 16.6% in 2006 to 31.3% in 2015 (MINEDUC, 2017 cited in OECD, 2017). Data from CASEN 2003 shows a significant increase for both non-indigenous and indigenous youth in Chile, reaching 38.1% and 32.7%, respectively (see Figure 5.1). Increasing average years of education also show generational advancements, which in 2015 stood at 10.1 years for indigenous populations, compared to 11.1 years for the non-indigenous, each having increased from 7.4 and 9.6%, respectively, in 1996.

Such data ought, however, to be assessed with caution given that many are based on beneficiaries of the indigenous grant (*beca indígena*).

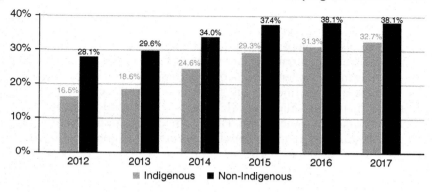

Figure 5.1 Access to higher education

This grant is open to applicants who are three generations removed from an indigenous ancestor, meaning not all these students necessarily self-identify as indigenous. Although it certainly indicates a positive step for indigenous enrolments at this level, these are still disproportionately lower than those of non-indigenous Chileans. An OECD document states that the "higher education participation rate of indigenous Chileans also remains less than 80% that of non-indigenous Chileans" (OECD, 2017, p. 182).

In 2008, just 20.7% of (indigenous and non-indigenous) students who completed technical-vocational education went on to higher education (including professional institutes), whilst in 2017, this had risen to 43.8% (MINEDUC, 2020). This in part is owing to the vast private educational market available in Chile, but still offers important pathways to young indigenous students. These rates are still inferior to those who study on the humanities and sciences curriculum, of whom approximately 63% went on to higher education in the same year (a figure that had previously reached as high as 69% in 2012). As I discuss in greater detail below, a further instance of inequality stems from the types of institutions reached. In 2016, 74.9% of the students who studied humanities and sciences and went on to post-secondary education, studied at a university, compared to just 31.6% of those who had studied technical-vocational (MINEDUC, 2020). This is significant because indigenous students are overrepresented in the latter type of establishments. Blanco and Meneses (2011) provide data showing 61% of indigenous students in 12th grade were in technical-vocational schools, compared to 43% non-indigenous (2011, p. 103).

Added to this, one of the critical issues in Chile is access to post-secondary education for rural families; just 1.3% of rural indigenous and 2.2% rural non-indigenous in 2003 had completed higher education (CASEN, 2003). Access to elite universities, in which students from private schools are overrepresented, is also limited given that only 1% of indigenous students attend private secondary schools, compared to 9% of non-indigenous students (Blanco & Meneses, 2011). Finally, according to these authors, indigenous students – despite achieving similar grades to their non-indigenous classmates – also tend to score lower on the university entrance exam. Part of the explanation offered is that indigenous students are more densely concentrated in poor quality, rural, technical-vocational education, meaning they are less well-prepared for higher education, and that expectations are lower among these students in terms of their possible inclusion in these establishments. All of these cumulative disadvantages add up to some discouraging outlooks for Mapuche youth.

On the one hand, then, access to tertiary education is increasing for the current generation compared to the opportunities afforded to previous generations of indigenous students. These are more readily available to those residing in urban areas attending state-funded private secondary establishments, or those following a humanities and sciences curricular. On the other, there seems to be little disruption to the hierarchical privileges of white upper-middle class Chileans attending private schools (9% of non-indigenous Chileans) in terms of reaching the most prestigious universities and courses.

In the following sections I provide Mapuche youth narratives about their pathways towards, and time within, higher education as a form of storytelling. I underscore the importance of cultural capital and the identity resilience expressed by Mapuche youth who reached and remained in post-secondary education. This storytelling, I suggest, problematises the logics of new racism and the ideological suppositions of an equal playing field in higher education.[1]

Expectations of Higher Education

For previous generations of indigenous families in Chile, reaching higher education was exceptional rather than a normative expectation. Since the return to democracy this has gradually changed. Throughout the duration of the research conducted in high indigenous composition schools, I often heard Mapuche youth speak matter-of-factly about parental expectations and the continued emphasis in the family home about reaching post-secondary education. I begin with some of the future aspirations of those who were interviewed while approaching the end of their secondary education, before continuing with those already in post-secondary education. In Chapter 3, I cited Julia's thoughts on indigenous territory, schooling, and higher education, and she was clear about the sacrifices that would have to be made to reach university but was undeterred:

JULIA: "In the countryside it's like, empty, it's not like it was before when there were more young people, more people, but not any more. Apart from that, there are no more schools and no universities. And I think us youngsters are aiming higher … at least I'm not thinking of finishing school and leaving it at that, but rather to keep studying. If I go [back] to the countryside, I'm not going to go there to study picking potatoes." (11th grade, Campos Verdes School)

Julia was not alone in holding expectations about higher education. Despite the low quality of education imparted in their underfunded schools many spoke optimistically about reaching university or vocational higher education. As the first generation from their family to do so, students emphasised its potential benefits for all the members of their household:

EDUARDO: "I want to make my mum proud; she wanted to go to university but couldn't, so I want to carry on. My passion is culinary studies, and I wouldn't change that for all the world." (12th grade, Lihuén School)

MARTÍN: "I'm studying accounting now as my technical qualification, but then I'd like to study further, perfect those skills, because I want to be able to help out the family. Nobody else [in the family] has gotten beyond 12th grade." (12th grade, Lago Profundo School)

DAVID: "I'm planning to work, but then go back to studying [higher education] so that I can give back to my family [*devolverle la mano a mi familia*] what they've given to me, because now I'm able to stay in school because they've given me everything … I want to [keep studying] so I can be an example to my younger sister, and to help her out [financially]." (11th grade, Raimilla School)

David's case was similar to many others, for whom financial restraints meant postponing a desire to go on to higher education in order to resolve more immediate concerns. It is fairly well established that financial restraints are the main barrier to higher educational opportunities, and that these socioeconomic conditions affect ethnic minority participation rates (Chen & Desjardins, 2010).

Whilst expectations to reach post-secondary education are common, Mapuche youth differed greatly regarding the opportunities they thought this would create. Some students were sceptical about how much it would change their life chances, noting that more general social inequalities prevent many from either accessing or benefitting from higher education. The following extracts are taken from conversations that took place during 2012, a year after the mass student demonstrations demanded free higher education:

JULIO: "Maybe later I could go [to university], but this country is pretty tough, only the rich get richer … so first I need to get together some money, and I don't know what I'd study." (11th grade, Tres Montes School)

EDITH: "Education isn't great [in Chile], I mean there isn't enough financing, because a lot of students don't have the finances to go on studying, they reach 12th grade and then they can't continue because of a lack of funds and scholarships." (10th grade, Raimilla School)

NELLY: "The [higher education] protests are to study for free, but I'm concerned many who have money will take advantage of that. The Mapuche and others, who have less resources, who want to go on ahead [with education] can´t because they´re always giving the privileges to those with more money." (12th grade, Raimilla School)

GONZALO: "Some people say that people used to be able to study for free [at university] and in other countries people do study for free, but the Chilean universities are among the most expensive so I've no chance for now." (12th grade, Campos Verdes School)

PAOLA: "The bad thing about this country is that studying what interests you doesn't make you any money." (10th grade, Castañeda School)

Material inequalities, then, are plain for most to see, but reaching higher education remains on most participants' horizons. This notwithstanding, a key issue is that reaching post-secondary establishments does not guarantee these young people the opportunity to participate on a level playing field with students from more privileged backgrounds. As Bourdieu and Passeron wrote in *The Inheritors*, reaching higher education is just the first structural barrier; staying in and completing one's studies is another. Universities, they affirm, operate according to a purposively vague and quasi-magical cultural capital, which requires individuals to gain a feel for the game that is absent in all but the most elite secondary schools (1979). Predisposition to higher education success, then, involves the match between previous accumulation of capital and those of higher education establishments. This makes progression onto, and the capacity to advance within, tertiary education a "natural" transition for some because the individual actors involved understand the rules of the field and possess the necessary symbolic capital to adjust to it.

A vital aspect of this, I argue, is that these fields do not operate solely premised on class-based symbolic capital or dispositions. Certain bodies, phenotypes, identities, and backgrounds do not fit neatly or seamlessly into university spaces. That is, ethnic minorities are also out of place because they embody a non-white habitus. Following Courtney (2017), this constitutes a "de-privileged habitus [that] is left chronologically stranded, its dispositions out of sync with the new rules" (2017, p. 1056). However, as noted earlier, Bourdieu's writings also include the possibility of adapting one's habitus to new fields and power relations where a mismatch occurs. Under these conditions, individuals can exercise resilient and creative agency, incorporating their own capital to get by, and by adapting to the rules of the new field. Higher education requires middle-class cultural capital to navigate academic writing, time management, understanding professors' expectations, critical thinking, and self-confidence in abilities or performance (Collier & Morgan, 2008; Leathwood & O'Connell, 2003). Much like primary and secondary establishments these are spaces that typically exclude indigenous expression, knowledges, or recognition.

Overcoming Structural Barriers

Almost every student identified ethnic discrimination at one level or other of their educational trajectories; some in primary, others in secondary, and also some in higher education. In the latter, participants recalled how lecturers had been reproducers of implicit racism and microaggressions (Yosso et al., 2009):

AILÍN: "Having to listen to how they [lecturers] speak about the Mapuche people is really tough, but also how they bypass it. For example, they only cover indigenous property in one class, they say it's not a seizable asset, then that's it. So if you go and ask them about it afterwards, they say it's not their area of expertise. I'm interested in that, and they just told me to go look up the law such and such. But if another student goes and asks about problems of inheritance, they say send me an email, we'll talk it over. I think all this talk about pluri-culturalism in Chile is a farce, just a total lie … We really need a Mapuche university, because this papering over the cracks isn't going to change anything. It's all colonial." (24 years old, Law, elite university)

ALISON: "A lecturer who I remember … when he spoke about the Mapuche People did it sarcastically, like as if he was making fun, and he knew I have a Mapuche surname, so he spoke sarcastically and would look at me. I didn't know if I was just paranoid, until a friend who was sat next to me realised and said, 'they're making fun of you'. That was a really bad experience." (20 years old, Sustainable Tourism, private institute)

For the most part, however, students described universities as less racist than previous educational levels. This does not equate to saying that racialised inequalities do not exist, since many of the obstacles that the students faced to reach post-secondary education, and then remain there, were described in relation to intersectional and accumulative disadvantages that carried through from their secondary education. One such barrier had been a lack of prior knowledge about how to choose a discipline or course subject (Bourdieu & Passeron, 1979, p. 13), or the right institution to apply to. Some participants indicated that neither schools nor family had been able to provide support in this matter:

LORENA: "I never knew what to study, I wanted Law but ... many people I spoke to made me too scared to try because they said it was only for those with connections, ... [I] registered for a Librarian career, but I didn't know much about that course either." (23 years old, Library Science, technical institute)

FELIPE: "In the school there was a university fair, and I just saw the stall and thought 'that sounds interesting'. My family didn't know anything about it, but my brother supported the idea, so that's what I studied." (22 years old, Health and Safety, technical institute)

CARLOS: "I chose [my course] because ... they didn't ask for a PSU [entrance exam score], it wasn't expensive like other universities, so I took it as the option to hand at that time." (28 years old, Gastronomy, technical institute)

These examples confirm that inequalities operate even prior to entering higher education. Many of the schools involved in the research, with their technical-vocational curriculum, are not set up to advise students on how to reach post-secondary education. An OECD report concluded that, "just as troubling as the features of potential racism that can be observed in Chilean dominant culture was the fact that some of the very institutions designed to support the success of Mapuche students appeared to be preparing them to assume subservient roles in society" (2004, p. 260). The evaluation teams' observations of technical-vocational schools found that, "the focus was not to prepare students for college entrance" and that these establishments promote "a school culture of low academic expectations where students were engaged in low-order cognitive tasks" (2004, p. 261). My research found similar trends, and, as I described in previous chapters, the lack of teaching quality in these schools disproportionately affects indigenous students, many of whom are enrolled in these types of schools.

However, since accessing post-secondary education is only the first hurdle, students must find a way to stay in these establishments. Family and work obligations, structural and bureaucratic obstacles, and the sociocultural climate and content of higher education mean specific social groupings experience these institutional environments differently. Michelle Fine (1993) demonstrates how *dropping-out* is framed as a personal choice, of individual interest and self-motivation rather than as a structural stratification, enabling white, middle-class privilege to prevail. A number of the students talked about having considered this option of abandoning their studies, while others confirmed they had suspended their studies for a year in order to resolve these pressing family and work obligations. Others had fought through while managing difficulties outside their studies. Carlos (cited above) who was studying in the evenings whilst holding down a full-time job missed the first and last minutes of all his classes due to his work hours and the need to catch the last bus. Others faced similar challenges:

JAIME: "I realised most of my course mates have much less complications [in life] but I leave the house at six in the morning, study on the [long] bus ride in, I don't lose time in social gatherings – if I go it's just for a short while to say hi ... I organize my time ... I work in a cooler storage, and I have a son too so I have to give time to him too." (25 years old, Health and Safety, private university)

BENJA: "My half-sister has two kids and she suffered domestic violence and left the father. Then they all had to come live with us because her mum threw her out ... imagine, our house is 32 m². It's a neighbourhood with lots of drug trafficking. On top of that, I had to start to work in a packing factory at weekends, bank holidays, during holidays to help support us, so I had no days off." (24 years old, Social Work, elite university)

Besides these difficulties, Bourdieu's theories of cultural and linguistic capital also suggest that universities operate so as to sift out and exclude those who do not possess the arbitrary symbolic codes required to succeed in higher education. These, Bourdieu and Passeron (1979) note, are mystical rules of the game, framed in a deliberately nebulous and abstract academic discourse so as to perpetuate privilege. The elite culture of universities requires certain knowledge, know-how, and tastes that translate into particular habits, routines, and organisational requirements. For some of the young people, these requirements inhibited their participation and success during their first years of higher education:

GABRIELA: "I was a good student during secondary school ... but when I got to university I realised everything was different; the people were different, the ideas were different ... the workload was much higher. I was always scared of failing my courses, and having to pay more. I found the material so difficult, and one semester I was seriously asking myself if I was good enough or not." (20 years old, Obstetrics, technical institute)

RICKI: "For a student who comes from a school where you are trained to be a [blue collar] worker, in those industrial schools with lots of Mapuche, and to change your expectations from being a worker to studying is already difficult. You realize you don't know how to read or write and there I found them asking me to read Hegel and Aristotle. I didn't know the difference between a comma and a full stop so that was really complicated." (26 years old, Sociology, private university)

The *cultural obstacles* (Bourdieu & Passeron, 1979, p. 8) that the universities create for students from less privileged backgrounds are often misrecognised at this level as a lack of intelligence, gifting, or ability, rather than a process of cultural elimination. The issue at stake here is that meeting the cognitive demands of higher education is not reported as a problem by any of the Mapuche youth; instead cultural, social, and environmental factors inhibit or restrict their opportunities to participate on an equal footing with students from more privileged educational backgrounds.

Developing Resilient Capital

Cultural habits, as noted earlier, are not entirely static and the Mapuche youth I spoke to developed different coping strategies and alternate forms of capital that compensate for the lack of preparation from their low-quality secondary establishments. In all these instances, the young people narrated their own strategies and adaptations to higher education, often drawing on different kinds of capital, such as family resources, cultural stocks of knowledge, personal resilience, community networks, and new study techniques. Two students studying in the highest ranked Chilean universities narrated their own experiences of adaptation following early struggles during their first year, and the resources social capital had provided:

HORACIO: "All my life has been a fight ... I had course mates who were from the Germany School, National Institute ... (prestigious secondary schools) and you could tell the difference, some were really, really bright ... but then I found others like me from peripheral neighbourhoods of Santiago, our social backgrounds united us ... so we helped each other, supported each other." (35 years old, Doctoral Studies, elite university)

AILÍN: "First year I was lost ... I never stepped inside the library ... I got the worst grades. I realized Law is an elite subject but there are poor students too. Once I found them, we could relate to each other and things became much easier ... It really helped me to have this group ... I learnt by copying their studying techniques, their rhythms, I did whatever others were doing because I didn't have a clue ... they were all so disciplined." (24 years old, Law, elite university)

Both students make reference to what Bourdieu and Passeron refer to as the "gift;" comparing themselves to those misrecognised as naturally talented or bright. However, they compensated through social capital and the mutual emotional and academic support this provided. Other students detailed more individualised strategies that they were able to develop to overcome the deficiencies of their earlier educational trajectories. Jaime – cited earlier – avoided spending any length of time in social gatherings, sometimes just going along to say hello so as to maximise his time on other responsibilities, while Jorge overcame the barriers of linguistic capital privilege in university by using a dictionary:

JORGE: "I remember my life was just work and study, work and study, ... I used to get home, grab a dictionary and start by looking up all the words that I didn't understand." (26 years old, Anthropology, private university)

In all these cases, students must meet institutionally defined forms of merit and ability through creative forms of survival such as studying on the bus, using a dictionary, copying others' study techniques, and seeking support from peers. All are crucial forms of capital accumulation enabling the students to get on in higher education, and overcome the structural inequalities that limit access to elite (white) knowledge, language, and academic capital.

Other students drew on social capital in order to survive higher education; whether parental, sibling, or friends' advice, or to resolve accommodation issues:

ANGELICA: "I went through a crisis – I didn't want to go back [to university] for the following year ... I started to evaluate it by myself, and my brother told me something that really made a difference; he started to make a table of benefits and costs, all mathematical." (22 years old, Social Work, technical institute)

LEONOR: "I felt totally out of place ... my course mates were all totally posh ... Before starting university, my close Friends [from school] told me it was a space that had to be taken advantage of; 'even if they are posh you should get to know them because at some point you will have to work with them, they might put you in touch with people in other parts'." (23 years old, Anthropology, elite university)

ALISON: "My sisters were already studying here in Santiago, and they said if I ever had any problems I could move in with them. It proved really useful after things broke down with my flatmates." (20 years old, Sustainable Tourism, private institute)

AILÍN: "I was going to suspend my studies and my dad just said no, that I couldn't do that, and he was really strict with me, like for the first time ever, because normally he's really flexible in everything. He said you're no good to the family down in the south (of the country) and that broke my heart ... he said they need someone who can defend their rights. There aren't many Mpauche lawyers who can do that ... That talk changed everything." (24 years old, Law, elite university)

The resilience needed to stay in higher education means drawing on resources to, "survive, recover, or even thrive after stressful events"

(Stanton-Salazar & Spina, 2000, p. 229). Mapuche students frequently narrated how family support, and their own development of psychological toughness, had gotten them through difficult periods, particularly during the first years of university. However, an additional aspect to this, beyond individual motives for surviving and completing their courses, was the moral incentive mentioned by Ailín in the previous interview quotation. She specifically mentioned that her community was depending on her to see her studies through to completion, and that her future profession would have a broader vocational purpose and significance. I now turn to other examples of this, and how Mapuche identity was strengthened – and in some cases even awoken – through the incorporation of indigenous knowledges and practices into their courses.

Indigenous Identities: Studying with a Purpose

Numerous authors have recognised the role that higher education plays in contemporary indigenous cultures for provision, self-determination, empowerment, and cultural revindication (Ottmann, 2017). Smith (2007), drawing on Bourdieusian terminology, has called this an "appropriation of the game" (2007, p. 416). That is, students willingly participate in the unequal field, but adapt the goals of doing so for their own purposes. As observed by Frawley et al., "the challenge for universities is to create socially just pathways" (2017, p. 4). Likewise, Battiste, Bell, and Findlay (2002) call for an end to the "cognitive imperialism" (2002, p. 83) of knowledge production in universities that only serves to reinforce eurocentric and whitened economic development. Intercultural universities have been proposed as a means of tackling these inequalities, and as the only intellectual arena in which decolonial education can truly take place (Earl, 2017). Whilst these are vitally important debates, I also wish to underscore the importance that individual agency plays in creating spaces for recognition, identity, and empowerment from the margins of these institutions.

In a country like Chile, which has been historically resistant to the recognition of the status and rights of indigenous Peoples, and is only beginning to address interculturalism at primary school levels, broader structural reforms to university systems are unlikely to be introduced in the near future. Given this rather grim forecast, I suggest that Mapuche youth are currently the bastions of interculturality in these spaces. In countries such as Canada, New Zealand, and Mexico, these issues are contested at meso and macro levels, but in Chile – as I demonstrate below – they are led by the individual practices of institutional agents and students.

A number of the students who were interviewed indicated that, like Ailín, they were motivated to study higher education not merely due to the promise of individual prospects, but the opportunity to benefit their family and community:

SAYEN: "Since we had always been active as Mapuche, and were educated this way, we knew our studies had to be useful for the Mapuche people." (20 years old, Primary Teaching, elite university)

GABRIELA: "I always wanted to study something related to helping my people. I want to go to the South when I finish and help my people; those with few resources, because there are many Mapuche people with precarious health issues." (20 years old, Obstetrics, private university)

The role of higher education, for these young people, cannot be limited to the provision of learning opportunities, but must create a cultural and social environment in which they can develop resources that benefit their communities. In this regard, many of the retention policies designed to keep indigenous students in higher education misunderstand young peoples' intentions to study. It may not be about individualised social mobility or obtaining professional credentials, but about having tools to transform society. Indigenous students may feel out of place due to a lack of cultural and political recognition in these spaces, or frustration at a lack of voice. Ottmann suggests that universities ought to be, "an act of social justice that encourages movement from survival, to recovery, to development" (2017, p. 102).

In certain instances, students spoke of universities as having provided them with the cultural tools that they had previously lacked in secondary education to develop a more nuanced self-identity:

ISABEL: "I always saw the Mapuche as belonging to the past, because that's what schools teach. But in my third year [of university] they gave us different options for our seminary presentation. There was one on the Mapuche and I said, 'well Ím Mapuche and I've never explored this' ... That's when I started getting involved, and it's gone on in stages. Then I started to feel obliged to study *mapuzungún*. That experience has helped me see the Mapuche world as something diverse rather than static." (25 years old, Linguistics, elite university)

RUBÉN: "I knew nothing about Mapuche culture, beyond what I saw on television and some family traditions ... I always had a sense that I was different to others, but then I started to study Anthropology which gave me tools to take forward a process of vindication. It taught me to value being different. I think that was its contribution, more than teaching me any kind of cultural knowledge or worldvision ... I started to participate in an organization here at the university, called *Trawün* (meaning assembly or meeting). I got to know students from other courses like Psychology, History and Political Sciences. We developed networks, to see ourselves in the university space as Mapuche, to inquire more about the culture. In higher education there are resources available that are missing at secondary level, like the books available, and course mates who value that culture and say, 'it's great what you are doing, keep going'. That created a context for me to start to feel I belonged to something." (26 years old, Anthropology, private university)

Despite the absence of explicitly intercultural curricular in post-secondary education, a few university courses appear more open to other worldviews when compared to the narratives presented by Mapuche youth about their secondary education. Following Stanton-Salazar (2011), it is also possible to identify the role that certain institutional agents (in this case, lecturers) play in providing direct or indirect support to the development of these kinds of Mapuche student interests:

RICKI: "I think [my identity development] had to do with maturing after finishing school. When I started uni I met a lecturer Mr. Gonzalez who spoke on Social Economics and Solidarity. It wasn't a course or anything, but it was a topic he liked to speak on in a sociology module. With a coursemate we decided we wanted to write a thesis on rural cooperatives, and that helped me develop new ideas for the [Mapuche] cause and made me realise how much it meant to me." (26 years old, Sociology, private university)

Whilst not subverting the system and its inequalities, these individuals still provide resource-generating information for their students. Stanton-Salazar mentions practices that offer counter-stratification to hierarchical dominance, by motivating students to *go against the grain* (2011, p. 1087). In the absence of intercultural curricular or specific policies at tertiary level, these individuals provide intellectual spaces for indigenous students to take greater control over their environment and studies. One example of this was Rodiz, whose idea to break with the monocultural hegemony of western dress code and vernacular was supported by her course tutor:

RODIZ: "For the final coursework we had to hand in a report on gaps in the constitution. My course-mates suggested the Mapuche conflict, and that's what we did. But I said to my professor, 'for me formal dress is not what you call formal dress, and I want to come to the exam in my traditional clothes.' He was fascinated by the idea and agreed, then I said, 'and another thing, if I'm going to speak about this issue, I want to do it in my native language.' He looked at me for a long time then said, 'excellent, do it'." (20 years old, Public Administration, state university)

Other students had broader ideas for social justice, diversity, and inclusion on their campuses, and some students talked about how they had benefited from them. Horacio suggested this had proved difficult in a predominantly white university, but Gonzalo and Rubén emphasised the importance of the multiple social identities and diversities expressed by peers on campus:

HORACIO: "What happened to me when I first studied at the Universidad de Chile (the oldest state university in Chile), we were so few Mapuche students in social sciences, like two of us in the generation. I spoke to Enrique about [Mapuche] issues but very informally because it was difficult to organise anything at that university being so elitist and all ... indigenous issues were rarely touched on, only as an exception, it wasn't integrated into the subjects." (35 years old, Doctoral Studies, elite university)

GONZALO: "I didn't have a Mapuche identity prior to university. I was totally chilenized by education, and my family didn't have many connections with the culture. But at university there were all sorts of cultural groupings, and I participated in a Mapuche collective to which I still belong. I haven't felt Chilean in a long time now. That experience led me to my *lof* (Mapuche community in a specific territory), to find out where my grandfather's land was, to project my life with a new meaning, and to understand a lot of the past racisms that operate even within the Mapuche – certain essentializing discourse." (27 years old, Philosophy, private university)

RUBEN: "I think universities are more prone [than secondary schools] to help Mapuche students to develop an identity because they are cauldrons for every type of cultural and political activity: hippies, anarchists, musicians, bohemians, vegans ... there's a bit of everything, especially at this [private university] which has a reputation for being political. The Mapuche are no exception." (26 years old, Anthropology, private university)

In some cases, students looked to transform university spaces and make them more inclusive. Two students spoke directly about these initiatives and their empowering potential:

LEONOR: "We called ourselves Trafkintu, with the idea of creating a space to spread ideas and Indigenous people's thinking within the university, because we realized that nobody knew anything about these peoples .... So we started to give talks. I was the one who presented most of the time, even though I never thought of myself as a leader or anything ... over the course of [doing this] I met other people with similar interests and that my studies could be useful, my thinking evolved so now I constantly question how I can link it to Mapuche culture." (23, Anthropology, elite university)

AILÍN: "I started to participate actively in the group and they helped me a lot. We talked through issues that you can't talk about with other friends, no matter how nice they are, it's different with a Mapuche student because the others can't see it from your perspective, they don't criticize the same things as you ... last year I remember we went to a march, a student march about education and we went as *Chilkatufe* [Mapuche group name] dressed as Mapuche students to put forward our demands."

It is evident, from the previous chapters, that the development of Mapuche youth identities is not age-specific or dependent on particular maturational life stages. As noted in Chapter 2, secondary school student organisations have historically promoted indigenous recognition in public arenas. In this sense, there is nothing unique about the university students' comments, except that these spaces seem to afford more opportunities for self-organization and expression than prior education levels. When we consider institutional agents, specific course content, subversionary practices against colonial education, and the organisational capacities of post-secondary indigenous students, we find an encouraging picture of the pathways that these young people are able to forge for themselves in a deeply unequal education system. Social capital plays a crucial role in this, offering both mechanisms for continuing in higher education (despite racism and classism), and for developing support networks with a view to transforming these racialising white-majority spaces into opportunities for indigenous identity formation or development and social justice.

Partial Success Stories

To date there are virtually no education policies to ensure greater indigenous inclusion and equality of opportunity in higher education, except the indigenous grant and special talent programmes. Although these help with access to higher education, it is questionable whether education policies have considered indigenous students' experiences of applying to, and then getting on in higher education. This chapter has demonstrated the versatility and resilience of Mapuche youth to overcome barriers of social and cultural exclusion in predominantly white higher education institutions, including the potent intersections of classism, sexism, and racism. Despite gradual improvements, inequalities remain across most comparisons with non-indigenous Chileans in issues of literacy, educational coverage (especially in Mapuche heartlands like the Araucanía Region), average years of education, access to quality education, and participation in post-secondary education (particularly elite universities and high-status career paths).

Higher education should be a meritocratic opportunity for all but, as we have reviewed in this chapter, it seldom is for ethnic minorities who face cumulative disadvantages as well as intersecting gendered and class-based inequalities (Ball et al., 2002). In a new racism era, these are seldom explicit forms of bias or discrimination. Quotas and inclusionary policies ensure that historic trends of excluding ethnic minority groups from higher education are changing for the better (Crozier et al., 2016; Modood & Acland, 1998). The dangers of these improving outlooks are that they divert attention away from the microaggressions and everyday forms of discrimination that remain in higher education, impeding young people from getting on in their education. They may even lead to young people deciding that higher education in white-majority institutions isn't for them, thus perpetuating the lower retention levels of ethnic minorities, misrecognised as "dropping out" (Fine, 1993).

With little promise of advancements in intercultural education at tertiary level in the foreseeable future, Mapuche students are left to resist assimilatory tendencies from the margins of their establishments. There is some room for optimism, given their own cultural wealth, resilience, and abilities to draw on institutional agents' and family support to get on in post-secondary education. Social capital remains a pivotal part of avoiding the educational death rates that govern most of Chilean education. In some cases, higher education also offers spaces for identity formation; whether through specific course modules, or forming and participating in indigenous organisations. I suggest that these counternarratives are crucial amidst the unequal pathways that push so many Mapuche youth towards blue-collar professions after attending low-quality technical-vocational secondary schools.

The current generation of Mapuche youth are well-positioned to continue a long history of Mapuche intellectuals who have transformed indigenous rights and recognition through post-secondary studies. On the other hand, cautious optimism is required since good intentions are clearly not enough to subvert colonial structures of oppression (Gorski, 2008). Schooling, whether at primary, secondary, or tertiary levels, currently limits the types of knowledges and identities that are valid in the classroom. Mapuche youth are forced to continue to resist the norms, values, and microaggressions that occur in these spaces. In addition, the most straightforward and easily accessible options available to Mapuche youth in a neoliberal, heavily privatised, and vocational secondary and post-secondary education marketplace, are pathways towards blue-collar and lower-income white-collar occupations. These young people's educational trajectories are partial success stories, and it remains to be seen where future educational policies and broader Chilean politics of recognition take us; a matter I return to in the concluding chapter.

Note

1 Some of the data was previously cited in Webb (2019) and Webb and Sepulveda (2020).

References

Augostinos, M., Tuffin, K., & Every, D. (2005). New racism, meritocracy and individualism: Constraining affirmative action in education. *Discourse and Society, 16*(3), 315–340.

Ball, S., Reay, D., & David, M. (2002). 'Ethnic choosing': Minority ethnic students, social class and higher education choice. *Race Ethnicity and Education, 5*, 333–357.

Bathmaker, A.M. (2015). Thinking with Bourdieu: Thinking after Bourdieu. Using 'field' to consider in/equalities in the changing field of English higher education. *Cambridge Journal of Education, 45*(1), 61–80.

Bathmaker, A.M., Ingram, I., & Weller, R. (2013). Higher education, social class and the mobilisation of capitals: Recognising and playing the game. *British Journal of Sociology of Education, 34*(5–6), 723–743.

Battiste, M., Bell, L., & Findlay, L. (2002). Decolonizing education in Canadian universities: An interdisciplinary, international, indigenous research project. *Canadian Journal of Native Education, 26*(2), 82–95.

Blanco, C., & Meneses, F. (2011). *Estudiantes indígenas y Educación Superior en Chile: Acceso y beneficios*. Chile: Equitas.

Boliver, V. (2016). Exploring ethnic inequalities in admission to Russell Group universities. *Sociology, 50*(2), 247–266.

Bonilla-Silva, E. (2006). *Racism without racists: Color-blind racism and the persistence of racial inequality in the United States* (2nd ed.). Oxford: Rowman & Littlefield Publishers.

Bourdieu, P., & Passeron, J. (1979). *The inheritors: French students and their relation to culture*. Chicago: University of Chicago Press.

CASEN. (2003). *Encuesta de Caracterizacion Socioeconomica*. Santiago of Chile: Ministerio de Desarrollo Social.

Chen, R., & DesJardins, S. (2010). Investigating the impact of financial aid on student dropout risks: Racial and ethnic differences. *The Journal of Higher Education, 81*(2), 179–208.

Collier, P., & Morgan, D. (2008). "Is that paper really due today?": Differences in first-generation and traditional college students' understandings of faculty expectations. *Higher Education, 55*, 425–446.

Courtney, S. (2017). Corporatising school leadership through hysteresis. *British Journal of Sociology of Education, 38*(7), 1054–1067.

Crozier, G., Burke, P., & Archer, L. (2016). Peer relations in higher education: Raced, classed and gendered constructions and othering. *Whiteness and Education, 1*(1), 39–53.

Earl, A. (2017). Inclusion or Interculturalidad: Attaining equity in higher education for indigenous peoples in Mexico. In R. Cortina (Ed.), *Indigenous education policy, equity, and intercultural understanding in Latin America*. New York, NY: Palgrave Macmillan.

Espinoza, O. (2017). Acceso al sistema de educación superior en Chile. El tránsito desde un régimen de elite a uno altamente masificado y desregulado. *Universidades, 74*, 7–30.

Fine, M. (1993). *Framing dropouts: Notes on the politics of an Urban public high school*. New York, NY: State University of New York Press.

Frawley, J., et al. (2017). Indigenous pathways and transitions into higher education: An introduction. In J. Frawley, S. Larkin, & J. Smith (Eds.), *Indigenous pathways, transitions and participation in higher education*. Singapore: Springer.

Gorski, P. (2008). Good intentions are not enough: A decolonising intercultural education. *Intercultural Education, 19*(6), 515–525.

Hollinsworth, D., Raciti, M., & Carter, J. (2021). Indigenous students' identities in Australian higher education: Found, denied, and reinforced. *Race Ethnicity and Education, 24*(1), 112–131.

Ingram, N. (2011). Within school and beyond the gate: The complexities of being educationally successful and working class. *Sociology, 45*(2), 287–302.

Leathwood, C., & O'Connell, P. (2003). 'It's a struggle': The construction of the 'new student' in higher education. *Journal of Education Policy, 18*(6), 597–615.

Lehmann, W. (2009). University as vocational education: Working-class students' expectations for university. *British Journal of Sociology of Education, 30*(2), 137–149.

Manzi, J. (2006). Segmented access to higher education in Chile. In P. Díaz-Romero (Ed.), *Avenues for equity in access to higher education* (pp. 187–204). Santiago: Fundación Equitas.

Maton, K. (2005). A question of autonomy: Bourdieu's field approach and higher education policy. *Journal of Education Policy, 20*, 687–704.

Ministerio de Educación (MINEDUC). (2020). *Estudio sobre trayectorias educativas y laborales de estudiantes de educación media técnica-profesional*. Santiago: Gobierno de Chile.

Modood, T., & Acland, T. (Eds.). (1998). *Race and higher education*. London: Policy Studies Institute.

Navarrate, S., Canadia, R., & Puchi, R. (2013). Factores asociados a la deserción/retención de los estudiantes mapuche de la Universidad de la Frontera e incidencia de los programas de apoyo académico. *Calidad en la educación, 39*, 44–80.

Organisation for Economic Cooperation and Development. (2004). *Reviews of national policies for education: Chile*. Paris: Organisation for Economic Cooperation and Development.

Organisation for Economic Cooperation and Development. (2017). *Education in Chile*. Paris: Organisation for Economic Cooperation and Development.

Ottmann, J. (2017). Canada's indigenous peoples' access to post-secondary education: The Spirit of the 'new Buffalo'. In J. Frawley, S. Larkin, & J. Smith (Eds.), *Indigenous pathways, transitions and participation in higher education*. Singapore: Springer.

Pilkington, A. (2013). The interacting dynamics of institutional racism in higher education. *Race Ethnicity and Education, 16*(2), 225–245.

Reay D, Crozier G, Clayton J. (2009). 'Strangers in paradise'?: Working-class students in elite universities. *Sociology, 43*(6), 1103–1121.

Reay D, Crozier G, Clayton J. (2010). 'Fitting in' or 'standing out': Working class students in UK higher education. *British Educational Research Journal, 36*(1), 107–124.

Reay, D., David, M.E., & Ball, S. (2005). *Degrees of choice. Social class, race and gender in higher education*. Stoke on Trent. Trentham Books.

Sabzalian, L. (2019). *Indigenous Children's Survivance in public schools*. London: Routledge.

Santelices, M.V., Horn, C., & Catalán, X. (2019). Institution-level admissions initiatives in Chile: Enhancing equity in higher education? *Studies in Higher Education, 44*(4), 733–761.

Sleeter, C., & Delgado, B. (2004). Critial pedagogy, critical race theory and anti-racist education. In J.A. Banks (Ed.), *Handbook of multicultural education research* (pp. 240–257). San Francisco: John Wiley & Sons.

Smith, H. (2007). Playing a different game: The contextualised decision-making processes of minority ethnic students in choosing a higher education institution. *Race Ethnicity and Education, 10*(4), 415–437.

Solórzano, D., & Yosso, T. (2002). Critical race methodology: Counter-storytelling as an analytical framework for education research. *Qualitative Inquiry, 8*, 23–44.

Stanton-Salazar, R. (2011). A social capital framework for the study of institutional agents and their role in the empowerment of low-status students and youth. *Youth & Society, 43*, 1066–1109.

Stanton-Salazar, R.D., & Spina, S.U. (2000). The network orientations of highly resilient Urban minority youth: A network-analytic account of minority socialization and its educational implications. *The Urban Review, 32*, 227–261.

Webb, A. (2019). Getting there and staying in: First-generation indigenous students' educational pathways into Chilean higher education. *International Journal of Qualitative Studies in Education, 32*(5), 529–546.

Webb, A., & Sepulveda, D. (2020). Re-signifying and negotiating indigenous identity in university spaces. *Studies in Higher Education, 45*(2), 286–298.

Yosso, T. (2005). Whose culture has capital? A critical race theory discussion of community cultural wealth. *Race Ethnicity and Education, 8*(1), 69–91.

Yosso, T.J., Smith, W.A., Ceja, M., & Solorzano, D.G. (2009). Critical race theory, racial microaggressions, and campus racial climate for Latina/o undergraduates. *Harvard Educational Review, 79*(4), 659–690.

Zemblayas, M. (2012). Pedagogies of strategic empathy: Navigating through the emotional complexities of anti-racism in higher education. *Teaching in Higher Education, 17*(2), 113–125.

Conclusions
Schooling, Indigeneity, and New Racism

This book has asked what role education plays in the articulation of indigenous identities and the reproduction of racial hierarchies. I have explored these questions from a sociological perspective in the context of Chilean educational establishments. Given historical processes of indigenous exclusion and colonialism, as well as neoliberal-oriented educational reforms during the last four decades, today's indigenous youth must navigate their educational trajectories amid a complex interweaving of racial lines, structural inequalities, complex ethnic categories, and possible self-identities. Additionally, with the rise of anti-discrimination laws in schools, a key issue is whether racism is really being eradicated or is merely taking other forms. Drawing on qualitative interviews and focus groups with indigenous youth and school staff in urban and rural primary and secondary schools, and post-secondary education, I have addressed the ways implicit forms of discrimination impinge on, and inform, contemporary forms of indigenous belonging.

Amid the diverse ethnic options available to ethnic youth in contemporary societies, I have stressed that cultural and social capital are important assets for re-positioning indigenous status. However, these resources remain tenuously balanced within structures that maintain indigenous youth on the margins of school life and within racialised hierarchies. Whilst there is considerable optimism surrounding the political voice that Mapuche communities have achieved in recent decades, in these concluding thoughts I query what the future holds for the next generations of indigenous youth socialised in Chilean mainstream schooling. Unquestionably there will be those who continue the legacy of Mapuche intellectuals educated in Chilean schools during the twentieth century, who used these institutions as platforms for furthering indigenous causes such as self-determination, autonomy, and the recuperation of ancestral lands. For others, schooling offers a less resolute pathway.

My conclusions are ordered first by recapping the content reviewed throughout the book. I then summarise what I see to be some of the key conceptual perspectives and empirical findings, before continuing to indicate some of the challenges that lie ahead in the Chilean context.

DOI: 10.4324/9781003090700-7

A Summary of Core Issues

Chapter 1 provided an overview of how indigenous identities can be theorised within the broader lens of ethnic identity and new racism. In particular, I drew attention to the importance of approaches that focus on "everyday ethnicity." I then addressed some characteristics of indigenous identities in Latin America and specifically the role of mestizaje as a political and self-making project. I linked this to empirical data gathered from Mapuche youth narratives in reference to racial taxonomies in Chilean society and their place within them. I discussed the ways students navigate certain ambiguity regarding in-group and out-group categories, and how they are able to simultaneously embrace group similarity and individual difference.

I continued in Chapter 2 with a broad-strokes review of the historic and sociopolitical implications of Chilean schooling for indigenous youth. Many generations of Mapuche youth suffered overt and crude forms of discrimination during these periods. However, hope also dawned from the political interventions that Mapuche intellectuals and organisations made during the twentieth century, resisting schooling as a colonising and explicitly racist vehicle of assimilation. I showed that IBE's roots come from broader indigenous demands for equity and social justice, which eventually resulted in the state-led implementation of a national programme, and indigenous grants. I then presented data from students who attended two IBE schools as examples of the potential benefits to be derived from education that breaks with colonial patterns of excluding or marginalising indigenous identities. However, I also argued that although IBE is held up as the model for a more inclusive education in Chile, paradoxically, IBE schools are spaces in which new racism can flourish.

Chapter 3 addresses Mapuche students' experiences of schooling in the Araucanía Region. I used Bourdieusian concepts of field, capital, and habitus to demonstrate the extent to which new racism is a latent tension for their own self-understandings and notions of belonging. I gave specific examples of how neoliberal educational arrangements fit into a new racism logic to justify school choice and the selection of low-quality, rural, technical-vocational schools with high indigenous compositions. I emphasised the role that racialised habitus plays in the repetitive work of schooling to adjust young Mapuche students' expectations towards a normative monocultural education. I also showed how these environments reproduce peer harassment and discrimination, despite being described as safe havens from racism. I finished by providing examples of how a minority of students are able to resist these racial projects through critical narratives that interrupt colonial ideas of inferiority and backwardness.

Chapter 4 presented teacher expectations and perceptions of working in these schools and with their student populations. I demonstrated how racialising structures of schooling find expression through the colour-mute and colour-blind tendencies of teaching staff. In this context, day-to-day constructions surrounding academic achievement underscore the ways racialised hierarchies are maintained as the normative status quo. This occurs through the pathologising of indigenous youth – especially those categorised as rural and socioeconomically vulnerable. These "gentler" neoliberal forms of new racism move away from biologising explanations for low academic achievement, but attribute poverty and limited home environments to personal or family failures, rather than broader structural issues. I argued that in these educational settings where indigenous youth are overrepresented – constituting as many as two-thirds of the school composition – the lack of explicit reference to indigeneity as a "causal" factor does little to avert the implications of these racialising discourses.

Finally, in Chapter 5 I addressed the partial success stories of Mapuche youth who have gone on to reach higher education institutes. All narrated having experienced some form of structural barriers, discrimination, and microaggressions during their educational trajectories, including elite university settings. However, they also voiced the personal resilience and indigenous capital that they drew on to overcome these inequalities. This chapter offers renewed but cautious optimism regarding certain advances in Chilean society, and the promise of a brighter future for indigenous youth in this country.

Conceptual and Empirical Contributions

Patricia Richards' (2013) outstanding monograph addresses the issue of indigenous rights, identity, and neoliberalism in Chile. I have sought to provide an institutionally specific example of this national situation. Richards demonstrates the influence that state policies have had in a racialising system, whilst noting that race and cultural difference are rarely addressed in public discourse. The theoretical perspective adopted in the book draws mainly on "neoliberal multiculturalism" to express a form of governance that increasingly recognises or names difference, but does little to transform or empower minority (indigenous) cultures. As numerous Latin American scholars have noted, there is an internal paradox between reforms that adhere to international standards of greater inclusivity and redistribution, and continuing state practices of exclusion. Scepticism about these reforms have led to questioning the extent to which states use minor reforms as makeweights to continue governing and to maintain the monopoly of power.

Although I am appreciative of work on neoliberal multiculturalism, I follow Richards (2013) in deeming it theoretically restrictive as it places too much emphasis on an economic and political logic that seems ahistorical. This framework does not go far enough in outlining how systemic racism continues to function, particularly beyond economic and political spheres. Richards acknowledges her debt to authors like Omi and Winant and Bonilla-Silva, though her work is less focused on an explicit theory of *how* national ideas about race are transmitted below the policy level. I have presented a sustained and detailed case for how new racism operates as an ongoing racial project within the cultural spheres of schooling, acting upon the lives of young Mapuche people today. This is important since systemic racism must be shown across macro, meso, and micro levels. In particular, colour-blind and colour-mute racism offer a lens through which to understand how Chilean teachers avoid addressing differences in their pedagogic practices in order to uphold more progressive ideas about racial difference, which in turn create ambivalence for indigenous youth growing up with conflicting ideas about indigeneity.

Much of the book has been dedicated to analysing new racism; whether through people's narratives or actions. New racism is founded on concepts that in other contexts are praiseworthy cornerstones of western democracy; freedom, individual rights, and personal merit, making them seem more palatable and tolerant (Augostinos et al., 2005). Since the late twentieth century, new forms of racism have replaced the former explicit and hostile associations of biological inferiority with cultural and civilising narratives, espousing politically correct vocabulary whilst alluding to liberal and individually based fairness and equality (Barker, 1981). My aim has been to develop an empirically led examination of new racism in Chilean schools where indigenous youth comprise an important presence. If there are any schools in this country where one would expect the most progress, it is in these establishments. I have been particularly indebted to Bonilla-Silva (2006), Pollock (2005), and Lewis's (2003) accounts of new racism, and their attention given to the ways these discourses are present among white teachers. Hence, whilst there is a clear intention on behalf of the adult staff involved in the research schools to provide a positive formative experience for their students, a number of unintentional, implicit processes can be simultaneously observed that affect the indigenous young people's identities.

In addition, I have reiterated that one way of moving new racism forwards is through Bourdieu's work, by addressing the ways specific material and symbolic violence continue to reproduce inequalities that are misrecognised and internalised as non-racial, irrelevant, or improving. This helped me frame these issues as unequal educational fields in which racialised habitus and misrecognised racism coexist with the tensions of agency and alternative cultural capital. Schooling cannot be conceptualised as merely a one-way process of socialisation and cultural reproduction. Numerous school ethnographies have given accounts of student resistance and counterculture, including among ethnic minorities (Carger, 1996; Carter, 2005; Cummins, 1996; Fine, 1993; Lewis, 2003). These are vital contributions, but I believe it is also important to provide evidence of the young people who are negatively affected by, and remain oblivious to, new racism's pernicious effects. I have shown that some students are better positioned to resist, while others are caught in more ambiguous territory of accepting the doxa of school life and incorporating it into their schooled habitus through pedagogic work. The persistence of new racism in day-to-day routines, then, is a vital aspect of cultural reproduction. The crucial crossing point between these two perspectives is that the cultural capital associated with educational success and as valued by society remains firmly rooted in white, middle-class urban and national categories. However, this continues to be misrecognised in educational fields precisely owing to the advances that have been made in overcoming previously explicit and offensive colonial forms of schooling.

At the beginning of the book, I referred to Burke's (2016) work which emphasises the need to press on towards looking at the material effects of new racism, rather than merely confirming its existence. The most important aspect of this materiality is how these schools are presented by staff as merely composed of socioeconomically vulnerable youth, and its racially coded meanings. In these spaces, indigeneity is always exceptional, different, or folkloric. Most of the school calendar and its curricular content profess to be "non-racial," in so far as they treat everyone as equal in the very strict sense of being the same. Equally troubling is that issues of structural racism and institutional discrimination are continually sidestepped or ignored altogether. Wherever there are school climate problems or instances of peer harassment (when they are not downplayed as jokes), they are dealt with as individual problems.

Teachers play a central role in reinforcing taken-for-granted notions of cultural background, school achievement, and ethnic belonging. Many assume an incompatibility between the cultural capital of the average families in the surrounding communities and educational success. Although the teachers believe socioeconomic factors are responsible, there is an unwillingness or resistance to considering how implicit forms of structural racism and exclusion might also be responsible. Misrecognition means that these issues are never dealt with in school curricula or activities, thus further reproducing a monocultural norm that intersects with social class, allowing these inequalities to continue unchallenged. The young people attending these schools are therefore caught up in environments where official discourses affirm that everyone is equal, treated with respect, where anyone can achieve, and where all cultures are valued. However, these staff perspectives actually consign indigeneity to an inferior position in relation to the nationalised and whitened normality.

Staff generally prefer to ignore indigeneity all together – a colour-blind approach to avoiding racism – thereby establishing culturally naturalised justifications for their inferior educational achievements or labour market prospects. Intercultural initiatives in schools also transmit mixed messages to the young people about the role and relevance of indigenous knowledges and practices in its stratified relationship to mainstream "education." Some young people are alert to these kinds of schooling, and discursively resist these practices. I also addressed some of the ways the young people actively resist racism and structural barriers to educational achievement, having reached higher education institutions. Many draw on cultural community wealth (Yosso, 2005) and also social capital to remain in these fields, and to develop their own cultural identity.

On the other hand, the young people are also socialised into pejorative media representations of the Mapuche and are encouraged to see the state as positively benefitting their educational pathways through grants. I have exemplified how these muddled and often contradictory signals cause very mixed and ambivalent responses among indigenous youth. It is certainly difficult to develop positive identities capable of discerning and challenging new racism's detrimental material and ideological effects in these environments. That is, ongoing structural inequalities tend to be misrecognised as personalised school choice, a lack of motivation or gifting, or disinterest in school curricula. Mapuche youth identities, then, inhabit an ambivalent day-to-day space of becoming.

Schooling is not the only institution or structural factor responsible for these dilemmas. Family influence, social media, television, local politics, and community also play important roles, and affect how young people manage and develop their identities. However, my research sheds light on the role of schooling (rather than education) and the multiple ways it influences young people's conceptions of belonging. In particular, I have shown how young people come to naturalise and accept poorer school conditions within a neoliberal educational marketplace, and their own cultural exclusion or marginalisation within it. I have also provided evidence of in-group discriminatory practices that reproduce wider racial values, but which also function to negotiate the complex meanings associated with racial mixture (*mestizaje*).

Given the relatively small amount of research conducted in high-indigenous composition schools, or the effects of racialised schooling on indigenous youth, I see this book as extending the current dialogue about the quality and equality of education offered to indigenous youth. Whilst there are commonalities with Latin American research on intercultural bilingual education programmes, and also critical works on colonial schooling in different former-settler societies, I trust these conceptual and empirical specificities will contribute to this field.

Advances and Ongoing Issues

Structurally speaking, there are some encouraging signs of improved opportunities for Mapuche youth and more equitable educational trajectories in Chilean education. Gross expenditure on education in Chile continues to rise year by year, and Chile spends 6.3% of its GDP on primary to tertiary institutions, and 1.2% on early years education and childcare; both are among the largest contributions of the OECD countries (OECD, 2019). Since 2016 higher education in public institutions (and some private) has been free of tuition costs for those from families with lower income levels are important advances. Likewise, since 2011 there have been formal procedures in place to educate on, and eradicate, discrimination, ensuring more students in Chile are protected from violence and harassment. Although it is too early to be overly optimistic, the referendum success in 2020 for a new constitution also promises reforms to the way the education system is structured. A nationally representative survey carried out by the Centre on Indigenous and Intercultural Research (CIIR) suggests discrimination towards the indigenous in Chilean society is decreasing while general support in the public domain for their rights is increasing (CIIR, 2019). Finally, as detailed in Chapter 2, there have been a number of advances in regard to the construction of a more culturally inclusive curriculum in Chilean education, as well the continuing special grants programme for indigenous students. IBE continues to expand, thus providing increasing numbers of indigenous students with at least some exposure to alternative knowledges and languages. In 2011 just 3,133 students participated in indigenous language classes, compared to 29,371 in 2016 (MINEDUC, 2017). However, this still only constitutes 24.5% of indigenous youth in Chile so there is a long path ahead, including extending intercultural content to secondary and tertiary levels. The quality of this education and the limited number of hours that are assigned to the subject matter are even greater concerns.

Amidst all these advances, a degree of tempered optimism is required. The issues raised in this book about new racism suggest Chile is not free from more implicit structural forms of inequality. Although IBE is an important way forward for subverting and eradicating newer structural forms of implicit racism in Chilean schools and universities, I have argued that a more pressing issue is teacher training. Following St. Denis (2007), I would be cautious about recommendations for all teachers to be versed in indigenous languages and traditions since these often have superficial results that, "encourage the development of a cultural hierarchy with notions of 'real', 'traditional', and 'assimilated'" (2007, p. 1081). However, teachers do need training in culturally sensitive pedagogies that discourage the reproduction of discourses of blame and stereotyping, and – equally damaging – the silencing of racial oppression and the present-day effects of colonial histories.

The latest OECD report for Chilean education (2017) acknowledges the invisibilisation, exclusion, and inequalities surrounding indigenous people's participation across all levels of schooling, cited at length here:

> Among categories of exclusion, indigenous communities and immigrants are perhaps the most overlooked and underserved groups in

Chile. Exclusion is particularly evident in the school system... Net enrolment rates among indigenous students are similar to those of their nonindigenous peers in pre-primary and primary education. This may be explained by the fact that roughly three-quarters of indigenous Chileans live in urban areas that provide greater educational options. However, indigenous students appear to face particular challenges in progressing. They have lower participation in upper secondary (71% versus 74%) and tertiary education (Ministry of Social Development, 2015). At the policy level, indigenous and immigrant students remain either invisible or pushed to the margins. While some efforts by the Ministry of Education have sought to bring attention to indigenous cultures and immigrant students, they remain marginal and disconnected from the overall educational improvement agenda. Ethnic, racial and immigrant identities are remarkably absent from the data collection and reports created by the Ministry of Education. This makes it challenging to estimate the extent to which the Chilean education system offers indigenous and immigrant students adequate educational opportunities. It also underlines the magnitude of the challenge of doing so.

(2017, p. 104)

In accordance with the OECD report cited above, Chile is ill prepared for effective teaching in classrooms with indigenous and ethnic minority youth on a national scale. IBE schools offer a solution for specific demands from indigenous communities able to manage schools autonomously (Luna et al., 2018), but this will not resolve the issues faced by the majority of Mapuche, or other indigenous youth, in Chile. The data presented by the OECD gives further credence to the general argument of this book; that structural racism continues to operate through education, against indigenous youth. I have been at pains to emphasise that unequal opportunities have consequences for indigenous young peoples' experiences of education and their own identities. It is not merely a matter of how their achievement levels are affected, as important an equality issue as this is, but also how education affects their outlook on their futures, on their communities, and on their participation in Chilean society in general as citizens.

Reforms to Chilean textbooks for the mainstream curricula have, over the last three decades, steadily become more inclusive, and less abrasively racist (Crow, 2006). However, the inclusion of indigenous peoples and different knowledges remain largely concentrated in the History, Geography, and Social Sciences textbook (a combined subject). Much more needs to be done to incorporate indigenous knowledges into mathematics, the natural sciences, and language.

This book provides a caveat for Chilean literature that is overly emphatic about the potential of IBE curricular programmes to overcome post-colonial forms of schooling. I have stressed that even in schools where IBE is implemented, there are no guarantees that staff perspectives will necessarily be transformed by these pedagogic devices. Instead, I have drawn on critical education literatures that articulate the need for culturally sensitive pedagogies and a willingness among staff to confront their own implicit perceptions of difference that perpetuate new forms of racism. Without these, IBE literature risks falling into utopian notions of school reform.

Mapuche Identities and the Future of Chilean Schooling

My intention has been to show the complex and diverse meaning behind being defined, and identifying oneself, as Mapuche in today's society, and in particular, the ways in which these definitions come to be socially constructed vis-à-vis dominant society through the education system. The historical context of discrepant power relations and the central role that schooling has played in this process is of utmost relevance to an understanding of contemporary identification and categorisation in a new racism era. I have tried to avoid a well-meaning academic intention of presenting Mapuche identities as something that all the young people must adopt. This remains a matter of personal choice, but schooling – as a process that takes away this choice – must be interrogated as a complicit structural arrangement in ongoing racial formations (Omi & Winant, 1994).

Younger generations' attitudes about what it means to be Mapuche suggest they will continue to shift the boundaries of what can legitimately be identified as "Mapucheness," especially in a time when *mapuzungún* remains an endangered language. However, as I also discussed earlier in the book, further research will be required to refine and deepen understandings of why – in some instances – affiliations to the Mapuche remain strong despite identification with traditional Mapuche ways of life being dropped. Generally, I would be reluctant to suggest that young people's identities will change much in the coming years, unless the training of pre-service teachers undergoes radical reform. Of course, intercultural bilingual education holds out some hope of more widespread change, but to date it remains concentrated at primary education levels, and as a sporadic or additive top-down model. Exceptions exist in some locally – and community-administered schools by indigenous groups and organisations, but are limited in scope.

There is, of course, no crystal ball for assessing the future identities of Mapuche youth, or what course schooling might take in the coming years. There is no indication that senses of belonging among Mapuche communities are waning, even among the young; rather they need to be understood from perspectives able to account for increasingly variable and flexible (even elastic) affiliations, which I have suggested are founded upon a more solid and permanent sense of self which derive from ingrained moral codes and pride in a historical but ongoing struggle. The CIIR (2019) survey suggests that identifications are in fact now stronger among indigenous youth, but are founded on complex variants and interplays of skin pigment/phenotype, mestizaje, and indigeneity.

However, there are a number of implications that future research needs to address, such as these young people's transitions to the labour market and their experiences of these institutional (and non-institutional) settings in which further instances of new racism may occur. Although beyond the scope of the book, there is some (limited) evidence to suggest that racialised structures continue to hinder Mapuche youth upon completion of their education (whether secondary or tertiary) (Cerda, 2017), meaning we need to consider the ways these young people's lives are affected across multiple life stages.

Some Implications for Moving Forward

The most urgent reform needed is to pre-service teacher training. Quintriqueo and Arias-Ortega (2019) propose that the current mechanisms and programmes for teacher training are so firmly entrenched within enlightenment, rationalist logics, as well as imported western curricular content, that it is currently impossible to think of an epistemologically plural education that can respond to the contextual and cultural realities of different localities (Atacameña, Mapuche, Huilliche, Rapa Nui, etc.) in Chile. To date, such programmes are scarce: the Universidad Católica de Temuco and Universidad de Tarapacá have some modules for intercultural teacher training (Espinoza Sanchez et al., 2018). Given the international evidence surrounding the possibilities of positively changing pre-service teacher expectations through critical and culturally sensitising workshops, interventions, and targeted field placements (Civitillo et al., 2018; Wiggins et al., 2007), I suggest that more encompassing measures are long overdue in the Chilean context, especially in universities located in Santiago. The capital remains largely overlooked in terms of research into teachers' attitudes towards indigenous students, which is surprising given the number of pre-service teachers trained there, as well as the number of indigenous children and youth who attend schools and post-secondary institutions in Santiago.

I also recommend that more monitoring of indigenous inequalities in Chilean education be provided, given the scarcity of academic or policy-based research on this matter. In this book I have drawn on the few studies available, but even less is known about other indigenous groups in Chile. This monitoring should ideally be oriented towards establishing how class-based, gendered, and racialised criteria operate simultaneously to create more intense experiences of inequalities for certain sections of the population than for others. Attention should also be given to the ethnic (indigenous and migrant) compositions of schools, with a view to considering additional funding and grants for these establishments, as well as means of attracting better-qualified teachers who are trained to work in multicultural classrooms. My reasons for proposing this are not to set up some kind of Foucauldian panopticon of neoliberal governmentality, but rather in an attempt to overcome what Romm (2010) has described as aversive racism. That is, a passivity that learns to tolerate and live with ongoing inequalities that unfairly restrict one group's opportunities. According to Romm, establishments need not operate with any intention to harm minority group members, but the lack of political will to transform these kinds of environments are a modern form of institutional racism.

There is a conspicuous absence of workshops or use of "citizenship" modules in the curriculum to hold formal discussions about the detrimental effects of institutional racism in Chile, in both IBE and non-IBE schools. Formal discussions about portrayals of the Mapuche in the media, as an instance of discrimination noted by the students themselves, could be held to re-educate and to move away from these misrepresentative moral panics. At school and regional levels, discussions about how racialised expectations of schoolchildren's futures affect their academic performance should also be held between parents and teachers.

I mentioned at the beginning of the book that if there are any schools in Chile where these processes should begin, it is in those where indigenous students (in this case Mapuche) are most present. I insist that this is not merely about incorporating IBE programmes, which over the last three decades have proven that top-down policies are no guarantee of producing intercultural relations in schools. Instead, reforms that introduce more critical forms of pedagogy are needed; specifically, those capable of addressing systemic and structural racism – in their sociohistoric and political contexts – through dialogues that draw on Mapuche students' own experiences. It is vital that these initiatives avoid becoming another school protocol or manual, but that they remain centred in the everyday lives of those who face these structural barriers, and that they be combined with critical educators' abilities to interrupt and challenge whitened normative categories and subtle forms of racism, together with their students. Only in this way will schooling be converted into a truly educational experience that makes a difference to these young people's lives in times of new racism.

References

Augostinos, M., Tuffin, K., & Every, D. (2005). New racism, meritocracy and individualism: constraining affirmative action in education. *Discourse and Society*, 16(3), 315–340.

Barker, M. (1981). *The new racism*. London: Junction Books.

Bonilla-Silva, E. (2006). *Racism without racists: Color-blind racism and the persistence of racial inequality in the United States* (2nd ed.). Oxford: Rowman & Littlefield Publishers.

Burke, M. (2016). New frontiers in the study of color-blind racism: A materialist approach. *Social Currents, 3*(2), 103–109.

Carger, C. L. (1996). *Of borders and dreams: A Mexican-American experience of urban education.* New York: Teachers College Record.

Carter, P. L. (2005). *Keepin' it real: School success beyond black and white.* New York: Oxford University Press.

Cerda, R. (2017). Situación socioeconómica reciente de los Mapuches: 2009–2015. In I. Aninat, V. Figueroa, & R. Gonzaléz (Eds.), *El pueblo Mapuche en el siglo XXI: Propuestas para un nuevo entendimiento entre culturas en Chile* (pp. 405–434). Santiago: Colección Centro de Estudios Públicos. Memorias del Primer Encuentro Interuniversitario de Educación Intercultural (pp. 121–139). Santiago de Chile: Lom.

CIIR. (2019). *Estudio longitudinal de relaciones interculturales: Resultados de segunda ola.* Santiago: CIIR.

Civitillo, S., Juang, L., & Schachner, M. (2018). Challenging beliefs about cultural diversity in education: A synthesis and critical review of trainings with pre-service teachers. *Educational Research Review, 24,* 67–83.

Crow, J. (2006). *Rethinking national identities: representations of the Mapuche and dominant discourses of nationhood in twentieth century Chile.* PhD thesis, University of London.

Cummins, J. (1996). *Negotiating identities: Education for empowerment in a diverse society.* Ontario, CA: California Association of Bilingual Education.

Espinoza Sanchez, E., Díaz Araya, A., Mondaca Rojas, C., & Mamani Morales, J.C. (2018). Formación inicial docente, prácticas pedagógicas y competencias interculturales de los estudiantes de carreras de pedagogía de la universidad de tarapacá, norte de chile. *Diálogo Andino, 57,* 21–38.

Fine, M. (1993). *Framing dropouts: Notes on the politics of an urban public high school.* New York: State University of New York Press.

Lewis, A. (2003). *Race in the schoolyard: Negotiating the color line in classrooms and communities.* Piscataway; NJ: Rutgers.

Luna, L., Tekechea, C., & Caniguan, N. (2018). Mapuche education and situated learning in a community school in Chile. *Intercultural Education, 29*(2), 203–217.

Ministry of Education (MINEDUC). (2017). *Programa de educación intercultural bilingüe 2010–2016.* Santiago: Ministerio de Educación.

Omi, M., & Winant, H. (1994). *Racial formation in the United States.* New York, NY: Routledge.

Organisation for Economic Cooperation and Development (OECD). (2017). *Reviews of national policies for education: Education in Chile.* Paris: OECD Publishing.

Organisation for Economic Cooperation and Development (OECD). (2019). *Education at a glance: Country note on Chile.* Paris: OECD Publishing.

Pollock, M. (2005). *Colormute: Race talk dilemmas in an American school.* Princeton, NJ: Princeton University Press.

Quintriqueo, S., & Arias-Ortega, K. (2019). Educación intercultural articulada a la episteme indígena en latinoamérica. el caso Mapuche en chile. *Dialogo Andino*, *59*, 81–91.

Richards, P. (2013). *Race and the Chilean miracle: Neoliberalism, democracy and indigenous rights.* Pittsburgh, PA: Pittsburgh University Press.

Romm, N. (2010). *New racism: Revisiting researcher accountabilities.* New York, NY: Springer.

St. Denis, V. (2007). Aboriginal education with anti-racist education: Building alliances across cultural and racial identity politics. *Canadian Journal of Education*, *30*(4), 1068–1092.

Wiggins, R., Follo, E., & Eberly, M. (2007). The impact of a field immersion program on pre-service teachers' attitudes toward teaching in culturally diverse classrooms. *Teaching and Teacher Education*, *23*(5), 653–663.

Yosso, T. (2005). Whose culture has capital? A critical race theory discussion of community cultural wealth. *Race Ethnicity and Education*, *8*(1), 69–91.

Appendix

Below I provide a summary of the schools involved in the research, including indigenous compositions as recorded in each establishment's administrative records at the time of each research project. I refer to schools as semi-rural when they are located outside towns or within a village, and as rural when they are more than a reasonable walking distance (albeit a subjective criteria) of one kilometre from the nearest amenities, or the town/village limits. Urban refers to any school located within city limits. It will be noted that indigenous compositions are significantly lower in Santiago than in the Araucanía Region, but since most schools in the capital have indigenous compositions of 3% or lower, the research schools can be considered high by comparison. Some of the schools had boarding facilities for students travelling from remote areas, while all operate on extremely limited budgets, and have limited pedagogic resources. All these factors speak of historic and enduring structural inequalities that disproportionately affect indigenous populations. After decades of developmentalist policies, many of the so-called gaps (a rather neutral term to describe outcomes of colonial histories) have been reduced, but this book has demonstrated that young Mapuche people's experiences of schooling is ambivalent, expressing tensions between negation and affirmation, indifference and proactive construction, and resignation and resilience. Some of the more critical voices that we have heard denounce the role of schools in reproducing societal racism, whilst others are more accepting of the status quo.

The schools diverged on how they identified Mapuche students. Some counted the number who applied for indigenous grants, others by surname. Both are problematic (compared to asking their self-identity), since the latter fails to account for all the families whose surname goes back two generations on the maternal side of either parent, so students with a Mapuche grandmother would not be identifiable using this selection process. In sum, this means Mapuche families could make up an even greater proportion of the school than indicated.

Table A1 Participating schools

School (pseudonym)	Location	Establishment type (M = municipal, SP = state-funded private)	Secondary curriculum (TP = technical-vocational, HC = humanities and sciences)	School size	Indigenous composition (Mapuche)
Lihuén	Araucanía – semi-rural	SP	TP	405	88%
Tres Montes	Araucanía – rural	SP	HC	316	83%
Campos Verdes	Araucanía – semi-rural	SP	TP	240	70%
Nacional	Araucanía – urban	M	TP	592	59%
Campaña	Araucanía – urban	M	TP	709	39%
Lago Profundo	Araucanía – semi-rural	M	TP	132	77%
Raimilla	Araucanía – rural	SP	TP	110	80%
Acevedo	Araucanía – semi-rural	SP	HC	473	25%
Quelentaro	Araucanía – semi-rural	SP	HC	235	67%
Linterna	Araucanía – rural	SP	HC & TP	302	71%
Castañeda	Araucanía – urban	SP	HC & TP	381	18%
Mapocho	Santiago – urban	M	N/A (Elementary only)	561	7%
Clorinda	Santiago – urban	SP	N/A (Elementary only)	227	14%
Neblina	Santiago – urban	M	N/A (Elementary only)	624	17%
Cerro Bajo	Santiago – urban	M	N/A (Elementary only)	574	11%
San Pablo	Santiago – urban	SP	N/A (Elementary only)	489	7%

Source: Author's own elaboration

Research Projects and Methodology

I began researching issues relating to Mapuche youth identity and schooling experiences for my doctorate studies, conducting fieldwork for a one-year period in 2008–2009 in five schools (two urban: Nacional and Campaña, two semi-rural: Campos Verdes and Lihuén, and one rural: Tres Montes). I was the sole researcher on this project, but I worked from the (then named) Institute of Indigenous Studies (*Instituto de Estudios Indigenas*) at the Universidad Frontera in Temuco. Staff working there advised me on ethical research methodologies appropriate for working with Mapuche youth. I conducted focus groups with a total of 116 self-identified Mapuche youth between 7th and 12th grade and 16 follow-up individual interviews. The participants were selected through the school's administrative records based on surname and who were then asked whether they identified as Mapuche before being selected to participate, and prior to discussing and signing informed consent forms. Much of the focus group discussions were based on supporting visual aids, providing stimulus material as icebreakers to provoke conversation. The images presented both traditional and contemporary hybrid expressions and representations of "Mapucheness." This enabled me to address complex issues of identity management and cultural symbols using immediately familiar and concrete examples which participants could relate to from their everyday stocks of knowledge. Concepts such as identity, ethnicity, and racism were not addressed directly during the focus groups or interviews, given the complexity and ambiguity surrounding these terms. Instead, I asked more general questions about their own experiences of school life so as to capture these subjectivities in my analysis.

In 2012 I carried out a follow-up study (postdoctorate) researching IBE and non-IBE schools and whether these special programmes made any difference to Mapuche identity or experiences of schooling. Sarah Radcliffe was the principal investigator, and Natalia Caniguan, a self-identified Mapuche researcher, was the research assistant on this project, who carried out approximately half of the interviews. This project was carried out in four semi-rural schools, two of which participated in the first research project (Lihuén and Campos Verdes) and the other two for the first time (Lago Profundo and Raimilla). On this project, 103 self-identified Mapuche students from 10th to 12th grade participated in focus groups, and I conducted interviews with 18 individual students, 12 teachers, and 16 Ministry of Education, all over a one-year period.

In 2015 I was the lead researcher on a project funded by the Pontificia Universidad Católica de Chile, with a research team of three researchers (one of whom, Rukmini Becerra, also has extensive experience working with indigenous communities) and one research assistant, Simona Mayo, who self-identifies as Mapuche. The aim of the research was to address different perspectives on the educational quality of high indigenous composition schools. Four schools participated in the project (Acevedo, Quelentaro, Linterna, and Castañeda). On this occasion, teachers and parents were interviewed as well as focus groups with students. My main responsibility on this project was the analysis of interview data.

In 2017 a small research project was conducted with a total of 26 post-secondary, self-identified, Mapuche students, with financial support from the Center for Intercultural and Indigenous Research (CIIR) at the Universidad Católica de Chile. Macarena Sepulveda acted as the research assistant on this project on account of her previous experience working with Mapuche communities, and her proximity in age to the interviewees. I was a co-interviewer on eight occasions. Snowball sampling was used to contact the interviewees, whilst purposefully selecting a maximum variation of institutions and courses (in total 14 different institutions, and 11 courses were included). Life course interviews were conducted with a view to understanding their educational trajectories as a whole, and any barriers that they had overcome to reach post-secondary education.

Finally, in 2018 I began research looking into school climate issues in schools with high compositions of ethnic diversity in Santiago, with a specific focus on schools with medium and high indigenous compositions. In 2019 this culminated in a Fondecyt Regular (national Funding) project in collaboration with Sandra Becerra who is an expert on school climate in contexts of the Araucanía Region, Andrea Canales, Santiago Irribarra, and Macarena Sepulveda. We conducted interviews and focus groups with students from 7th to 8th grade, and interviews with school staff (school climate committee members and teachers) in Santiago and Temuco with a view to understanding different experiences of ethnic discrimination, school climate measures, and how they affect educational achievements.

Quality and Ethical Considerations

As I mentioned in the introduction, it would be egregious as a white British researcher living in Chile to claim any role other than that of an ally to the inequalities that Mapuche youth face. I cannot claim to speak for any of the young people involved in the research and have never experienced the power asymmetries or racism that they have undergone, either as a one-off event or across my life course. Nor do I share a working-class background or experience of low-quality educational establishments. As a sociologist, I see my role as reflexively understanding and interpreting intersectional inequalities in view of theories that help make sense of these phenomena. Whilst social actors will themselves have their own ideas about racism and schooling, I believe that the role of a critical researcher is to examine the social mechanisms operating beyond the immediately perceivable circumstances of everyday life.

To this end, my contribution is simply to offer a different perspective to those of indigenous people in general and indigenous scholars in particular. I recognise, for example, that objections could be made to the use of Bourdieu's theories, of French origin, and new racism literature from North America, as further examples of western interpretations and constructions of indigenous experiences. I have cited Mapuche scholars who are authorities on decolonialism, Mapuche worldviews, and community-based proposals for autonomous education (Quilaqueo 2012; Quilaqueo and Quintriqueo 2008; Carihuentro 2009, for example). My contribution, far from being a final word on these matters, aims to compliment insiders' perspectives by exposing inequalities that are captured and explained by western sociological theories.

Regarding the decision to conduct the research in Spanish rather than *mapuzungún*, it is worth noting that none of the students from across the research projects that I conducted described *mapuzungún* as their first language, and less than 5% spoke it semi-fluently as a second language. While there are ethical issues connected to my own interpretations of these interviews – as an outsider – I do not believe that language has been a detracting issue, given my fluency in Spanish. I do not know of any study carried out by a Mapuche scholar directed towards Mapuche youth (at any level of education) to have been conducted in *mapuzungún* due to the declining levels of fluency among younger generations. I would also repeat a point made at the beginning of the book; that the research presented throughout is not focused on indigenous language use, intercultural pedagogies and methodologies, or on decolonial knowledges, despite sporadic references to these issues. Finally, all the research projects were approved by the relevant university ethics committees prior to commencement, and informed consent was given by all schools and participants, including students' parents/guardians wherever the participants were minors (under 18 years of age).

A majority of young people who participated in the research were not actively involved in, or politically motivated by, Mapuche movements for national/territorial autonomy. This in part has to do with where the research was carried out. That is to say, the research was not carried out in Mapuche communities or in areas of the Araucanía Region where Mapuche political organisation is strongest. Were the research to be carried out in *comunas* like Ercilla, Galvarino, or Lumaco, conversations may well have been different. We heard from young people like Mateo in the Nacional School, who have been brought up to understand the political context of post-colonialism, historical conflicts between the Mapuche and the Chilean state, Mapuche *cosmovisión* (worldvision), and the legitimate claims for autonomy in *Wallmapu* (Mapuche territory stretching across the Chilean–Argentinian border) and how it ought to be administered and governed. This is one meaningful way of being Mapuche today, and I would add that it is perhaps the most empowering in terms of self-realisation and developing a clear and meaningful pathway for their futures. Yet clearly it is not the only way of *becoming* Mapuche, and this is precisely the point of this research. By interviewing Mapuche youth in less politicised areas, I was able to capture more of the everyday and banal elements of ethnic belonging and meaning. That is, how young people make sense of their indigenous identity in schools where being Mapuche is "normal" and accepted, but mostly as part of an assimilatory Chilean category of belonging. This is worthwhile taking into consideration since my research is not representative of all Mapuche – or, of course, indigenous – communities. I leave this as an issue for future research.

Index

Page numbers in **bold** indicate tables, page numbers in *Italics* indicate figures and page numbers followed by n indicate notes.